THE MEDIEVAL EROTIC *ALBA*

structure as meaning

JONATHAN SAVILLE

THE MEDIEVAL EROTIC

ALBA ~~~~~ *structure as meaning*

COLUMBIA UNIVERSITY PRESS   NEW YORK & LONDON

1972

This study, prepared under the Graduate Faculties of Columbia University, was selected by a committee of those Faculties to receive one of the Clarke F. Ansley awards given annually by Columbia University Press.

To my mother and father

ACKNOWLEDGMENTS

MY GREATEST DEBT is to W. T. H. Jackson of Columbia University, whose sensitive critical approach to medieval literature served as a model for the kind of study I have tried to write. Mr. Jackson read the entire manuscript, as did Joan Ferrante, Lawton P. G. Peckham, and Jeffrey Ford, all of Columbia, and my colleagues at the University of California, San Diego, Ronald Berman, Thomas Dunseath, and Martin Wierschin. I am grateful to all of these scholars for the patience and thoroughness with which they read my book, and I am indebted to all of them for valuable suggestions. In addition, I have discussed various points with Jaime Alazraki, Michel Benamou, Bernhard Blume, Joaquín Casalduero, David Crowne, Robert Durling, Claudio Guillén, Victor Harris, Roman Jakobson, Fredric Jameson, James Monroe, and Gian Roberto Sarolli, to all of whom I express my gratitude for their time and help. Sacvan Bercovitch and Edwin Fussell patiently answered my questions on technical points, and I take this opportunity to thank them. I also want to acknowledge my general intellectual indebtedness to the late Andrew Chiappe, Howard McP. Davis, Robert Hanning, John C. Nelson, and Maurice Valency, all of whom have influenced me in profound ways. Mrs. Tommye Smith did an admirable job in preparing a difficult manuscript, and I am also grateful to Mrs. Betsy Dyer for her help. Part of the writing was done under a Summer Faculty Fellowship at the University of California, San Diego. I want to express my warm thanks to Robert C. Elliott and Roy Harvey Pearce for helping me to obtain this fellowship, as well as for many other kindnesses. Finally, I wish to thank my parents, whose generosity and encouragement made a crucial contribution to the writing of this book.

La Jolla, 1970

CONTENTS

. . . there occurs the leave-taking; namely, the departure of the lover or of the beloved: and this truly is a terrible spectacle, and a difficult situation, in which the resoluteness of the most resolute is broken . . . and the strength of every perspicacious person is gone, and when every never-weeping eye sheds tears . . . .

And by my life, if a fine-feeling person died in the hour of leave-taking, he could be excused, if he died because he remembered what will be his lot after that hour in the way of shattered hopes, and appearance of fear, and change of joy into grief. . . .

—Ibn Hazm [1]

Ach scheiden, immer scheiden . . .

—Anonymous *Tagelied* [2]

THE *ALBA* "SÎNE KLÂWEN"

by Wolfram von Eschenbach

"SÎNE KLÂWEN," discussed at length in this book, is both a representative example of the genre and one of its crowning masterpieces. It is placed here, in original and translation, for easy reader reference.

I

"Sîne klâwen   durh die wolken sint geslagen,
er stîget ûf mit grôzer kraft,
ich sihe in grâwen   tägelich als er wil tagen,   3
den tac, der im geselleschaft
erwenden wil, dem werden man,
den ich mit sorgen în verliez.   6
ich bringe in hinnen, ob ich kan.
sîn vil mangiu tugent michz leisten hiez."

II

"Wahtaer, du singest   daz mir mange fröide nimt   9
unde mêret mîne klage.
maer du bringest,   der mich leider niht gezimt,
immer morgens gein dem tage.   12
diu solt du mir verswîgen gar.
daz gebiute ich den triuwen dîn:
des lône ich dir als ich getar.   15
sô belîbet hie der selle mîn."

III

"Er muoz et hinnen   balde und âne sûmen sich:
nu gib im urloup, süezez wîp.   18
lâz in minnen   her nâch sô verholne dich,
daz er behalte êr und den lîp.
er gab sich mîner triuwe alsô,   21
daz ich in braehte ouch wider dan.
ez ist nu tac: naht was ez dô
mit drucke an brust dîn kus mirn an gewan."   24

IV

"Swaz dir gevalle,   wahtaer, sinc, und lâ den hie,
der minne brâhte und minne enphienc.
von dînem schalle   ist er und ich erschrocken ie: 27
sô ninder morgensterne ûf gienc
ûf in, der her nâch minne ist komen,
noch ninder lûhte tages lieht,   30
du hâst in dicke mir benomen
von blanken armen, und ûz herzen nieht."

V

Von den blicken,   die der tac tet durh diu glas,   33
und dô der wahtaer warnen sanc,
si muose erschricken   durch den der dâ bî ir was.
ir brüstelîn an brust si dwanc.   36
der rîter ellens niht vergaz
(des wolde in wenden wahters dôn):
urloup nâh und nâher baz   39
mit kusse und anders gab in minne lôn.

I

"His talons   have struck through the clouds,
he climbs upward with great power,
I see him becoming gray,   dawn-like, as if he will dawn,   3
the day, who intends to turn the worthy man away from
          companionship,
the man whom I let in with such worry.   6
I will bring him away from here, if I can.
His very many virtues have called upon me to do that."

II

"Watchman, what you are singing   takes much joy from me   9
and increases my lamentation.
You always bring news   that unhappily does not suit me at all,
always in the morning towards day-break.   12
You must be completely silent with me about these things:
I order you by your faithfulness.
I will reward you for it as I dare,   15
if my companion remains here."

III

"He really must get away from here   immediately and without
          delay;
now give him leave to depart, sweet woman.   18
Let him make love to you   at some later time, secretly,
so that he may keep his honor and his life.
He entrusted himself to my faithful promise   21
that I would also bring him out again.
Now it is day; it was night then,
when, as you pressed him to your breast, your kiss won him from
          me."   24

IV

"Whatever pleases you,   watchman, sing! But leave him here
who brought love and received love.
By your clamor   he and I have always been frightened,   27
when no morning-star at all was rising
upon him who came here seeking love,
nor was daylight gleaming anywhere.   30
You have often taken him
from my white arms, but not out of my heart."

V

Because of the glances   that the day was sending through the
          window-panes,   33
and when the watchman sang his warning,
she was forced to become alarmed   on account of him who was
          there beside her.
She pressed her little breast against his breast.   36
The knight did not lose the battle-zeal
from which the watchman's song wanted to turn him aside.
Their parting, coming near and yet nearer,   39
with kissing, and other things, gave them the reward of love. [3]

THE MEDIEVAL EROTIC *ALBA*

structure as meaning

INTRODUCTION

TWO LOVERS, a knight and a highborn lady who is not the knight's wife, are lying abed in the lady's chamber, enjoying a night of ecstatic love-making. Suddenly their joy is interrupted: the dawn, announced by the song of birds or by the voice of the castle watchman resounding from the ramparts, has come to put an end to the night of love. The lovers, particularly the lady, protest. They berate the watchman, they curse the sun, they deny that day is really at hand. But in the end they must give way. With grief and tears at the separation, and with promises that they will soon meet again, they part; the knight goes off into the outer world; the lady remains behind, in anguish and longing.

Such is the plot of the *alba*, a form of lyric poetry which, along with several other genres of vernacular lyric, made its first appearance in Southern France around the middle of the twelfth century. The *alba* subsequently took part in the extraordinary international career of these newly created genres, a career in which the inventions of the twelfth-century Provençal troubadours became the dominant lyric forms in all the European vernaculars for the following five-hundred years. Including several subclasses or variants of the genre, we possess nineteen medieval *albas* written in Provençal (the literary language of Southern France in the High Middle Ages); five in the language of Northern France, where the genre was known as the "aube"[1]; and over one hundred in Middle High German, where the poems were variously called "tageliet" or "tagewîse." The *alba* eventually found its way into narrative poems, notably the *Filostrato* of Boccaccio and Chaucer's *Troilus and Criseyde*; Shakespeare used it in a narrative (*Venus and Adonis*) and in two plays (*Romeo and Juliet* and *Troilus and Cressida*); and, as a lyric or as part of a larger form, it has made occasional reappearances throughout the later history of European literature—in Donne, Goethe, Wagner, and Yeats, to mention only the best-known examples.

In spite of its prolonged international success, the *alba* is commonly—and, in certain ways, legitimately—thought of as a "minor" genre in the lyric poetry of the High Middle Ages. The major genre is the *chanson*,[2] the poem of hopeless, endless, frustrated love by a humble and faithful lover for an exalted and inaccessible lady. Later on, it is the *chanson* which, through the medium of its great fourteenth-century master, Petrarch, becomes the universal staple of Renaissance love poetry. When Astrophel pines for the unobtainable Stella, when Ronsard laments his emotional enslavement by Hélène, when Shakespeare's Jaques mocks the lover "sighing like a furnace, with a woful ballad / made to his mistress' eyebrow," all these lovers and ladies are still acting out the roles set down for them in the twelfth-century *chanson*. The *alba* does indeed recur in the Renaissance, but it remains a special and unusual delicacy, while the *chanson*, with its particular dramatic situation and love ethos, is served up with every common poetic meal. Even in the Middle Ages the number of *albas*—in all languages—is far inferior to the number of *chansons*. Furthermore, the medieval *alba* attained a degree of popularity only in Southern France and in Germany. Northern France and Italy, the other great continental centers of vernacular love poetry, seem to have shown very little interest in this particular form. The *chanson*, on the contrary, was popular everywhere on the continent. The great productivity of the *chanson* genre, its wide dissemination, and the fact that it subsequently underwent so many interesting developments and expansions (in Dante, for example), have all combined to make scholars feel that this is the genre most in tune with the ideals of medieval vernacular lyric in general, and most representative of its poetic techniques. The *alba* is looked upon as less characteristic and more idiosyncratic. It is clearly related to the *chanson* in that it too is an aristocratic love poem and in that the *albas* and *chansons* were written by the same poets. But it is quite different in its techniques, and seemingly different in its meanings as well.

These judgments about the relations of the *alba* and the *chanson* are not so self-evident as they may appear. They require looking into. First of all, the minority status of the *alba* as a genre can be admitted without dispute only in regard to the relatively small quantity of *albas* written in the Middle Ages and the relative restrictedness of its later influence. The quality of the best medieval *albas* is in no way inferior to that of the best *chansons*, and a number of the very greatest lyric poems of the Middle Ages belong to this "minor" genre. In the elegance and musicality of their diction, the poignance of their emotional expressiveness, and the dramatic power of their structure, the best *albas* (such as Wolfram von Eschenbach's "Sîne klâwen") belong with the masterpieces of medieval literature. Surely, the capacity of the *alba* form to foster such individual masterpieces must be taken into account when we are deciding how characteristic or representative the *alba* is, how much it may reveal of the general intentions of medieval lyric poetry. And as to techniques and meaning, the apparent differences between the two genres cannot be taken for granted. Many important categories of technique have scarcely been touched upon in studies of either genre, and the meanings of the *alba* and the *chanson*—the values they express, their attitudes toward love, reality, and human destiny, their relation to real ideologies in the society that produced them—need to be defined much more precisely than they have been before any meaningful statements about their differences or similarities can be made. The present study focusses on the *alba*, but it always has in mind the *chanson* as well. It aims to understand the *alba*'s techniques and meanings not only for the sake of the *alba*— the "minor," though no less splendid, of the two genres—but also for the light such understanding throws on the *chanson* and its later derivatives. Although only the last chapter deals specifically with this comparison, it is implied throughout.

In attempting to increase our understanding of the *alba*—and, implicitly or explicitly, of the *chanson*—this book occasionally digresses into other areas of literary history, and sometimes out of the specifically literary altogether. These digressions have two aims. One is to suggest—in an unsystematic but, hopefully, provocative way—that certain categories of the imagination which find expression in the medieval *alba* are characteristic of the medieval mind in general, and that they may be detected in many other—not necessarily literary—manifestations of medieval culture. The *alba* thus becomes a means of ingress into the historical understanding of the Middle Ages, of what is specifically *medieval* about the way men of that period perceived and evaluated experience.

A second aim of those parts of the book that do not deal directly with the medieval *alba* is to point out the persistence of some of these imaginative categories in later periods of European literature, and to suggest that they undergo a radical—if not total—change somewhere in the eighteenth century. These suggestions make no pretense to do anything but add slightly to the already overwhelming evidence for the profound alteration of the European mind at the end of the Enlightenment. However, the comparisons of some nineteenth-century poems with the medieval *alba* have the advantage of making a number of these alterations strikingly evident; and I believe that our understanding of the later poems themselves is significantly enhanced by their being juxtaposed with a medieval treatment of similar themes.

There are a number of other methodological principles under-lying this study, some of which may require a preliminary justification. In the following few pages I deal with the most important —and perhaps the most controversial—of these. First, two method-ological problems of particular concern to students of medieval literature: the problem of the continuity of literary traditions, and the problem of "origins." Then, two problems of more general application: the relationship of a literary work like the *alba* to the culture that produces it (or, more precisely, how one may legiti-mately go about establishing such a relationship); and the use of psychoanalytic concepts in literary studies of this sort. A subsequent paragraph explains my criteria in singling out exemplary *albas* from the considerable number of extant poems in the genre. Finally, I attempt a brief justification of the very fact that I have used certain methods of analysis not ordinarily applied to literary forms so brief —and so apparently "simple"—as the *alba*.

CONTINUITY OF THE "ALBA" AS A LITERARY TRADITION

The brief account I have given of the *alba* and its literary history is based on an assumption which is by no means beyond dispute, namely the existence of a clear-cut literary tradition con-necting the various poems or sections of poems I have mentioned. There seems to be little doubt that many of the Middle High German examples were based on Provençal models, or that Chaucer (in the *alba* of *Troilus and Criseyde*) was using Boccaccio's *Filostrato*, directly or indirectly, as his source. The other interconnections cannot be established so readily, however. Some of the twelfth-century German poems have been claimed for the creative genius of the German people and have been declared to be free of any Provençal influence.[3] The *alba*-like scenes in *Romeo and Juliet* have been referred to a Dutch source going back to a German original,[4] and to an English ballad translated from the French.[5] The *alba*-like speeches in the *Filostrato* itself might be explained as derivations from a poem of Ovid (*Amores* I.xiii, to be discussed later) without any reference to the medieval *albas*. And there are sufficiently large divergences from the plot I have described above to give grounds for thinking that, even in the Provençal *albas*, we are dealing with not one but two or more separate literary traditions. *Albas* in which the dawn is announced by the song of birds may have no direct connection with *albas* in which it is a watchman who gives the warning. *Albas* in which the lovers curse the sun may go back to one source, while *albas* in which they reproach the watchman may go back to another, and *albas* in which the lovers simply express their grief without placing the blame on anyone or anything may belong to a third and quite distinct tradition.

Although some of the theories as to the line (or lines) of derivation of the *alba* are due mainly to Romantic nationalism and others are patently absurd,[6] the doubts they express as to the existence of a single tradition are to a considerable extent justified. These doubts have been reinforced by the recent publication of a book devoted to the dawn-song as a universal literary genre (A. T. Hatto's *Eos*[7]). A collection of more than five-hundred poems in dozens of languages, all portraying the parting of lovers at dawn, this remarkable work gives ample evidence that the *albas* of the European Middle Ages need not be considered as necessarily belonging to a single literary tradition. If cultures as diverse as the Kurdish, the Malayan, the Votyak, and the Quechua can produce dawn-songs which are clearly not interdependent, there seems no logical reason to deny this creative independence to the various peoples of medieval Europe. The association of love-making with nighttime and separation with dawn is evidently part of the general stock of human experience. If these same notions appear in Provençal lyrics and German lyrics and Italian narratives and English dramas it may very well be that in each case we have to do with a separate, indigenous literary tradition—or, now and then, even with a completely new creation based on observation and experience and having no literary source whatsoever.

Nevertheless, there are certain elements of certain European *albas* which, on the evidence of the poems collected in *Eos*, occur virtually nowhere else: the watchman is the most salient example.

Most of the German *Tagelieder* resemble certain of the Provençal *albas* much more closely than they do any of the other dawn-songs in Hatto's collection. More importantly, whatever the ultimate sources of the various European dawn-songs, whatever the truth about interrelationship or lack of interrelationship, these poems are ipso facto related to each other by their community of culture. The medieval European *albas*, no matter what their language, were all written in the same context of ideas and associations. Certain ways of looking at the world, of organizing reality, are shared by the great majority of them; and these ways of looking at the world are also to be found in other manifestations of medieval culture. If we may not speak accurately of a single literary tradition, we are nevertheless justified in seeing a unity based not on lines of literary derivation but on a general cultural ambiance common to all the various types of European *alba*. The present study, therefore, will be limited entirely to the dawn-songs of medieval Europe, on the grounds that it is possible to speak about them as a group, to make critical statements that apply to most of them, and to show affinities between them and other aspects of medieval thought. For the sake of convenience I will refer to them generically as *albas*, and will usually use this term when speaking of individual poems, even though they may be German or Northern French. The use of the term is not meant to imply a belief in a single literary tradition for this type of poem. It merely indicates that these poems have enough in common, in their structure, in their ideas, and in their relation to medieval culture in general, for it to be productive to treat them as a single genre.

THE PROBLEM OF ORIGINS

The problem of the origins of the *alba* is distinct from the problem as to whether the *albas* constitute a single literary tradition. Solutions of the problem of origins often presuppose a belief in the existence of a single tradition, entirely derived from a single source, but it would be quite possible to believe that the medieval *albas* belong to several different traditions, and to attempt to trace each to a source of its own. What is common to all the theories of origins which have been advanced in regard to troubadour poetry is precisely their assumption that poems do have origins, that these origins may be found, and that the later poems may be largely explained in terms of their derivation from their source. The method of such theories is basically a good one: a poem, or a set of poems, is compared with the supposed source, sometimes with acute critical insight. But the results of the comparison, however stimulating they may be for an understanding of the individual poems or of the art of poetry in general, are always treated as way stations on the road to the real goal, which is the establishment of a clear case of paternity: one poem is the engenderer, the other is the engendered. This procedure is based on a fallacious notion as to how poems are created and how they express meaning. Poems cannot really engender poems; what *can* happen is that poems may influence poets, who, in the context of their own particular culture and with their own particular intentions, then create new poems. The real relation between a supposed source and its supposed offspring is thus not essentially different from the relation between any poem and any other poem. When two poems treat the same subject, what is important for an understanding of both poems is to see how they are similar and how they are different in their treatment of the subject; the assertion that one of the poems is the source of the other tells us nothing whatever about the poems themselves.[8] Consequently, in this study I have attempted to avoid the concept of sources, and have focussed rather on the *comparison* of different poems, with only the most cursory regard for how they may be related genetically.

I have not, however, ignored the problem of origins entirely. For the *alba*, as for troubadour poetry in general, a number of origin theses have been championed: the thesis of folk origins, the liturgical thesis, the Ovidian thesis, the Arabic thesis, the "realistic" thesis.[9] I have not sought to judge all of these theses on their merits, but I have occasionally found it illuminating to compare the *albas* with some of the works that have been posited as their sources. My purpose has not been to confirm or reject any of the theses of origins—in the sense in which they use the word "origins" I suppose

I must reject them all—but to aid in the understanding of the *alba* by comparing it with other works which share one or more elements with it or which treat the same theme.

THE "ALBA" AND MEDIEVAL CULTURE

In comparing these poems, and in treating individual *albas*, I have often gone outside the poems themselves to point out analogies with other literary works, with certain aspects of theological and philosophical thought in the Middle Ages, and with universal human experiences. These analogies are intended to throw light on the structure and meaning of the *alba*, on its ethics, its concept of reality, and its concept of human nature. Some of them, as I have already stated, are also intended to indicate the ways in which these poems are distinctively medieval productions: the specifically medieval problems they deal with, the specifically medieval forms of thought they share. There is always a danger in analyses of this type that they may shade off into allegorization. Let me say at once that, except for those few late *albas* that plainly declare themselves allegories, I do not consider any of the erotic *albas* allegorical, in the sense that the elements that make them up conceal a specific hidden meaning which can be penetrated only by those who have an esoteric key. I do not, for example, believe that the lady and the watchman, those two ubiquitous characters of the *alba* drama, are really masks for the poetic representation of psychological faculties or metaphysical principles or Biblical personages. On the other hand, I do believe that the *relations* between these two fictional beings can be shown to parallel certain structures of thought found in medieval philosophical works and in Biblical story. Furthermore, I believe that the characters in the *alba*, the situation itself, and all the elements which compose it, although in one sense standing in isolation in a self-sufficient work of art, in a broader sense are also implicated in the complex of social usages, religious and philosophical notions, and literary traditions that gave shape to the minds of the *alba* poets and their audiences. Their meaning, therefore, involves resonances beyond the literal level, though the literal, dramatic action always remains the main carrier of the meaning. Although the *alba* is not allegorical, it is symbolic—as I propose to show.

PSYCHOANALYTICAL CRITICISM

Among the various thought-structures in which I see analogies to the *alba*, a number are of the sort generally called "Freudian" —that is, they are thought-structures arising from supposed infantile experiences as they persist in the adult psyche. Many readers bridle at the mere mention of Freudian criticism, and often with a good deal of justification. Much orthodox Freudian criticism tends toward the same kind of reductionism that appears, in a somewhat less striking way, in the theories of "origins" I spoke of earlier. For the proponents of origin-theories, one literary work is thought of as the source of a second literary work, that is, as its cause; the second work is a mere effect, reducible to the source. Similarly, Freudian psychologists speak of infantile experiences being the source and cause of adult experiences; the adult experience is reduced to its cause, the infantile experience; and all the things that make the adult experience unique, all its actual, particular circumstances, are pared off until nothing is left but the bare infantile core. This kind of reductionism, when applied clinically, may succeed in clearing up the mysterious nature of an adult experience. But when it is applied to a work of literature it runs the grave risk of discarding most of the individuality, most of the reality of the work, just as positivistic source-criticism frequently does. Complex works of art are ruthlessly metamorphosed into a formula, usually a very unpleasant-sounding one like "oral-genitalism" or "polymorphous perversity." And even when a commitment to Freudian theory is attenuated by a more subtle and complex understanding of literature, this ghastly jargon, which is characteristic of so much psychoanalytical writing on the arts, often makes the criticism seem reductionist when in fact it is not.

Another objection often advanced against the psychoanalytical method in literary criticism comes from the point of view of literary scholarship. This objection is that psychoanalysis tends to speak of universal human experiences, experiences that are biologically given, and that are thus independent of time and place and culture. Modern literary scholarship has conventionally—and this is all to the good— been rooted in the idea of history, the idea that works of art are culturally conditioned, that they grow out of a particular period with its particular climate of ideas, its particular artistic traditions, its particular social circumstances. This has been especially true of the study of the art of the Middle Ages, where the cultural conditions are so different from our own that a deep study of the extra-literary culture of the period seems a *sine qua non* for an understanding of the art. Does not psychoanalytical criticism, with its emphasis on universal, biologically conditioned experiences, run counter to the cultural and historical orientation of literary scholarship?

I do not see why the historical approach and the psychoanalytical approach should be contradictory, either in theory or in practice. Let me give an example of how they may be harmonized. In the great thirteenth-century romance by Gottfried von Strassburg, *Tristan*, there is a famous episode in which the two adulterous lovers retire to a kind of cave-temple in the midst of a forest, where they live for a while in solitary, erotic bliss. I shall have occasion later on to discuss various analogical meanings of this "Minnegrotte" and what they can tell us about the *alba*. Now, if we suggest that the idea of the isolated grotto of erotic love in Gottfried's *Tristan* is analogous to the story of the Garden of Eden, we are keeping within the framework of historical criticism. This Biblical story, so crucial to the whole Christian world-view, was a living part of the particular culture out of which Gottfried's *Tristan* sprang. If, on the other hand, we show analogies between the *Minnegrotte* and the infant's experience before it is separated from its mother, we are speaking of a universal biological experience and comparing it with a particular work of art. In the one case we are comparing two literary plots, two literary thought-structures (the *Minnegrotte*-story and the Eden-story). In the other case we are comparing a literary, fictional thought-structure (the *Minnegrotte*-story) with a real and universal experience (infancy). But these two procedures do not exclude each other. To all the historical-cultural analogies that have been adduced to this literary structure of Gottfried's—and let it be noted that much criticism of medieval literature is explicitly or implicitly concerned with pointing out such analogies—we have simply added another analogy, an analogy with a universal psychological experience. One analogy does not exclude the other, as the Middle Ages, with its vast systems of multiple analogy for everything, well understood. On the contrary, each additional analogy illuminates all the others. In adducing psychoanalytical analogies to the *alba* and its various elements I have aimed precisely at this kind of mutual illumination.

This means that, at least so far as literary criticism goes, I have rejected the psychoanalytical notion of causation, just as I have rejected the similar notion in the treatment of "sources." The difference between an approach to literary criticism by means of causation and an approach by means of analogies is fundamental, whether we are dealing with the relations between literary works (the problem of sources) or with the relations between a literary work and an infantile experience (psychoanalytical criticism). I should like to give another example, to make this difference perfectly clear. It has been said that the religious mysticism of Saint Bernard and the erotic *chansons* of the troubadours (phenomena of twelfth-century thought which are, roughly, contemporaneous) have many significant points in common. The most striking of these similarities is the picture, found in both Bernard and the troubadours, of the individual soul longing for union with a supremely high and virtually inaccessible ideal—in Bernard's case God, and in the *chansons* a beautiful and disdainful lady.[10] This seems to me a very productive comparison: it throws light on Bernardine mysticism and on troubadour love poems and ultimately on all of literature, because it shows us a certain thought structure taking a number of different and yet similar literary forms; it tells us something about the variety and the unity of literature in general. But to say that troubadour love poems *derive* from Bernardine mysticism[11] is to talk about history rather than about literature, and, in talking about history, to make assertions which cannot be satisfactorily proved by the methods of historical demonstration. Of these two kinds of historical criticism, the first is based on analogy, a method which has proved extremely fruitful; the second kind is based on causation, a critical concept I feel cannot be justified either theoretically or practically.

So, too (to return to my first example), I think it is most productive to note analogies between, on the one hand, Biblical story or erotic poetry, and, on the other, infantile experience. This kind of psychoanalytical criticism tells us something valuable about the human imagination in general: the forms the human imagination likes to take. But to go on to declare, as orthodox Freudian criticism usually does, that the infantile experience (for example, the infant before weaning) is the basic one and that the literary structures (for example, the Garden of Eden and the *Minnegrotte*) are mere elaborations of it, is, it seems to me, to introduce notions extraneous to literary criticism and indeed injurious to it. The notion of causation, once we admit it, can be applied with frightening abandon. We may maintain that the story of the garden of Eden is the origin of Gottfried's *Minnegrotte* (historical causation). We may maintain that the infant's experience before it is separated from its mother is the origin of both the *Minnegrotte* and the garden of Eden (psychoanalytical causation). Indeed, if we want to speak in terms of causation we might just as easily say that the basic experience was the experience of Eden and that all later imaginative experiences of paradise, including that of the infant in its mother's bosom, are elaborations of *it*—a way of thinking that would have been quite congenial to the Middle Ages. (Let us remember that Augustinian thought, following the Book of Genesis quite literally, derives even such a purely biological fact as that of woman's pains in childbirth from the original sin of Adam and Eve. This, of course, is *theological* causation.) To speak of a primary cause is always to introduce some sort of belief of the critic's own as to the governance of the universe, and that is an intrusion on literary criticism that I believe ought to be avoided. The insights of psychoanalysis can be applied to literary criticism without any commitment to the psychoanalytical notion of what constitutes reality. Literary criticism, as I see it, is not the study of the universe, with the universe's structure and causal processes, but the study of the imagination, which has its own structure and its own processes—not processes of causation, but processes of analogy. Consequently, in those parts of this study where I have used the insights of psychoanalysis, I have done my best to use them in the service of criticism rather than in the service of psychological science; and along with this I have tried to express psychoanalytical ideas in the language of normal discourse rather than in the technical language of a psychoanalytical monograph.

I should add, lest it be misunderstood, that this is not, in any narrow sense, a psychoanalytical study of the *alba*. Certain psychoanalytical concepts are brought in on a par with concepts from medieval philosophy and theology and purely aesthetic analyses. The psychoanalytical sections form only a part of the whole, and by no means the chief part.

CRITERIA OF SELECTION

In applying these various methods of criticism to the *alba* I have had to steer a line between large generalizations and detailed treatment of individual texts. Because many of my analyses proceed from close attention to the poetic text, I have necessarily had to select a restricted number of *albas* as the basis for what I have to say about the genre. Therefore, I cannot claim that all my arguments are true for all *albas*. The elements that go into the *alba*—the watchman, the knight, the lady, their interrelations, the dawn, the setting, and so forth—are different in each *alba*. Some *albas* omit one or more elements. Some emphasize one or another at the expense of the rest. Furthermore, it should be said that each of this fairly large group of conventional poems is a work of art in itself, in which a particular structuring of the elements produces a meaning particular to that poem. Because the *albas* are so conventional, the differences in meaning among them are usually not great (though a number of the main variations, as we shall see, have more than a merely trivial significance); but even the slight differences produced by—to give an example—the decision of the poet to make the watchman an intimate of the woman in one case or of the man in another [12] alter the effect of the poems in a real if not a striking way. Each of the medieval *albas*—not a few of which are of considerable poetic quality—could be analyzed in detail, and no two analyses would be quite the same because no two *albas* are quite the same. But such an undertaking would of course be impossibly long, and each successive analysis would contribute less and less to an understanding of the *albas* in general. My procedure, therefore, has been to isolate some of the elements characteristic of the genre as a whole, and to study these elements in a few specific poems. I might add that the *albas* I have chosen are, in my opinion, the very best poems in the group.

MEDIEVAL LYRICS AND MODERN CRITICISM

This brings me to a final point I feel I must deal with before proceeding to the study itself. A number of the *albas* are wonderful poems, as I have said, and are worth looking at for this reason alone. But how legitimate is it to subject this small literary form to a barrage of high-powered critical techniques, to look in it for ideas of reality and value, to draw analogies to passages in the *Patrologia Latina* and to universal infantile experiences? This is the question posed by A. R. Nykl in his critique of Leo Spitzer's approach to troubadour poetry:

One wonders why . . . Saint Augustine, Saint Bernard, Santa Teresa, Pascal, Valéry, Freud, Husserl and Heidegger should have been dragged into the joyful twelfth-century Aquitanian atmosphere, represented by such jolly singers like [sic] Guilhem IX of Poitiers, Peire d'Alvernhe, and Jaufré Rudel.[13]

Surely it does not show a great poetic or human sensitivity to call the ineffably melancholy Jaufré Rudel a jolly singer, but Nykl's doubts about treating the troubadours seriously cannot be ignored. In a later section I will touch upon the problem as to whether the ideas in the *alba* are to be taken as serious expressions of medieval belief. But that there *are* ideas in the *alba*, that the *alba* has a meaning, and that this meaning can be discovered only by critical investigation into how the poems are put together, are points I must maintain from the very beginning. The *alba* is not a *Divina Commedia*, but it is a work of literary art; a work of literary art must have a structure; and such a structure must convey a concept of what is good and a concept of what is true. This is so of all literary productions, from the lengthiest epic down to the most modest epigram. Indeed, I have chosen this brief lyric form as a subject not only because of its historical and poetic value but also because it *is* a small form, one which, however great its capacity to produce brilliant poetry, scarcely seems capable of conveying complex ethical and metaphysical ideas. This study of the medieval *alba* is an intentional demonstration of what modern techniques of criticism can do, even with a genre that makes so little explicit claim to philosophical statement. The techniques are used to investigate the *alba*, and at the same time the investigation of the *alba* is used as a means of exposing, through practical criticism, a theoretical framework that I believe could be profitably applied to many other literary works—lyrics and nonlyrics, medieval and nonmedieval. It is a theoretical framework that involves various hypotheses about the relation of poetic structure to the structure of the imagination and about the relation of the imagination to culture and history; and one of its fundamental assumptions—an assumption common to social and cultural history, historical stylistics, anthropology and archeology—is that *any* product of a culture exhibits all sorts of profound linkages with the whole culture that produced it. Investigated carefully and with imagination, a coin, a fashion in gardens, a superstition, a potsherd, each can reveal the life of a people. The *alba*, as a work of refined (and sometimes sublime) literary art, has far greater intrinsic importance than a coin or a potsherd. But it resembles them in that its network of linkages to its culture is in large measure invisible to the uncritical eye. Indeed, it may be that precisely because of its apparent status as "pure" poetry, as a superb artifact of brief compass and purely aesthetic intention, a poem such as the *alba* may tell us more about some of the basic thought processes of the civilization in which it flourished than a more explicitly philosophical work could do.

To learn whatever it is the *alba* has to tell us, however, we must not treat it as a delightful but meaningless bit of literary fluff produced by jolly singers in joyful medieval courts. We must take it seriously as a work of art. And that is what I have tried to do in the following study.

All translations, except where otherwise indicated, are my own. My aim, in the translation of the poetic texts, has been to aid the reader in following the originals; consequently, these translations are perfectly literal—often word for word—and make no claim to reproduce the artistic excellences of the various poems quoted.

ONE

𝕿HE TWO WORLDS OF VALUE

THE SITUATION portrayed in the *alba*, while it has certain contacts with a possible reality, nevertheless has a considerable air of the unreal about it. The lady's chamber from which all other persons in the castle are excluded, the watchman shouting from his position on the ramparts to alert the lovers to the danger of their being discovered, the strange emptiness of the social environment—these are elements not of a realistic portrayal of real events, but of an idealized, typical, illusionistic portrayal of an archetype. We are shown not a real event but an archetypal fiction; what is important is not particular individual details of the scene— no such details are given—but a basic, more or less abstract structure, which corresponds to a typical medieval way of structuring reality. The structure of the *alba* situation is a contrast between two worlds of value, the world of love with all of its values, and a world composed of everything that is not part of that love, a world that not only does not share the values of the world of love but is strongly opposed to them.

This contrast of two worlds of value, which reappears at all levels of meaning in the *alba*, is shown in its most concrete form in what we may call the topography of the situation. We see a universe divided physically into two distinct parts, an enclosed chamber, an *inside*, in which everything of value is to be found, surrounded by a hostile *outside* of much lower value, composed explicitly or by implication of the lady's husband; the watchman; all of society with the exception of the two lovers; all of nature, including the creatures of earth and the astronomical bodies, with all their various movements and processes; the Catholic Church, with the moral law that it administers; and in a certain sense even God Himself. The lovers wish to remain together in their inside world, which is the only world that really counts for them. But the outside world, represented by the sunrise and the watchman's announcement, impinges on the interior world of the chamber of love. The knight must eventually go outside, into the world of lesser value, and he feels this physical exit from the inner world into the outer world to be a loss of all joy, a separation from all that is good and real. All that sustains him in the moment of separation is the expectation that he will soon return to that inner world and recover the joy which he is leaving behind there and which it is impossible for him to find anywhere on the outside. For him, as for the lady, the world of true value is nothing but that single, small, enclosed room; this is the moral center of the universe; and all around it, up to the very heavens, moves another world, inferior, deprived, inimical.[1]

That a love scene should be imagined as taking place inside a room scarcely calls for notice. But the clear topographical contrast in the *alba* between a highly valued inner world and an outer world of inferior value is an extremely frequent structuring principle in medieval thought and art. To begin with, it is the structuring principle of the concept of the Garden of Eden, the ideal place of joy and plenty, surrounded by the fallen world of work and pain. The Garden of Eden is persistently associated in medieval exegesis with the enclosed garden—the *hortus conclusus*—of the Song of Songs, and this in turn is treated allegorically to represent various aspects of the Christian life. The Church, a center of true value in a world of wickedness, is both Eden and the *hortus conclusus*. So Honorius Augustodunensis, in his exegetical treatise on the Song of Songs, defines the allegorical meaning of the *hortus conclusus* as "Ecclesia," and then goes on to describe it in terms drawn from the description of Eden in Genesis iii:

> *Hic hortus est conclusus . . . scilicet praesidio angelorum contra daemones munitus. Hic etiam conclusus . . . quia munimine doctorum contra haereticos est circumseptus. . . . Ecclesia hortus Dei est, divino praesidio et igneo muro circumdata, et angelica custodia munita, ut nec daemones nec mali homines ei ad nocendum praevaleant.*

> This garden is enclosed . . . being protected by a garrison of angels against the demons. It is also enclosed . . . because it is circled around by the ramparts of the learned men of the Church against heretics . . . . The Church is the garden of God, surrounded by a divine garrison and a wall of fire, and protected by an angelic guard, that neither demons nor wicked men may have the power to harm it.[2]

The actual church building is thought of in a similar way, with a world of inferior value surrounding it, and a particular focal point of true value at a more or less central position inside it: the altar.[3] The monastery, too, is thought of in terms of Eden, the earthly paradise: it is a "paradisus claustralis," an inner, better world in the midst of the outer, fallen world, within whose walls the monks strive to rise to the heavenly Jerusalem, the "paradisus supercoelestis."[4] All of these "insides" are also allegorically interchangeable with the soul, which itself is thought of as an inside of great value opposed to the exterior corruptibility of the flesh and the world. The *hortus conclusus* is an inner paradise of the soul, a foretaste, while we are on earth, of the joys of the heavenly paradise:

> *Haec est paradisus in qua versatur anima, cujus deliciis et amoenitate delectatur. Hanc paradisum in terra possidet, de hac ad coelestem migratura. . . . Hanc paradisum emittit hortus devotae animae, et de hoc horto emittitur ad hortum conclusum supernae civitatis Hierusalem.*
>
> This [city] in which the soul finds itself is a paradise, whose pleasures and charms it delights in. It possesses this paradise while it is on earth, and will migrate from it to the heavenly paradise. . . . The garden of the faithful soul makes this paradise, and from this garden the soul is sent forth to the enclosed garden of the heavenly city of Jerusalem.[5]

Saint Bernard, who in his interpretation of the Song of Songs did not reach the *hortus conclusus* passage, equates paradise and the soul directly, without the intervening image of the *hortus conclusus*—the soul is a spiritual paradise, delightful, full of riches, and secluded from the inferior, earthly world:

> *Habet fidelis anima paradisum suum, spiritualem quidem, non terrenum: et idcirco priori illo delectabiliorem et secretiorem. In hoc delectatur anima, sicut in omnibus divitiis.*
>
> The faithful soul has its own paradise, but this paradise is spiritual, not earthly, and for that reason more delightful and secluded than that earlier paradise. The soul delights in it as the sum of all treasures.[6]

And Hugo of Fouilly supplies us with an extremely detailed allegorization of the cloister as the soul within the body; the columns, the doorways, even the refectory, all are given a spiritual meaning.[7] Honorius Augustodunenis (*Expositio*, cols. 423–24) sums up most of this series of equivalent images as follows: the *hortus conclusus* interpreted *literally* is the garden of Adam and Eve;* *allegorically* it is the Church; *tropologically* it is the virtuous soul; and *anagogically* it is the heavenly paradise.

* It is interesting that the *hortus conclusus* of the Song of Songs was assumed *literally* to be the Garden of Eden, while we would take this identification of the two to be already an allegorization.

Each of these images contains the topographical (and moral) structure we noted in the *alba*: an inside of great value, an outside of inferior value in opposition to the inner world. Let me repeat that I do not intend to add the *alba* to Honorius's list of allegories. The love chamber of the *alba* is not an allegorical representation of the virtuous soul or of the Church. What we *can* say is this: that as the Garden of Eden is to the fallen world, and as the Church is to the society is exists to save, and as the monastery is to the world of the laity, and as the virtuous soul is to the flesh, and as the heavenly paradise is to earthly life, so the inner love chamber of the *alba* is to the world of society and nature—that world that surrounds it, and is inferior to it, and is opposed to it.

We may note even closer analogies between some of these images and what we find in medieval erotic poetry other than the *alba*, especially since this poetry owes so much to the Song of Songs interpreted not as a spiritual allegory but in its literal erotic sense. The Song of Songs does not give us an enclosed chamber, as does the *alba*. It does give us an enclosed garden, however, and this enclosed garden, as a scene for love-making, is in many ways equivalent to the enclosed chamber. A number of the earliest *albas* set the scene not inside a room but in a garden (with certain effects on the meaning of the *alba*, as we shall see later on). But the inner chamber of love itself often has something of a garden about it. In a Latin poem from the eleventh-century *Cambridge Songs*, "Iam, dulcis amica, venito,"[8] which is not an *alba* but which shares with the *alba* the image of the chamber of love, the girl is invited to enter "in cubiculum meum"[9] in order to make love. The inner room of love has been so richly decorated with flowers and fragrant herbs, however, that it closely resembles a garden: it is the *hortus conclusus* brought within doors, so to speak.

The word "paradise" as a metaphor for love-making or the scene of love-making is not unusual in medieval erotic poetry, but I am speaking here of a more concrete use of the metaphor, a use which merges into a literal presentation of the love chamber as the enclosed Garden of Eden. A version of this image which seems to hang perfectly balanced between the literal and the metaphorical is found in a strophe apparently added by a later poet to the *alba* of the late twelfth-century troubadour Giraut de Bornelh (a poem we shall be referring to frequently). A friend of the knight—here taking the role of the watchman—has been calling to him from outside the love chamber, warning him of the imminence of dawn. The knight replies:

> *Bel dolz compan, ben auzi vostre cant,*
> *Molt me pesa ke tu m trabalhas tant,*
> *Car tu me trais del fon del paradis*
> *Mon leit ai fah, combra me flor de lis,*
>   *E ades sera l'alba.*

> Handsome sweet comrade, I have heard your song quite well,
> It vexes me very much that you disturb me so,
> For you are drawing me back from the depth of paradise
> [Where] I have made my bed, [and] lilies are crowded around
>   me,
>   And in a moment it will be dawn.[10]

In this case we evidently have not only a general structural analogy between the *alba* and the *hortus conclusus* or Garden of Eden (the inside-outside structure), but a specific identity of content as well; not only is the relation between inside and outside in the *alba* analogous to the relation between inside and outside in the *hortus conclusus* image, but the inside room of the *alba* is to a certain extent identified with the earthly paradise.[11] Later on we shall consider just what significance identifications of this sort have for the meaning of the *alba*.

Another type of medieval allegory exhibiting the inside-outside structure is the allegorical castle.[12] Occasionally the castle allegory is related to the *hortus conclusus* allegories we have been speaking of, as when the Virgin is allegorized both as a castle and as an enclosed garden, each of these enclosed places bearing the source of all goodness within it, that is, the unborn Christ.[13] (The allegorical reading of the *hortus conclusus* passage in the Song of Songs as referring to the Virgin is extremely common.) But the usual castle allegory is of the soul within the body, surrounded and besieged by the vices. In the *Castrum humani corporis*,[14] for example, the human body is allegorically represented by a castle; the chief palace of the king is the human heart, or "Animus"; the five gates of the castle represent the five senses; and so on. Outside lurk evil and death, against which body and soul must be constantly vigilant. One of the most elaborate of these allegories, quite medieval in spite of its late date, is that of the castle of Alma in Book Two of Spenser's *Faerie Queene*. Canto XI of this book shows us the castle (the body) and its presiding mistress (the soul) being besieged by the seven deadly sins along with other vicious enemies. The outside-versus-inside structure is perfectly analogous to that of the *alba*: the highest values, the noblest creatures, the source of everything that is good and meaningful, within; and, all around, a second world of values, wicked values, opposed to the inner world and actively trying to destroy it.

The allegorical battle of vices and virtues is a literary device that goes back to the *Psychomachia* of Prudentius, but the castle allegory, while presenting a similar sort of battle, changes its meaning by changing its structure. The structure of the *Psychomachia* is that of two armies drawn up for battle in rigid lines, facing each other. There is a simple one-to-one contrast of the good and the bad, which is reiterated in the series of combats, each between a single vice and a single virtue; the same one-to-one structural principle is repeated over and over. The castle allegory, in Spenser and in his medieval predecessors, shows us not good *facing* evil but good *surrounded by* evil. We are given the sense of the good world's being isolated, attempting to protect itself against the evil world by enclosing itself, yet remaining subject to constant danger from all directions. The opposed vices and virtues in Prudentius' poem are more or less equal beings; they are all warrior ladies, of varied attributes but nonetheless of fairly equal stature. The allegorized castle, the individual human body and soul, is a single small focal point of the good; the world of evil which is all about it is enormous. What is emphasized in this kind of allegory is the immensity and enormous force of the hostile evil world as it tries to destroy the small world of true value; and, conversely, the enormous moral triumph of the small world if it manages to maintain itself against such a universe of attackers. It is just this sort of picture that the *alba*, with its virtually identical topography, gives us—although its way of defining the content of the two worlds of value differs radically from what we find in, for example, Spenser.

Another castle allegory by Honorius Augustodunensis imparts—at the price of some confusion—an added subtlety to this structure of thought. Here the castle is the body, as usual; its prince is the soul; its populace is made up of the virtues; and a war is being waged against the vices. But that is not all:

> *Cujusque autem fidelis corpus hujus civitatis castellum praedi-*
> *catur, quod ab anima principe et populo virtutum inhabitatur,*
> *in qua contra exercitum viciorum decertatur. Hoc castellum a*
> *turba hostium exterius obsidetur, a factione civium interius*
> *commovetur, dum proximi exteriora damna ei inferunt, vicia*
> *autem et carnis desideria interiora bona obruunt.*

> And the faithful Christian's body is represented by the castle
> of this town, which is inhabited by its prince, the soul; and
> its populace, the virtues. A battle against the army of vices is
> going on. The castle is besieged from the outside by a crowd
> of enemies, and agitated within by the factionalism of the
> citizens. Its neighbors wreak external damage on the castle,
> and vices and carnal desires overthrow what is good within.[15]

Not only is there a hostile army without, but there is insurrection within the castle itself. The external army, which we would expect to be made up of the vices, is merely a crowd of unspecified enemies, neighbors who harm the external body. (Perhaps these hostile neighbors represent the wear and tear on the body of sickness, accident and old age, but we are not told this.) Within the castle, however, a factious battle is going on among the citizens themselves, who had previously been identified as the virtues. Now it appears that in the midst of the population of virtues the destructive vices and fleshly desires also reside—and all this *inside*, in the place the usual castle allegories reserve for the higher and better world in all its purity.

Of course, the psychological and moral ideas expressed by these two kinds of castle allegory are very much the same. The vices, the sins, are indeed *within* a man. Spenser's allegory shows us the vices attacking from outside the castle, but Spenser does not intend for us to believe that vices are phenomena external to mankind; his allegory is merely a dramatic way of showing us the conflict of vices and virtues within the human heart, the multitude and power of the vices and the staunchness required of the virtues. Honorius expresses the same idea in an allegory which is less figurative, more consonant with the literal reality as it was conceived of in Augustinian Christianity. Nevertheless, the poetic effect of the two allegories is quite different. In one we have a clear division between the two worlds of value: the good world is inside, the evil world is outside. Even if the idea behind the drama is that both worlds are *inside* man, the drama itself, which is what we respond to most immediately, has a different structure and evokes a different kind of response. For the unlearned, an allegory of this sort may well seem to be putting all of the blame for sin on the Devil, an exterior force of evil, and to be slighting the Augustinian idea that man is himself corrupt, that evil need not be forced upon him from without, that it is there inside him already. And even for those who know better, the effect of the structure of the allegory is probably stronger than the meaning it is supposed to convey. The structure itself has a meaning, which in this case is more than a little in conflict with the ideas that lie behind the allegory. Honorius's allegory, in contrast, makes it dramatically plain that the enemies of the soul lie within, that human will, since the Fall of Man, is divided into a good part and a bad part which cannot be separated in the simplistic way of the inside-outside castle allegory. His allegory is therefore dramatically truer, and more subtle in its insight into human psychology.

The structure of the courtly *alba* resembles that of the conventional castle allegory. The two worlds of value are completely separate; the enemies to the all-valuable love are without exception exterior values; the love itself, locked in its inner chamber, is flawless. This structure is simplistic, and the idea of reality it conveys is simplistic. It was two hundred years from the time of the first

Provençal *albas* before an *alba* (Chaucer's, in *Troilus and Criseyde*) admitted the enemy into the chamber of love, and in so doing acquired the deeper and subtler sense of human reality conveyed by this particular castle allegory of Honorius Augustodunensis.

Allegories of the castle show a number of other analogies to the *alba* which we shall refer to in different connections later on. At this point I would like to turn from the castle allegory per se to the social phenomenon its structure and imagery derive from. Bernard's notion of the "paradisus claustralis" and the more extended figure of the soul described as a cloister, both of which we have already spoken of, correspond not only to a moral and theological contrast of inner and outer but also to certain facts of institutional and social history. Particularly during the early Middle Ages, but still to a notable extent in the twelfth and subsequent centuries, monasteries were centers of civilization in the midst of what was usually a wild and often a hostile environment. One thinks of Fulda, surrounded by Germanic barbarians, or the Cistercian monasteries, intentionally built in great tracts of wasteland (which the Cistercians soon turned to productive uses). The inside-outside structure we have noted in Biblical images and Christian allegories was not a figure of speech or a dramatic device, so far as these monasteries were concerned; it was a geographical fact.

Much the same thing is true of actual medieval castles, actual medieval cities. The city was a center of civilized life, of the values of social order and law that made community living possible. This little cluster of civilized usages existed entirely inside the castle or the town—the two were often identical—and it was surrounded by a wall which protected it from the uncivilized anarchy without. Numerous medieval towns that have preserved their original appearance present us strikingly with an idea of what this kind of topography must have meant to the imaginations of medieval men. Inside the walls: the town itself, with its houses, palaces, churches, squares, its architecture giving physical expression to the hierarchical structure of the society it enclosed and to the institutions that provided the organizing principles of medieval civilization. Outside the walls, for miles around, fields and forests, with an occasional peasant

following his oxen (or, nowadays, riding his tractor). This area outside the city walls, now peaceful and productive if still relatively
deserted, was subject in the Middle Ages to pillage and destruction,
to the ravages of enemy knights, to brigandage and barbarism, to all
the antisocial impulses of medieval man that medieval institutions
and medieval cities were organized to curb. That this topographical
structure should have been given a moral meaning and so transferred
to allegories of the soul is perfectly understandable; the castle, its
walls, and the surrounding countryside had a moral meaning to
begin with, although this meaning related to the moral good and
evil of society rather than to the moral good and evil of the individual
Christian. Even when factious ambitions brought the anti-social impulses within the town walls—as was so often the case, especially in
Italy—the ideal conception of the enclosed city as the place where
security and order reigned (or were expected to reign) remained.

It is probably this topography which, idealized and given a useful
mobility, lies behind the topographical structure of many medieval
epics and romances. One of the most frequent structural devices of
medieval narrative is the court or castle, a center of civilization and
its values, surrounded by a wild forest or wasteland full of danger
and ruled by hostile, evil, and uncivilized values.[16] In *Beowulf*, for
example, the mead-hall, Heorot, is pictured as a haven of light and
civilization surrounded by a wilderness full of evil and destructive
forces. This sort of image, evidently an accurate representation of
topographical reality among the Anglo-Saxons, is given an even
more extensive moral meaning in the famous simile in Bede's
Ecclesiastical History of the English Nation (Book Two, Chapter
XIII): the king's mead-hall, with its light, warmth, food, and con-
viviality, is likened to the life of man; the wintery rain, snow, and
darkness outside the hall are likened to the mysteries that lie before
birth and after death.

In Arthurian romance the "epic center" (as it has been called) is
usually represented by the Arthurian court itself, often no longer
tied down to a walled castle but made up rather of portable pavilions
which may be moved at the poet's will and brought to the geographic
center of things in any place that the narrative may require it. Here

the physical buildings themselves—the castle, the town, the walls—
are no longer considered necessary to symbolize the center of civilization, the world of values by which all exterior experience is to be
judged; the court alone, with its personnel and organization, suffices
to convey this symbolical meaning. Wherever the court may be
located, it is the center of the world of chivalry, the focal point of
chivalric values. Around it, outside it, lies the forest, the world of
disordered nature, non-chivalric values, felon knights, dwarfs,
dragons, giants.

Another epic center is the grail castle, in this case an actual
physical castle, placed in the midst of a mysterious wasteland. In
its various literary versions it is the home of a Christian society embodying the fullest moral perfection possible in the world; it is the
scene of the most intense mystical experience known to man, hence
of the greatest level of reality man can rise to in this life; and it carries with it the symbolic associations of all the real castles in real
wastelands, of all the real monasteries where men strive to make
themselves perfect, and perhaps of many of the allegorical representations of castle or cloister as well. All of these associations, along with
the grail castle itself, exhibit the same structure of inside versus outside we have found in the *alba*; though it must be added that the
structure of medieval romance is much less schematic and simplistic
than that of the *alba* or of the usual castle allegory. A romance may
contain two rival epic centers; the forest outside and around the epic
center may be less than wholly bad, offering to the hero, as it often
does, an opportunity for self-discovery and moral development; and
so forth. Nevertheless, although in one case it may be quite simple
and in another quite complex, at bottom we see the same imaginative form, the same structure of thought, working in all of these
varied genres. What is called the epic center in romance might well
be called the "allegorical center" in certain allegories or the "erotic
center" in poems such as the *alba*; in a large sense, all these works
are constructed according to the same pattern.

A good number of these different manifestations of the inside-
outside structure are summed up in the *Roman de la Rose*, which is
perhaps what we would expect in a work so conventional (in the

good sense of this word) and so encyclopedic. To begin with, the entire poem, with the exception of the very beginning, takes place within the enclosed garden of love, a garden of paradisiacal setting pictured as containing all of the highest values of life—at least of a life devoted, in the courtly manner, to love. The garden is clearly a *hortus conclusus*, and also something of a castle, for it is surrounded by a high battlemented wall of the sort appropriate to a medieval castle or town but most unusual for an ordinary garden. The contrast between the two worlds of value, here, does not quite observe the topographical conventions we have noted in other examples of the inside-outside structure, for the land surrounding the garden is not a wasteland or a battleground but a delightful spring landscape. The world of values put into opposition with the interior world of love *is* outside, however; it consists of the paintings of "vices"— vices from the point of view of romantic love—displayed on the outside of the garden wall. The two worlds of value are contrasted in something like the one-to-one pattern of virtues and vices we noted in Prudentius (though of course the structure of the contrast is of the inside-outside sort): for Poverty, painted on the outside, we have Wealth, strolling on the inside; Old Age outside and Youth inside; Avarice outside and Generosity inside; outside, all that is antagonistic to love and destructive of its values; inside, the higher, better world of love.[17]

An identical structure governs the description of the garden of paradise toward the end of the poem.[18] This garden—which is, so to speak, a Christian *contrafactura* or serious parody of the earlier garden of love—like the earlier garden is surrounded with a pictured wall. Pictured on the outside is nothing less than the whole world of nature; this is the whole vast inferior world, which is excluded from the garden within. And the world inside, the world of ultimate value, is the park of Christ, with the carbuncle of the Holy Trinity at its center. The *hortus conclusus*, more often used to represent the Garden of Eden or the earthly paradise (if the two can be distinguished), now serves as image for the heavenly paradise itself. The heavenly paradise is elsewhere in Christian literature figured as a city, the heavenly Jerusalem, following the vision in Revelation xxi.

The city, of course, is surrounded by a great high wall; the blessed dwell within it, and the damned are kept outside forever. Here the two worlds of value are at their most extreme polarity. In Jean de Meun's heavenly *hortus conclusus* and the holy Jerusalem of the Book of Revelation the inside-outside structure of the garden image and the city image thus reaches the height of its imaginative career.

In this connection we should mention an even loftier imaginative height attained by the inside-outside structure, independent of representations of it in garden and city imagery. This high-point occurs —as do so many of the high-points of medieval poetry—in Dante's *Paradiso*. The topographical structure of paradise, as Dante portrays it in all but one passage of the *cantica*, is Aristotelian and Ptolemaic. The earth is at the center, surrounded by a series of concentric spheres, each of which supports one of the planets and is moved by one of the orders of angels. The outmost sphere is the *primum mobile*, outside of which lies the non-spatial, non-temporal presence of God. This scheme is marvelously adapted to Dante's narration, but it runs contrary to the wide-spread medieval attitude toward the moral meaning of insides and outsides. It places the earth, the world of lowest value, at the very center of everything, while God, the highest reality and highest good, is placed at the utmost distance from the center, in an outside which surrounds the whole material universe. Dante must have found this reversal of the traditional roles of inside and outside quite intolerable. In *Paradiso* xxviii he re-establishes the traditional structure by an ingenious device. The Ptolemaic system is shown to be merely a physical model of the universe. The true moral model of the universe, which Dante, in his moral ascent, is now capable of seeing, is Neoplatonic. God is seen as a brilliant point of light, a center, around which the angelic orders circle in concentric orbits. The utmost goodness is now, as is proper, at the center. The orbits, going outwards from the center, represent a progressive descent in participation in the divine goodness. The earth, the place of least value, is not even represented in this vision. It is, presumably, at the greatest possible distance from the center. In other words, it has reassumed its proper moral place as an outside. Inside and outside have regained their proper relationship, according to medieval ways of thinking.

But to return to the *Roman de la Rose* and to the garden of love, which still has something to tell us about the structure we have been investigating and hence about the *alba*: the object of the lover in the *Roman de la Rose* is to win the rose (that is, the lady), whom he succeeds in kissing toward the end of Guillaume de Lorris's section of the poem. But before Guillaume ceased writing he had Jealousy, enraged by the kiss, erect a huge castle in which the rose is immured and made much more inaccessible than before.[19] This castle now constitutes an inside within the inside—the ultimate source of value, walled in inside of a garden which represents the world of love and is itself walled in. The imaginative construct which insists on all good things being on an *inside* is thus redoubled and reinforced. The emphasis is no longer on the two opposed worlds of value, represented as an outside and an inside, but rather on a penetration further and further toward the inside, toward the source and object of the values of the interior world. In the last witty, ecstatic, and pornographic lines of Jean de Meun's completion of the poem,[20] this entire progression toward the ultimate interior becomes an allegory of sexual intercourse. The lover moves further and further into the ivory tower of the now destroyed castle. He penetrates to a place described as a sacred shrine, an image which of course refers to the similar structure of religious buildings—Christian churches, the Biblical temple with its holy of holies in the inmost chamber—which we spoke of earlier. Finally he penetrates into the very center of the rosebud, and having achieved this ultimate depth of experience he awakens.

The fact that the higher world of value in Christian allegories, chivalric romances, and the *alba* lies on the *inside* thus presents an interesting analogy to the structure of the female anatomy, and more particularly to the values attributed to that anatomy by the male mind. And in the *alba*, at least, the analogy is not merely structural, since the interior in the *alba* is explicitly a place of sexual pleasure. According to Freudian theory, a man's sexual desire to penetrate to the inside of a woman (where, as Jean de Meun puts it, the sacred shrine of human experience is to be found) is related genetically to his subconscious memory of the womb. Whatever may be the truth about such a genetic relationship, it can hardly be denied that there is a certain analogical relationship between the two experiences. The experience of the womb, with its darkness, warmth, security, and automatic nourishment, is the first human experience of inside-ness; and the emergence, at birth, into a world of much less comfort must similarly be considered the first human experience of an outside. The contrast of a desired inside and an outside felt as hostile continues in the early stages of infancy, where the inside is the sphere of the mother's emotional and physical presence—the mother as source of all nourishment, protection, and love—and the outside is all the rest of the world, dimly apprehended at the surrounding edges of the interior world.

I want to emphasize once again that I am not saying that in the imaginative life of man the experiences of the womb before birth and of the mother's surrounding and enclosing presence in early infancy are the *origins* of all the other inside-outside structures we have noted. It would take a really excessive faith in psychoanalytical reductionism to believe that the topography of the medieval walled town resulted from unconscious memories of the womb on the part of its architects. What can be said is that all the various experiences we have been speaking of—social, infantile, sexual, religious, and poetic—reinforce each other in the medieval imagination, and that they do so because of their similarity in topographical structure.

Note, for a final example, the *Minnegrotte* or grotto of love in the *Tristan* of Gottfried von Strassburg. This is an interior world representing the highest of human values, love, surrounded by a wild and deserted forest and beyond that by the world of ordinary courtly life, ordinary chivalry, ordinary human attachments, conventional society, morality, and religion. Its setting is very much like a paradise garden; its architecture is like that of a church, and all of its architectural members are given allegorical meanings of the sort conventionally applied to the parts of a church; it is consecrated to a goddess of love; it is the scene of sexual intercourse; it enables the lovers to be nourished on nothing but love, without their having to take any other food. It is explicitly or implicitly analogous to the city, the *hortus conclusus*, paradise, the church building, the love chamber, the womb. It exists in an imaginative universe whose basic moral and metaphysical idea is a duality of worlds, and like so many other expressions of medieval dualism it insists on seeing the two worlds in the form of an inside and an outside.[21]

It might be objected that this kind of inside-outside structure of the imagination is merely a universal human commonplace and has nothing specifically medieval about it. Certainly, the notion of the inwardness of the womb cannot be said to be uniquely a characteristic of medieval thought. Nevertheless, by the nineteenth century we find a pervasive movement in literary thought toward the reversal of the roles of inside and outside. The old structure does not entirely disappear, but it is clearly characteristic of Romantic thought to use insides to symbolize all that is bad, bourgeois, oppressive, and deadly, and outsides to symbolize all that is good, humane, liberating, and alive. The city, once a symbol of order and civilization in the midst of a dangerous barbaric wilderness, is now thought of as a boring or terrifying prison; the wilderness, in the form of the forest or the jungle or the sea, is the medium in which one discovers truth, value, meaning, and oneself;* and the dominant image for the achievement of human desire is not one of enclosure and protection but one of escape.[22] The image of being suffocated in an enclosed room is frequent in psychological descriptions, and it sometimes appears as an actual narrative event.†

As for the enclosed chamber of love that we find in the medieval *alba*, Romantic love poetry does not reject it entirely, of course. Keats's *Eve of Saint Agnes*, for example, is topographically very much like the *alba*, with its warm sensuous inside and its hostile

---

* An idea already found to some extent in medieval romance, although generally without the corollary idea of the evil and oppressive city.

† A modern work in which there is a particularly vivid exploitation of this complex of images is Evgenii Zamyatin's anti-Utopia, *We*. The protective and oppressive totalitarian state is enclosed by a glass wall, a wall the revolutionaries wish to break through in order to reach the wilderness and instinctual freedom outside. The preferred means of torture used by the One State's secret police is, typically, suffocation inside a glass bell.

dangerous outside—a poem, we might note, with an expressly medieval atmosphere.* A cozy, happy sense of being enclosed; a desire to remain within the walls, within the town or castle, within the room, that inner world shaped by lovers' desires; a hatred of the larger, alien world that surrounds and threatens and is not subject to the lovers' wishes—this is the relation of space and love in the *alba*. But the Romantic portrayal of love psychology in terms of space can be quite different. It can show us the feeling of expansion, the sense of having escaped from a limited, hemmed-in world, that is so characteristic of the Romantic idea of love—in literature and in experience as well. What could show a clearer contrast to the topography of the *alba* and the psychology of love symbolized by that topography than the following lines of Goethe, describing a young man in love?

> *Er schaut umher, die Welt gehört ihm an.*
> *Ins Weite zieht ihn unbefangne Hast,*
> *Nichts engt ihn ein, nicht Mauer, nicht Palast . . . .*

> He looks around. The world belongs to him.
> An ingenuous rashness draws him into the distance.
> Nothing hems him in—not walls, not palaces . . . .[23]

---

* Yet even here there are significant variations from the *alba* topography. Madeline's chamber of love, the center of true value, is an inside-within-an-inside. Surrounding it, although still within the castle, is the hostile and dangerous world of society, filled with Porphyro's enemies. Outside of the castle lies the cold and stormy world of nature, poignantly contrasted with the sensual warmth in Madeline's room. Yet, at the end, the lovers flee out into the storm; it is only in the freedom of the outside world that they can preserve the love whose natural habitat is the inmost chamber.

TWO

THE ENEMIES OF LOVE

THE TWO WORLDS of value in the *alba*, the inner world and the outer world, are in conflict. The lovers and their love are beset by exterior enemies, and they themselves are in declared opposition to the forces outside. Who are these exterior enemies, and how do the lovers oppose them?

THE LOVERS VERSUS SOCIETY: THE KNIGHT'S IDENTITY

First of all, the lovers are in opposition to society. This opposition takes two forms, one tacit and passive, the other explicit and active. For the first, we should notice that within the context of the poem the knight's social function is virtually ignored. According

to the values of chivalry, a knight has certain social duties to perform, of which the main one is fighting. He fights for his honor, or
for that of his lord, or to protect the helpless, or merely to demon-
strate his prowess at arms. The *alba* makes a slight obeisance to this
notion of the knight's prowess, but only by means of perfunctory,
conventional epithets. He is often referred to specifically as being of
the knightly class—he is called "ritter" or "chevaliers"—but this
name serves not so much to define his role in society as to enable
the courtly audience to identify him as one of their own.[1] The conventional epithets commonly applied to him in the German examples
of the genre—"hôhgemuot," "guot," "wolgemuot," "gemeit"—
tell us mainly that he has the nobility and vitality of spirit to enable
him to do knightly deeds, but the deeds themselves are not mentioned. Only one of the commonly used epithets has a really strong
suggestion of knightly prowess: this is "küene" ("bold").[2] But so
far as the actual events of the poem are concerned, the knight's high
spirits and even his boldness might be interpreted as referring to his
deeds of love alone. (In one of his *albas*, Wolfram von Eschenbach
comically uses the heroic word "ellen" ["boldness in battle"] in
speaking of the knight's love-making.) From what we see of the
knight, he is mainly a lover and only vaguely and peripherally a
social being with a social function. He comes in from the outside,
where he has presumably been leading the more or less heroic life
of a knight in chivalric society. In the morning he must reluctantly
go back outside to that world and its responsibilities. But what
counts, so far as the *alba* and its audience are concerned, is not his
social existence outside, but his life as a lover inside. Heroism, skill
and strength in the use of arms, social responsibilities—these are not
condemned by the *alba*, not actively opposed, but they are tacitly
relegated to the outside world, the world of inferior values and inferior experiences. The ideal picture of itself the courtly class must
have seen and relished in the *alba* is a picture of courtly man finding
his reality, his being, his identity, entirely in his participation in a
love relationship with a woman. The idea, all-embracing in the
heroic epic and forming a prominent part of the ethos of much
courtly romance, that a knight must find his identity in heroic

social action, is simply ignored in the *alba*—and so, by inference, contradicted.

THE LOVERS VERSUS SOCIETY: ADULTERY

But the opposition of the lovers to society takes a much more active and specific form than this. The *alba* is the only form of troubadour lyric (and of its German equivalent, *Minnesang*) that consistently represents the love affair as adulterous. The husband, representative of the society whose social bonds are being infringed upon, is frequently mentioned—of the eight fully developed erotic *albas* in Provençal, for example, five mention the husband, the *gilos* —and where he is not specifically named, his existence is implied by the very plot of the *alba*. Why must the knight leave in the morning, if not for fear that the husband will return and discover his wife's infidelity? Adultery is of the very essence of the *alba*, and to understand the moral meaning of the poem we must look closely into this in many ways problematic fact.

From the lady's point of view, her husband and her lover represent two different kinds of relationship, and these two kinds of relationship are in painful conflict. The relationship to the husband is one made legitimate by society and the Church; the relationship to the lover is justified by the free choice of love. The relationship to the husband belongs to a world of objective, universally approved values; the relationship to the lover belongs to a world of values dependent on the subjective, unique emotional life of the individual. Nor is there any doubt in the *alba* as to which of these relationships, which of these worlds, takes precedence.

A similar kind of conflict and a similar kind of solution are to be found in one of the commonplaces of Christian thought. One of the prime messages of Christian writings, from the Gospels on, is that Christ, God, is the source of true value; that a man's relationship to God may be in conflict with his relationship to other men, to his family, even to his closest blood relations; but that the relationship to God must take precedence over all others, that one must leave one's family and follow Christ. Love for God cancels the obligations of all lesser relationships that might interfere with it.[3] Similarly, in the love poetry of the troubadours and their followers the love for the lady, who is considered the source of all true value, overrides all social, and hence inferior, relationships: the lover's relationship to the husband (in the Lancelot romances the lover's feudal overlord, in the Tristan romances his uncle); the lady's relationship to the husband; indeed, all relationships other than the erotic relationship between the lover and the lady.

The fact that the love in the *alba* is adulterous thus tends to reinforce the notion of two worlds of value, a superior and an inferior one, which we saw symbolized in the topographical structure of the poem. Leo Spitzer offers the following reason for the adulterous element of the Provençal *chanson*: the lady is thought of as married because that makes the consummation of the love that much the more impossible; it guarantees the love's ideal and chaste quality.[4] Whatever the truth of this in regard to the *chanson*, it is clearly not true for the *alba*. On the contrary, it might be said that the reason for the element of adultery in the *alba* is that the consummation of an adulterous love is that much the more in opposition to Christian morality and medieval social conventions, and thus the love is that much the more separated from all other value systems: it is made to constitute a value system in itself. The stronger the opposition to the love, and the more sources of opposition there are, the more powerful the love must seem if it dares to defy such enemies. Adultery is the perfect device to set up such an opposition—it opposes both society and the Christian sacrament of marriage that serves as one of the strongest binding forces of that society. A love that sets itself up against two such institutions achieves, by that very act, an exalted status that a legitimate love leading to marriage could scarcely attain. Furthermore, in its willful disobedience of social and religious law, adulterous love states or implies as its rationale and justification that it has its own society and its own religion and its own laws, all of which it holds superior to any other. Adultery, in a patriarchal, socially conservative, and Christian society, polarizes the world into two systems of values, two mighty competitors; it is a way of making the love affair of a man and a woman into an independent world of value, a competitor of that other, established world.

This is the literary effect of adulterous love, and it applies not only to the *alba* but also to almost all major literary love-affairs from the twelfth century on. When the love is not adulterous, as in *Romeo and Juliet*, the result is a considerable diminution of the anti-social, anti-Christian element—of the element of the forbidden. No matter how much the lovers may oppose and be opposed by churlish fathers, there is much less of a sense of their love as an attack on all established values of society and morality. The lovers in literary works of this sort tend to be seen no longer as heroic rebels or schismatics, as Prometheuses or Mohammeds of love in opposition to great gods, but rather as pathetic victims of petty social prejudices.

The fact that the love in the *alba* is adulterous adds another element that contributes to the emotional effect of the poem: the element of danger. If the knight were to ignore the watchman's warnings and remain with the lady after daybreak, if the husband were to return and discover them together, the result would not be merely a painful and embarrassing altercation. The knight may very well be risking his life for the sake of a night with his beloved. The danger is always implied, and sometimes explicitly stated:

> *Ein ritter der hat sînen lîp*
> *gewâget durch ein schoene wîp*
> *bî der er slief vil tougen.*

> A knight risked his life
> on account of a beautiful lady
> next to whom he slept in great secrecy.[5]

Danger to the hero's life is a frequent element in fictions of all sorts. It is this element that makes stories "thrilling," and it is universally relished. Why audiences should enjoy the vicarious experience of danger that is given them by so many literary works is a problem closely related to the problem of why audiences enjoy tragedies, and both problems require a much more extensive discussion than would be appropriate here. What concerns us in the *alba* is the close association of danger—potentially mortal danger—with sexual enjoyment. This is quite different from the mortal risks heroes are accustomed to take in order to save a defenseless woman from an attacker: the Perseus archetype which recurs so frequently in medieval and Renaissance romance. Here the hero risks death not in order to save the woman's life, but in order to enjoy a night of intimacy with her. The joys of love are at the same time dangerous risks, and it is this union of the two contrary experiences in the same situation that give the *alba*—along with many other narratives of adulterous love—its particular emotional quality, its particular excitement. A picture of idyllic love in a situation of total security would not provide the same experience at all.

Furthermore, we must note that the hostility of the *gilos*, which is expressed by the sense of danger the lovers are forced to submit to, is matched by an equal, though usually tacit, hostility toward the *gilos* on the part of the lovers. The *alba* of the Provençal poet Cadenet makes the hostility toward the husband explicit. The lady, like the *mal mariée* of numerous trouvère poems, relates how she has been given to a "vilan" because of his wealth, and she vows:

> *Ja per guap ni per menassa*
> *que mos mals maritz me fassa,*
> *no mudarai qu'ieu non jassa*
> *ab mon amic tro al dia.* . . .

> Not for any jibe or threat
> that my wicked husband may offer me
> will I refrain from lying
> with my lover till daylight. . . .[6]

Even when the hostility toward the husband is not so outspoken, it is there in the adulterous act itself, which is not only an act of love between the lovers but at the same time an act of aggression against the husband's prerogatives and ultimately against his masculinity. Frequently the lovers vent their hostility against the watchman or the sun; sometimes against the *gilos* himself; and always, by implication, in the fact that the *gilos* is being cuckolded; but the element of hostility on the part of the lovers is always there, closely tied up with their mutual love.

We may say, then, that the fact that love in the *alba* is adulterous offers an audience the vicarious experience of three kinds of strong emotion: love, fear, and hate. The tying together of the three emotions in one fictional experience, moreover, gives an added acuteness to each of them. The love is more exciting because of the fear that attends it; the fear of the husband's potentially aggressive actions is more acute because it is so closely associated with the lovers' own aggressive action toward him; and the lovers' hostility toward the husband and toward the representatives of the husband's world is more violent because the husband and his world are interfering with so intense an experience as sexual love.

I have spoken of three kinds of emotion as being involved in the experience of the adulterous love in the *alba*, but in a larger sense there are only two. On the one side we have love, on the other side hate, hostility, aggression, whether coming *from* the lovers or directed *at* them. And these two contrary emotions, which between them cover all the most intense experiences of life and of literature —which, indeed, according to Freud's instinct theory account for the entire life of the emotions—are neatly divided, in the *alba*, into the two moral worlds of inside and outside. The inside world, dominated by the lady, is the world of love, the emotion that seeks for unity and an increase in being; the outside world of society, symbolized by the husband, is the world of hate, the emotion that seeks for separation and destruction.

It is hard not to see in all this an analogy to that constellation of infantile feelings Freud saw as itself analogous to the legend of Oedipus. The emphasis on the fact that the beloved woman is married; the element of fear and danger, along with the suggestion that the knight is weaker than the husband (the knight, after all, does not stay to fight it out with his enemy); the division into two worlds of feeling, one associated with a beloved woman, the other with a hated man who is her husband; even the very emphasis on divisions into *two* that is found at all levels of meaning and structure in the *alba*—all might be seen as analogues to the archetypal family situation as it is emotionally experienced by the child. Or perhaps it would be better to say: to a simplified, schematized version of the Oedipal situation, which ignores any element of hostility in the attitude toward the mother and any element of love in the attitude toward the father.*

These analogies are more or less obvious. But it would be critically false and historically suspect to say that the child's Oedipal feelings are the origin and total explanation of the structure of the *alba* and of the reactions of medieval audiences to it. Even if we were to accept the notion of infantile experiences as the origin of all later productions of the imagination, we do not really know enough about the actual family relationships among mother, father, and child in feudal and courtly society to establish a genetic connection between those relationships and the relationships shown us in the *alba*.[7] But that the *alba* situation is, in its large outlines, *analogous* to the Oedipal situation scarcely seems to admit of doubt. And in assessing the function and meaning of adultery in the *alba* we cannot ignore this psychological analogy and the imaginative resonances it suggests, although we should be careful to perceive such resonances as possibilities rather than as facts.

The problem as to whether adultery in medieval poetry is to be taken as anything more than an imaginative construct—that is, whether it actually constitutes a moral code, a program for action, or even the ritual of an anti-Christian religion—will be taken up at a later point. At the moment our concern is with the *alba* as a work of the imagination, and with its values as fictional values in a fictional setting. We must, however, mention a medieval critique of the adulterous element in the *alba*, a critique that may at first sight appear to be treating this poetic genre as just such a moral code or program for action. The critique is contained in the so-called

---

* See Maurice Valency, *In Praise of Love: An Introduction to the Love-Poetry of the Renaissance* (New York, 1958), especially pp. 59–85. Pages 84–85 suggest, in addition to the psychological analogies I have been speaking of, that the adulterous relationship in troubadour poetry represents an imaginative projection of the actual authority relationships in society during the period of declining feudalism. This sociopsychological approach, it may be mentioned, also offers considerable insight into the meaning of adultery in the bourgeois novel.

"anti-*Tagelied*" of Wolfram von Eschenbach, a poem which seems to be offering its audience real moral advice on the conduct of their love-affairs; more precisely, it seems to be advocating *marriage* as a happier way of life than that of the adulterous lovers in the *alba*.

> *Der helden minne ir klage*
> *du sunge ie gen dem tage,*
> *daz sûre nâch dem süezen,*
> *swer minne und wîplich grüezen*
> *alsô enpfienc,*
> *daz si sich muosen scheiden:*
> *swaz du dô riete in beiden,*
> *dô ûf gienc*
> *der morgensterne, wahtaer, swîc,*
> *dâ von niht langer sienc.*

> *Swer pfligt odr ie gepflac*
> *daz er bî liebe lac*
> *den merkern unverborgen,*
> *der darf niht durch den morgen*
> *dannen streben,*
> *er mac des tages erbeiten:*
> *man darf in niht ûz leiten*
> *ûf sîn leben.*
> *ein offen süeze wirtes wîp*
> *kan solhe minne geben.*

Of the lament of knights' love
you always sang toward day-break,
the bitter after the sweet.
Everyone who has received
love and a woman's greeting in such circumstances
that they had to part from each other—
everything that you counseled them then,
when the morning star
arose: watchman, be silent!
Sing no more of that!

Anyone who has or has had the experience
of lying with his beloved
without being concealed from spies,
he need not, on account of the morning,
struggle to get away from there;
he can stay there awaiting the day;
he need not be guided out for his life's sake.
An avowed, sweet, married wife
can give such love as this.[8]

This poem may very well express an actual opinion of Wolfram's
as to the relative merits of adultery and married life. Both of Wolfram's major narrative poems, *Parzival* and *Willehalm*, show marriage in a very positive light and at the same time virtually ignore
adultery. All the love affairs in *Parzival* culminate in a socially
approved marriage; indeed, the final books of the poem present us
with a veritable flood of weddings.[9] On the other hand, Wolfram
wrote four *albas*—among the very best of all the genre—that treat
adulterous love in such a way as to exalt it to one of the pinnacles
of human experience. Taking all of these poems (the narratives and
the lyrics) as serious expressions of Wolfram's philosophy of love,
many Wolfram scholars have been concerned with reconciling them by
arranging them in an order that will show a chronological change and
progression in Wolfram's point of view.[10] The general idea has been to
show that the adulterous *Tagelieder* come earliest in Wolfram's production; that the present poem represents his farewell to adulterous
love; and that the epics show us his final opinions on marriage and
adultery. (*Willehalm*, which is incomplete, may have been broken
off at the poet's death, sometime in the 1220s.) Since there is no
unassailable external evidence for such a chronology, however, it
can only be based on various hypotheses about the development of
Wolfram's opinions. Aside from this speculative approach, we have
no reliable way of determining at what point in Wolfram's career
he wrote his adulterous *albas* or "anti-*Tagelied*," or what biographical significance these poems may have had, if any; so far as their
style goes, they could all have been written at the very end of his life.

I should like to approach the poem "Der helden minne ir klage" from a somewhat different point of view. Whatever this poem may or may not tell us about Wolfram's attitude toward adultery and marriage as they actually exist in society, it indisputably tells us what Wolfram saw to be the literary effect of adultery or marriage on the structure of the *alba*. Without excluding other interpretations we may certainly consider this poem as a piece of literary criticism, germane to what we have been saying about the function of adultery in the *alba*. When Wolfram, addressing the watchman, speaks of the love lament that the watchman has *always* sung toward daybreak— "du sunge *ie* gen dem tage"—he is thinking of the *alba* as a fixed, established poetic form, supposed to be sung in its entirety by the watchman himself. (The notion that the *alba*, in its fully developed form, is a song sung by the watchman is a fiction that becomes conventional in the thirteenth century and afterward.) Wolfram realizes, in his capacity as literary critic, that the whole drama of the *alba* is based on the element of adultery. All the characteristics of the genre —secrecy, fear of the light, danger, the need to part, the sorrow of the lovers at parting, the role of the watchman himself—depend on the fact that the love is adulterous. If adultery is eliminated, Wolfram notes, all of these characteristics disappear. Secretiveness is no longer necessary: the lover may lie abed, "den merkern unverborgen." He need no longer fear, or be at all affected by, the arrival of daylight: "der darf niht durch den morgen / dannen streben." There is no longer any danger: "man darf in niht ûz leiten / ûf sîn leben." Above all, there is no longer any need for the lovers to part: "er mac des tages erbeiten." The parting motif, which provides the basic movement of the *alba*, is thus eliminated; and the whole genre collapses. When Wolfram orders the watchman to be silent he is noting that, on the dramatic level, the fact that the knight is married to the lady makes the watchman's warnings superfluous. But what the watchman has sung is not only the words of warning to the knight at daybreak but also the whole *alba*, the whole literary form. Thus, Wolfram is also saying, in effect, that with the element of adultery eliminated from the *alba* the *alba* itself must disappear. The command "swîc" thus means both "no more warnings!" and "no more *albas*!"

The elimination of adultery at the same time eliminates the *alba* because the basic dramatic movement of the *alba* demands a change from a state of unity and happiness to a state of separation and grief. The movement of the *alba* is, precisely, "daz sûre nâch dem süezen" —the bitter after the sweet. This is, seen in its basic structure, the movement of tragedy; and the *alba* does in fact present us with a potentially tragic situation. But married love carries with it exactly the opposite dramatic movement. Marriage is the classical ending to a comedy. It is a movement of unification, unification of the lovers with each other and unification of their desires with those of society. The love relationship is brought into perfect harmony with the society that sanctions it and legitimizes it. That is why married love eliminates the *merker*, the spies, who play such a large role in the love poetry of the troubadours and *Minnesänger*. These spies, representatives of a society hostile to the lovers, show by their very existence the division of the world into two antagonistic camps: on one side the lovers, on the other all the rest of society. In comedy, of the sort suggested by Wolfram's "anti-*Tagelied*," the duality of worlds is resolved into one harmonious world, and the conflict that could have led to a tragic movement disappears in the general marriage feast. And for the reasons we have indicated above, following Wolfram's critique of the *alba*, adultery can never lead to this kind of comic literary resolution. Only "ein offen süeze wirtes wîp" can give such an ending as this.

THE LOVERS VERSUS NATURE: CONTRASTS OF FEELING AND PERCEPTION

In addition to the conflict we have been speaking of between the lovers and society, there exists a deep disharmony in the *alba* between the inner world of love and the outer world of nature. Wolfram, who more than any other writer of *albas* seems to have been aware of the numerous ethical and metaphysical meanings of the genre, gives us an explicit statement of this disharmony:

> *Den morgenblic bî wahters sange erkôs*
> *ein frouwe, dâ si tougen*

an ir werden friundes arme lac;
dâ von si hôher fröiden vil verlôs.
des muosen liehtiu ougen
aver nazzen. si sprach "owê tac,
wilde und zam daz fröit sich dîn
und siht dich gerne wan ich eine."

At the song of a watchman, a lady perceived
the light of dawn, where she secretly
was lying in her worthy lover's arms;
therefore she was deprived of much intense joy.
Because of this, bright eyes
once again had to become moist. She spoke: "Alas, day,
wild and tame creatures rejoice in you
and are glad to see you, except for me alone."[11]

All of nature rejoices in the coming of the dawn, but the human being in love has feelings opposite to those of all the rest of nature.

This contrast of the feelings of the lover with those of lesser creatures, or of the tone of the lover's feelings with the tone of surrounding nature, is common in literary representations of love. Vergil shows us Dido on the night of Aeneas's departure raging and lamenting in the grief of her spurned love, while all the rest of nature sleeps, silent and peaceful:

Nox erat, et placidum carpebant fessa soporem
corpora per terras, silvaeque et saeva quierant
aequora, cum medio volvuntur sidera lapsu,
cum tacet omnis ager, pecudes pictaeque volucres,
quaeque lacus late liquidos, quaeque aspera dumis
rura tenent, somno positae sub nocte silenti,
lenibant curas et corda oblita laborum.
At non infelix animi Phoenissa, neque umquam
solvitur in somnos, oculisve aut pectore noctem
accipit; ingeminant curae, rursusque resurgens
saevit amor, magnoque irarum fluctuat aestu.

Night: and tired creatures over all the world
Were seeking slumber; the woods and the wild waters
Were quiet, and the silent stars were wheeling
Their course half over; every field was still;
The beasts of the field, the brightly colored birds,
Dwellers in lake and pool, in thorn and thicket,
Slept through the tranquil night, their sorrows over,
Their troubles soothed. But no such blessed darkness
Closes the eyes of Dido; no repose
Comes to her anxious heart. Her pangs redouble,
Her love swells up, surging, a great tide rising
Of wrath and doubt and passion.[12]

The "at" ("but") in the eighth line of the Latin passage and the
"wan" ("except") in the last line of the passage from Wolfram both
serve to separate the emotional world of the grieving heroine from
the contrasting natural world around it. The actual contrast in each
of the two poems is different: in one we have the heroine's grief
contrasted with the joy of nature at dawn, in the other the heroine's
passion contrasted with the peacefulness of nature at night. But the
structure of the contrast is the same.

Medieval lyric gives us numerous examples of this kind of contrast. One of the most poignant is the following lament of a girl in
springtime:

> *Levis exsurgit zephirus,*
> *et sol procedit tepidus,*
> *iam terra sinus aperit,*
> *dulcore suo diffluit.*
>
> *ver purpuratum exiit,*
> *ornatus suos induit,*
> *aspergit terram floribus,*
> *ligna silvarum frondibus.*
>
> *struunt lustra quadrupedes*
> *et dulces nidos volucres,*

inter ligna florentia
sua decantant gaudia.

quod oculis dum video
et auribus dum audio,
heü pro tantis gaudiis
tantis inflor suspiriis.

cum mihi sola sedeo
et hec revolvens palleo,
si forte caput sublevo,
nec audio nec video.

tu saltim, veris gratia,
exaudi et considera
frondes, flores et gramina,
nam mea languet anima.

The west wind rises lightly,
and the warm sun moves along;
already the earth is baring its bosom
and abandoning itself to its sweetness.

Clad in purple, the spring goes forth
puts on its splendid clothing,
sprinkles the earth with flowers
and the forest trees with leaves.

Four-footed beasts build their dens
and the sweet birds their nests;
among the flowering trees
they sing songs of joy.

When I look at this with my eyes
and listen to it with my ears,
alas! in place of so many joys
I am taken hold of by many sighs.

When I sit all alone
and turn pale as I think of these things,

if by chance I lift my head
I neither hear nor see.

Do you, at least, for the sake of the spring,
hear and observe
the leaves, the flowers and the grass;
for my soul languishes.[13]

Here the contrast is between the vivid life of nature in spring, seen mainly in terms of sexuality, and the solitude, the sadness, and presumably the sexual deprivation of the girl. The earth, with a strong suggestion of personification as a sexually excited woman, bares her bosom and abandons herself to her own sweetness, while the girl merely sits. Animals and birds prepare dens and nests to house the results of their vernal sexual activity; the girl, cut off from motherhood and the community of family life, is all alone. Spring, clad in royal purple, sows the earth with life-giving moisture; the girl remains pale, lost in her unsatisfactory internal life. In the outer world of nature the inspiring, revivifying breeze rises; in the inner world of human emotion the only inspiration is one of sighs. And the internal sorrow is so great that it succeeds in blocking out the sights and sounds of spring altogether. The disharmony between the world of the emotions and the world of nature could not be shown more acutely.

Walter of Châtillon, in a different treatment of this disharmony, contrasts the cold of winter and the fiery heat of love:

Inportuna Veneri
redit brume glacies,
redit equo celeri
Iovis intemperies.
cicatrici veteri
squalet mea facies:
amor est in pectore
nullo frigens frigore.
Jam cutis contrahitur,
dum flammis exerceor. . . .

Troublesome to love-making,
the ice of winter returns.
Jupiter's bad weather
returns on a swift horse.
With an old scar
my face is rough.
Love is in my breast
And no frost can make it cold.
My skin is already shrivelled,
While I am tormented by flames. . . .[14]

The ice of winter presumably cools the sexual ardor of animals, those whose emotional life is governed entirely by the external world of nature. But the lover's emotions are independent of external nature, even though his body is subject to it. The outer skin may shrivel with the cold, but within, the flame of love rages.

The poem of Bernart de Ventadorn, "Tant ai mo cor ple de joya," shares motifs with both of the foregoing. As in Walter's poem, it is an external winter with which the lover's feelings are contrasted. As in the "Verna feminae suspiria," the lover's emotions are so strong that they overpower external nature. But in Bernart's poem, the emotion felt is the *joy* of love, which contrasts with the harshness of winter; and while the sorrow of the girl in the *Cambridge Songs* blinded her to the joys of spring, here the lover's joys so affect his perceptions that the winter seems a spring to him.

> *Tant ai mo cor ple de joya,*
> *tot me desnatura.*
> *flor blancha, vermelh' e groya*
> *me par la frejura,*
> *c'ab lo ven et ab la ploya*
> *me creis l'aventura,*
> *per que mos pretz mont' e poya*
> *e mos chans melhura.*
> *tan ai al cor d'amor,*
> *de joi e de doussor,*

per que·l gels me sembla flor
    e la neus verdura.

My heart is so full of joy
    that everything loses its natural qualities for me.
The frost seems to me
    white, red, and yellow flowers.
For with the wind and the rain
    my good luck grows,
so that my repute rises and climbs
    and my songs grow better.
 I have so much love in my heart,
    so much joy and sweetness,
that the ice seems like flowers to me
    and the snow like greenery.[15]

The power the lover's emotions have to transform his perceptions of nature is summarized in the word "desnatura."[16] But there is no question of transforming nature itself. The lover's perceptions are part of himself, subject to his feelings; the winter, not as it appears but as it *is*, is external and intractable. Thus, the various paradoxes in these lines—frost as flowers, snow as greenery, wind and rain accompanying good luck—serve not to indicate a magical unity between the lover and a natural world controlled by him, but, on the contrary, to reinforce the sense of disharmony between what he feels and sees and what is really there.[17] As in the *alba*, the contrast is between an inner, psychological experience (love and its desires) and an outer natural reality.

Numerous other medieval examples of this disjunction could be given. It occurs every time a joyous *Natureingang*—the conventional description of nature that medieval love lyrics so frequently open with—is followed by the lamentations of a suffering lover. For example, of the six songs by the twelfth-century Provençal master, Jaufré Rudel, five begin with a *Natureingang*; four of the five show us the lover in grief and longing while the natural world of spring or summer is rejoicing; and the other, which shows us the lover in a happy state, begins by telling us that his favorite season is winter.

Grieving while nature sleeps, burning while nature is cold, happy while nature is sad, sad while nature is happy—these lovers are always out of tune with the natural world around them. The same disjunction, although not confined to lovers, can be found in later poetry and narrative as well. In later examples, however, the complexities implicit in the disjunction of mind and nature, but generally ignored by medieval poets, often replace the simplified division into two worlds most medieval love poetry was satisfied with. We need only think, for example, of Coleridge's "Dejection: An Ode," or the opening of T. S. Eliot's *The Waste Land*.

The notion that nature and the lover are in disharmony, of course, is not the only way of representing the relationship between the two. There is a strong literary tradition which shows us nature and the lover as sharing the same mood, or, as it is often suggested, nature reflecting the feelings of the lover. When the lover is melancholy, the landscape is melancholy; if he is joyous, it is spring; if nature rejoices in the coming of the dawn, so does the lover. These two kinds of relationship between the lover and nature—the one in which they are alike and the other in which they are contrasted—create distinctly different poetic effects and imply different views of reality. When the relationship is one of likeness, we are given—with varying emphases—a sense of the unity of all created things; humanization and spiritualization of nature; a harmonization of man with nature so that he is seen as himself a natural creature, not radically different from other creatures or even from inanimate things; a general emotionalizing of everything, so that all reality seems to be a result, fundamentally, of feelings; and, as a consequence of all the above, a blurring of the demarcation between the interior, psychological world and the exterior world of natural phenomena. It is this that we find to a certain extent in Petrarch and his followers and, more fully developed, in Romanticism: one thinks of Musset, Wordsworth, Shelley, Lermontov, the early Goethe—among a host of others.

But where the relationship between the lover and nature is one of disjunction and disharmony, where the relationship, in short, is an ironic one, the effect is to set the lover apart from nature, and, at least in medieval love poems, to set him above nature. The lover's feelings, whether they are of joy or grief, are superior to whatever feelings are imputed to singing birds, lowing beasts, or the personified earth herself. The lover's judgments as to whether the dawn is good or bad, and as to whether frost is really frost or flowers, may not correspond to the opinions of all the other creatures in the world or to objective natural reality, but it is the judgments of the lover that *count*. He, after all, is human; and the human is superior to the inhuman; and the most human of human beings, according to the conception of man we see in medieval love poetry, is the man in love.

THE LOVERS VERSUS NATURE: THE SYMBOLISM OF NIGHT, DAY, DAWN, AND THE SUN

In this discussion of the disharmony between the lovers and nature we have so far spoken only of contrasts of feeling or perception. The disharmony in the *alba* goes deeper than that. Nature is not merely a different world of feelings, a world of lower creatures who cannot understand or share the lovers' higher feelings. It is also felt as an antagonistic force of great strength, opposed to the lovers and trying to destroy their union. Nature and the lovers are not merely contrasted in respect of their values and their kinds of reality; they are in active, bitter conflict. And the focus of this conflict is that indispensable element of the *alba*, the dawn.

The dawn—or, more properly, the sun—in the *alba* carries with it a number of functions and associations. It is, first of all, a great natural force. We have spoken of the two worlds of value in the *alba* and of their topographical separation into an inside and an outside: an inside world of love, and an outside world which for the present discussion we will speak of as the world of nature. These two worlds are separated by a wall, the wall of the castle. The outside world of values, symbolized by the sunlight, tries to break through that wall and penetrate into the inner world to which it is opposed. This penetration is felt as an act of spying or of violence: a peering through or bursting through of the wall barrier, generally by means of a window or window-like opening. In Chaucer's *Troilus*, to give a vivid example, the sun breaks in through the chinks in the wall:

> "*O cruel day, accusour of the joie*
> *That nyght and love han stole and faste iwryen,*
> *Acorsed be thi comying into Troye,*
> *For every bore hath oon of thi bryghte yën!*"[18]

In Wolfram von Eschenbach's "Sîne klâwen" (a poem I shall analyze in detail later on) the day is represented as peering through the window:

> *Von den blicken,   die der tac tet durh diu glas,*
> *und dô der wahtaer warnen sanc,*
> *si muose erschricken   durch den der dâ bî ir was.*

> Because of the glances   that the day was sending
> through the window-panes,
> and when the watchman sang his warning,
> she was forced to become alarmed   on account of him
> who was there beside her.[19]

But the somewhat gentle-sounding act of peering through the window-panes takes on greater force from its association with the more violent opening lines of the poem:

> *Sîne klâwen   durh die wolken sint geslagen,*
> *er stiget ûf mit grôzer kraft,*
> *ich sihe in grâwen   tägelîch als er wil tagen,*
> *den tac . . . .*

> His talons   have struck through the clouds,
> he climbs upward with great power,
> I see him becoming gray,   dawn-like, as if he will dawn,
> the day . . . .[20]

These mysterious and magnificent lines, one of the very few passages in any medieval vernacular before Dante that make one think of the splendor of ancient Greek poetry (Aeschylus especially), emphasize the great, violent power of the dawn and of the act of *breaking through*—although here it is the clouds, rather than a window, that the dawn is penetrating. The (for medieval poetry) quite astonishing metaphor strengthens the sense of the dawn as a great power of nature. This metaphor has been interpreted as identifying the dawn with a demon,[21] but I think it more likely that the reference is to an eagle. The eagle in the bestiaries is always spoken of in terms of his power, his lofty flight, and his various associations with the sun:

> *Therover he flegeth and up he teth*
> *Til that he the hevene seth,*
> *Thurh skies sexe and sevene,*
> *Til he cumeth to hevene.*
> *So rigt so he cunne*
> *He hoveth in the sunne;*
> *The sunne switheth al his fligt,*
> *And oc it maketh his egen brigt. . . .*[22]

> It is claimed that an eagle presents his young to the sun-beams, and holds the children up to them in middle air with his talon. And if one of them, when stricken with the sun's light, uses a fearless gaze of his eyes, with an uninjured power of staring at it, that one is made much of, because it has proved the truth of its nature.[23]

From the notion of the eagle mounting aloft to gaze on the sun with naked eye Wolfram has proceeded to a metaphorical identification of the eagle with the rising sun itself. The eagle's ferocity and his conventional associations with royalty are poetically transferred to the impression Wolfram wishes to give us of the dawn.[24] All of these images and associations then echo, however lightly, in the later passage of Wolfram's poem that describes the sun's sending its glances through the window.

In another of Wolfram's *albas*, this image of the daylight breaking in through the windows by force is presented more directly:

Der tac mit kraft al durch diu venster dranc.
vil slôze si besluzzen:
daz half niht: des wart in sorge kunt.

The day thrust powerfully through the windows.
Many locks they locked;
it did not help; because of this, care became known to them.[25]

Windows in literature are often symbols of the connectedness of two
different worlds. A window is a means by which those in one world
can obtain knowledge of the other world—by looking out through
the glass. The nineteenth century, especially, makes considerable
use of window symbolism (as it does of the symbolism of those in-
troverted windows, mirrors), often with ironic effect. In Wolfram's
poem, the window is the means by which the destructive power of
the outer world penetrates into the inside. The wall that separates
the two worlds cannot be completely solid; it *must* have a window
in it, because the two worlds cannot be totally separated. The inner
world of love, however much it may seek to be secluded, contained,
protected, remains a part of the larger world of society and nature.
The larger world cannot be locked out, no matter how hard the
lovers try. Furthermore, the sunlight results in the knight's having
to leave the inner world and go out into the outer world. The penetration of the dawn through the window thus causes a further break-
down of the barrier between the two worlds. The outside world
moves in; the inside world moves out.

The same kind of connectedness between the two opposed worlds,
with a window or door as the means of connection, is frequently
found in the castle allegories we spoke of earlier. The vices outside are
trying to penetrate within—that is, the world of evil impulses is trying to encroach upon the world of virtuous impulses. In *Piers Plowman*
(B text, Passus XX; C text, Passus XXIII), for example, Conscience
has retired into the castle of Unity-Holychurch to defend himself
against Antichrist; but the defenses of the castle seem virtually
overthrown when the friars—to Langland the worst corrupters of
the Church on account of their corruption of the sacrament of
penance—manage to wheedle their way in through the gate. Evil

forces who ought resolutely to be kept outside the community of faithful Christians, they penetrate into the inner world and seem on the point of bringing about its downfall. Another example: in the *Castrum humani corporis*, of which we have already spoken, the five gates of the castle—that is, the five senses of the body—"must be shut whenever there is danger that evil may enter." The body is open to the destructive moral forces of the world: "Death enters by the windows."[26] Much the same allegory, although perhaps a bit more graphic, is to be found in a sermon on the Abbey of the Holy Spirit, attributed to Richard Rolle. The cloister represents the conscience or the heart, and care must be taken "that no evil enter the cloister of the heart through the door of the mouth, or by the window of the eyes or of the ears."[27] The senses, like literary windows, are means by which we come to a knowledge of the outside world and at the same time means by which the destructive forces of the outside world—in this case, temptations to concupiscence—enter into the vulnerable interior world.

Windows, whether literal or allegorical, are thus in a sense empty symbols, in that they have no special ideational content of their own; they serve mainly to indicate relationships. Consequently, they can be used equally well in an erotic *alba* or a Christian allegory of a castle, since the structure of these two kinds of literary work is so similar and since the windows in them do little more than point up that structure. As for the actual content of the symbols that are connected by the windows, that is quite different in the two kinds of works. In fact, the difference can often be described as being close to a complete reversal. In the allegory of the Holy Spirit's Abbey, the destructive force that enters through the figurative windows is the sensual temptations of the world. In the *alba*, the life of the inner world consists precisely of unlimited indulgence in the sensual temptations of the world, and the force that enters through the windows has the effect of putting an end to that indulgence. In the *Castrum humani corporis*, death—that is, the spiritual death which is concupiscence—enters through the windows; in the *alba*, the sunlight entering through the windows acts as the enemy of concupiscence.

The fact that certain symbols in the *alba* have a meaning exactly opposite to that of the same symbols in Christian thought is fundamental for an understanding of the *alba*; and it is in the symbolism of the sunlight, along with the associated symbols of day and night, that this reversal of symbolic meanings appears most strikingly. To appreciate the significance of such a reversal, let us compare the associations and meanings attached to these symbols in various spheres of thought: naturalistic thought, medieval Christian thought, and the thought that lies behind the *alba*.

From the naturalistic point of view—which is to say the point of view of the mind or part of the mind that is concerned only with the natural realities of this world, and that is more or less independent of any other-worldly or eschatological system of thought—both day and night have two different kinds of meaning or value. The day is evidently the time of brightness, warmth, activity, the movement of animal and human life—those good associations that tend to make the day a symbol of life itself, with all its vitality and direction. On the other hand, day is the period of toil, of wearying activity demanded by economic necessity, of servitude to need and to duty. All of this is equally a part of life, but an unpleasant part. On a naturalistic level, then, daytime is closely associated with life, and it has two feeling-tones, one good and one bad.

Night, in a society which, like ancient, medieval, and primitive societies, has no cheap and easy method of providing general illumination when the sun is down, is a very powerful natural phenomenon, much more so than it ever can be in a modern, electrified, urban society. It contrasts with the day in a radical way. All societies without electricity, of course, have some way of providing light at night: camp-fires, hearth-fires, torches, and the like. But this is the kind of light that makes the night seem even blacker by contrast; let us recall King Edwin's mead-hall in Bede, for example. The fire provides a tiny focus of artificial day, but all around it is the great dark reality it can do almost nothing against. Consequently night, like day, carries with it a considerable freight of meaning and feeling—at least in those early periods of our civilization in which most of our poetic symbols were taking on their conventional meanings. (If the twentieth century had to invent all of its literary symbols anew they would be very different from those we have inherited from less comfortable ages.) On the one hand, night is the time of quiet, peace, rest from toil, sleep.* It thus has something of a desirable tone about it, but this tone differs from the good feeling-tone of day. Night is desirable not because of any positive good it may possess—not because of brightness, warmth, activity, all that we associate with life—but because of the disagreeable things it is free of: work, servitude, necessity. In its lack of most of the characteristics of life such as are found during the daytime, it resembles—even from a naturalistic point of view—death; but death seen in its aspect of absence and emptiness, or, at best, of a quiet and somewhat sad eternal repose, as in the *limbo* of Dante.

Night has another face, however—this one also associated with death, but with death in its more disagreeable aspects. Here the point of view we have called "naturalistic" shades over into the superstitious. This is the night that in its blackness conceals animals of rapine, evil demons, mysterious and frightening threats to life and soul. The association of night with something fearful and dangerous is, we may suppose, virtually universal, and thus it constitutes part of the general substratum of symbolical meaning upon which more lofty symbol systems are built.

Of these symbol systems, the one most important for medieval literature is of course that based on the Bible. The general naturalistic attitudes toward night and day which we have spoken of sometimes appear in the Bible without any symbolic overtones.† But

---

* See, for example, the passage from the *Aeneid* quoted earlier. This represents the general attitude toward night found in classical literature.

† For example, Psalm ciii.20–23 (Vulgate numbering):

Posuisti tenebras, et facta est nox: in ipsa pertransibunt omnes bestiae silvae,
Catuli leonum rugientes, ut rapiant, et quaerant a Deo escam sibi.
Ortus est sol, et congregati sunt: et in cubilibus suis collocabuntur.
Exibit homo ad opus suum: et ad operationem suam usque ad vesperum.

Thou hast appointed darkness, and it is night: in it shall all the beasts of the woods go about:

very frequently they are adapted, in metaphors, to theological concepts and doctrines. Furthermore, the Biblical emphasis on moral issues, on good and evil, results in a simplification of the more naturalistic scheme—a scheme which, as we have indicated, observes the processes of nature and of human life and draws its symbolism directly from these processes, along with the contradictions inherent in them. In both Testaments the meaning of light and day, when they are used as metaphors, has been narrowed in great part to those things that are good, the meaning of darkness and night to those things that are bad. The metaphors themselves are drawn from the life of nature, but the meanings given to them derive from the clear-cut moral and theological scheme that Judaism and, especially, Christianity impose on the world of natural life.

The Old Testament on several occasions speaks of God as light:

> *Quoniam apud te est fons vitae: et in lumine tuo videbimus lumen.*

> For with thee is the fountain of life; and in thy light we shall see light. (Psalm xxxv.10)

> *Dominus illuminatio mea, et salus mea, quem timebo?*

> The Lord is my light and my salvation, whom shall I fear? (Psalm xxvi.1)

In Isaiah, the redeemer of captive Israel—later interpreted by the Jews as the future Messiah and by the Christians as Christ—is portrayed in a series of light images:

> *Surge, illuminare, Jerusalem: quia venit lumen tuum, et gloria Domini super te orta est.*
> *Quia ecce tenebrae operient terram, et caligo populos: super te autem orietur Dominus, et gloria ejus in te videbitur.*

The young lions roaring after their prey, and seeking their meat from God.
The sun ariseth, and they are gathered together: and they shall lie down in their dens.
Man shall go forth to his work, and to his labour until the evening.

Et ambulant Gentes in lumine tuo, et reges in splendore ortus tui.

Arise, be enlightened, O Jerusalem: for thy light is come, and the glory of the Lord is risen upon thee.
For behold darkness shall cover the earth, and a mist the people: but the Lord shall arise upon thee, and his glory shall be seen upon thee.
And the Gentiles shall walk in thy light, and the kings in the brightness of thy rising. (Isaiah lx.1–3)

Darkness here is bondage and misery; the light of God, spoken of as the sun itself, is the initiator of the imminent rule of peace and justice.

In the Gospel of St. John the identification of Christ with light is a persistent image:

Iterum ergo locutus est eis Jesus, dicens: Ego sum lux mundi: qui sequitur me, non ambulat in tenebris, sed habebit lumen vitae.

Again, therefore, Jesus spoke to them, saying, "I am the light of the world. He who follows me does not walk in the darkness, but will have the light of life." (John viii.12)

That is, God is light, eternal life is light, damnation is darkness.

Hoc est autem judicium quia lux venit in mundum, et dilexe-runt homines magis tenebras, quam lucem: erant enim eorum mala opera.
Omnis enim, qui male agit, odit lucem, et non venit ad lucem, ut non arguantur opera ejus:
Qui autem facit veritatem, venit ad lucem, ut manifestantur opera ejus, quia in Deo sunt facta.

Now this is the judgment: The light has come into the world, yet men have loved the darkness rather than the light, for their works were evil.

For everyone who does evil hates the light, and does not come to the light, that his deeds may not be exposed.

But he who does the truth comes to the light that his deeds may be made manifest, for they have been performed in God. (John iii.19–21)

Christ, in the above citation, is the just judge, identified with light; and the evil deeds of men are darkness.

These notions are combined in the Pauline doctrine of salvation. The Day of Judgment is imminent; those who are not Christians and do not follow the laws of Christ are children of darkness, which is the world of evil identified with the present life on earth; followers of Christ, however, are children of light and of the day, which symbolizes both the virtuous acts of men in this life and the whole world of salvation which is to come:

> *De temporibus autem et momentis, fratres, non indigetis ut scribamus vobis.*
>
> *Ipsi enim diligenter scitis, quia dies Domini, sicut fur in nocte, ita veniet.*
>
> *Cum enim dixerint, pax et securitas: tunc repentinus eis superveniet interitus, sicut dolor in utero habenti, et non effugient.*
>
> *Vos autem, fratres, non estis in tenebris, ut vos dies illa tamquam fur comprehendat:*
>
> *Omnes enim vos filii lucis estis, et filii diei: non sumus noctis, neque tenebrarum.*
>
> *Igitur non dormiamus sicut et ceteri, sed vigilemus, et sobrii simus.*
>
> *Qui enim dormiunt, nocte dormiunt: et qui ebrii sunt, nocte ebrii sunt.*
>
> *Nos autem, qui diei sumus, sobrii simus, induti loricam fidei, et charitatis, et galeam spem salutis.*

But of the times and seasons, brethren, you have no need that we write to you,

for you yourselves know well that the day of the Lord is to come as a thief in the night.

For when they shall say, "Peace and security," even then
sudden destruction will come upon them, as birth pangs
upon her who is with child, and they will not escape.
But you, brethren, are not in darkness, that that day should
overtake you as a thief;
for you are all children of the light and children of the day.
We are not of night, nor of darkness.
Therefore, let us not sleep as do the rest, but let us be wakeful
and sober.
For they who sleep, sleep at night, and they who are drunk,
are drunk at night.
But let us, who are of the day, be sober. Let us put on the
breastplate of faith and charity, and for a helmet the hope of
salvation. (I Thessalonians v.1–8)

The contrast of day and night is thus used both for a description of
present morals, as in John iii.19–21, cited above, and for an image
of the dynamic temporal scheme of life and salvation which is the
dominant characteristic of Pauline thought. (It is this scheme that
is alluded to in John viii.12, also cited above.) The temporal scheme
carries with it an important addition to the symbolism of day and
night. A static description of good and wicked moral behavior need
only concern itself with day and night, if it is using this sort of
symbolism. Day and night are merely static categories. But the
temporal scheme of salvation gives these symbols a dynamic relationship in time: it is now night, but soon it will be day. The static
moral contrast is set in motion; and a great emphasis is naturally
thrown upon the moment at which night gives way before day, the
moment of the Second Coming of Christ. And this moment is
symbolized by the dawn:

> Et hoc, scientes tempus: quia hora est jam nos de somno
> surgere. Nunc enim propior est nostra salus, quam cum cre-
> didimus.
> Nox praecessit, dies autem appropinquavit. Abjiciamus ergo
> opera tenebrarum, et induamur arma lucis.

*Sicut in die honeste ambulemus: non in comessationibus, et
ebrietatibus, non in cubilibus, et impudicitiis, non in conten-
tione, et aemulatione:*

*Sed induimini Dominum Jesum Christum, et carnis curam
ne feceritis in desideriis.*

And this do, understanding the time, for it is now the hour
for us to rise from sleep, because now our salvation is nearer
than when we came to believe.

The night is far advanced; the day is at hand. Let us therefore
lay aside the works of darkness, and put on the armor of
light.

Let us walk becomingly as in the day, not in revelry and
drunkenness, not in debauchery and wantonness, not in strife
and jealousy.

But put on the Lord Jesus Christ, and as for the flesh, take no
thought for its lusts. (Romans xiii.11–14)

Let us note here the association of night with sins of the flesh and
day with renunciation of these sins; and let us also note that night
is associated with sleep, which is a spiritual sleep, an ignoring of the
moral and theological truth of Christ, and dawn is associated with
awakening, which is both a spiritual awakening, a perception of the
true way of Christ, and also a translation of the good Christian from
the present world of night to a higher heavenly world of salvation.

This heavenly world is a world of light, illuminated by God. In
the heavenly Jerusalem, night, with its Christian associations of
evil, sin, and ignorance, and with its naturalistic associations of
danger and demons on the one hand and empty, peaceful silence on
the other, is eliminated. It is a place of the utmost fullness of life
(cf. the naturalistic association of day with life), and of the utmost
moral goodness springing from God (the Christian symbolism of
goodness as light, and of God as light and as the source of light,
the spiritual equivalent of the sun):

*Et nox ultra non erit: et non egebunt lumine lucernae, neque
lumine solis, quoniam Dominus Deus illuminabit illos, et
regnabunt in saecula saeculorum.*

And night shall be no more, and they shall have no need of
light of lamp, or light of sun, for the Lord God will shed
light upon them; and they shall reign forever and ever.
(Revelation xxii.5)

By the fourth century, these various symbols and the doctrines
they were employed to communicate were consolidated into a tradition of conventional dawn-hymns, of which the most famous, and
apparently the earliest, are two by Saint Ambrose and two by
Prudentius.[28] Let us look at various sections of one of Prudentius's
dawn-hymns, commenting as we go along on the symbols and their
meanings.*

I

Ales diei nuntius
lucem propinquam praecinit;
nos excitator mentium
iam Christus ad vitam vocat.

"auferte" clamat "lectulos
aegros, soporos, desides;
castique, recti ac sobrii
vigilate, iam sum proximus."

The bird, herald of the day, proclaims by its song that light
is nearing; now Christ the awakener of minds, calls us to
life.

"Take away," he cries, "the beds of weariness, sleep, and
sloth; be awake, pure, upright, and sober; I am already very
near."[29]

A literal dawn, announced by a literal cock, is drawing near
(lines 1–2). Lines 3–4, parallel to the first two lines, give us the
same event with a spiritual meaning. Christ awakens us, as the cock
does. This is a spiritual awakening, however, and the day Christ

* In the following discussions of Prudentius's "Ales diei nuntius," the extracts
(numbered 1 to 7) in each case precede the analysis of their symbols.

is calling our minds to is the full life of heavenly blessedness after the sluggish partial life of this world, represented as night. But Christ is not presented only as one who, like the cock, awakens us. He is also—metaphorically—the dawn itself, because His coming, like that of the dawn, is imminent. Christ is light, in accord with the old convention; but He is at the same time the herald of the light, for it is He who has proclaimed (in numerous parables and direct statements) the imminence of the kingdom of God. The dawn He calls us to awaken to is His own Second Coming and the Last Judgment, to be followed by the endless day of the blessed (for those who receive a favorable judgment and are translated to heaven).

We should note the naturalistic attitude toward night and day that lies beneath the religious symbolism. Day is the time of life, here enlarged to mean the full spiritual life of the blessed in heaven. Night is the time of sleep, weariness, lack of movement, lack of vigorous life, here enlarged to mean the spiritual torpor of all life in this world.

2

tectos tenebris horridis
stratisque opertos segnibus
suadet quietem linquere
iam iamque venturo die,

ut, cum coruscis flatibus
aurora caelum sparserit,
omnes labore exercitos
confirmet ad spem luminis.

Covered as we are by horrible darkness and hidden under blankets of sluggishness, he urges us to abandon our rest, for day is just about to come;

so that, when dawn has sprinkled the sky with her shining breath, she may strengthen all those who have carried out their work and give them hope of light.

Here the night takes on some of the value-tone ascribed to it by the second kind of naturalistic attitude toward night. It is not merely a time of sluggish, slumbering natural processes; it is also horrible, frightening. The contrasting dawn is seen in its conventional classical personification. It is a beautiful natural phenomenon. But because we know what dawn symbolizes in this Christian symbol system, the physical light of dawn gives us hope of the spiritual light of salvation.

3
hic somnus ad tempus datus
est forma mortis perpetis;
peccata, ceu nox horrida,
cogunt iacere ac stertere.

sed vox ab alto culmine
Christi docentis praemonet
adesse iam lucem prope,
ne mens sopori serviat,

ne somnus usque ad terminos
vitae socordis opprimat
pectus sepultum crimine
et lucis oblitum suae.

This sleep, given to us for a time, is a symbol of everlasting death; sins, like a horrible night, force us to lie stretched out and to snore.

But the voice of Christ our teacher forewarns us from the high summit that the light is already near, lest our mind be enslaved to slumber,

and lest sleep weigh down our breast all the way to the end of a sluggish life—our breast buried in crimes and forgetful of its light.

Sleep, that is, the literal act of sleeping, is now specifically stated to symbolize death. But this is not the peaceful death associated with the naturalistic view of night as a time of repose from toil. It is the frightening, terrible image of death, associated with the superstitious view of night as a time of danger and demons. This is the eternal torment of punishment in hell, which from a Christian point of view is the only death that can truly be called death. (Death of the body followed by bliss in heaven is not everlasting death but everlasting life.) The symbolic equivalence of sleep and everlasting death (damnation) is carried through in the likening of night, which is the cause of sleep, to sin, which is the cause of damnation.

The voice of Christ warns us of the proximity of light. The voice comes from a high summit because Christ is speaking to us from His seat in heaven; because of His moral loftiness; because the word of Christ, which is to say the teachings of the Church that lead us to salvation, is preached from a raised pulpit; and because the cock, with whom Christ is identified at the opening of the poem, announces the coming of dawn from a high perch. (There is also a suggestion here of Christ as a metaphorical watchman, a discussion of which we will postpone to a later chapter.)

The light that is imminent is both the light of salvation for the virtuous and the Day of Judgment altogether, on which the virtuous will be granted eternal bliss (day) and the wicked will be condemned to eternal torment (night).

4

invisa nam vicinitas
lucis, salutis, numinis,
rupto tenebrarum situ
noctis fugat satellites.

hoc esse signum praescii
norunt repromissae spei,
qua nos soporis liberi
speramus adventum Dei.

For the hated nearness of light, salvation, and the Godhead, having broken the sluggishness of the darkness, puts to flight the servants of night.

They know by their prescience that this is a sign of the hope that has again been promised to us—that hope by which, free of slumber, we expect the coming of God.

The servants of night are the demons who, according to popular superstition, inhabit the night and flee at the coming of dawn. They are at once the instruments and the symbols of sin. As they know, the dawn symbolizes (on the level of eschatological history) the Second Coming, which will put an end to the whole fallen world. On the level of the individual human life, furthermore, it symbolizes the moment of personal death and salvation through Christ, when we are at last freed of devilish temptations and the power that sin has over us.

5

fit namque peccatum prius
quam praeco lucis proximae
inlustret humanum genus
finemque peccandi ferat.

For sin is committed before the herald of the coming light illuminates the human race and brings an end to sinning.

We have at least three levels of meaning here. Night, dominated by demonic forces, is literally the time of the commission of sins. The literal dawn, which drives the demons away, puts an end (if only temporarily) to the sins of the night. On a second level, which we might call the tropological, a man commits sins until his soul is illuminated by the true words of the Christian religion; having acquired this vital knowledge, he turns away from ignorance and sin (night) to knowledge and virtue (day). And on the level of eschatology, the anagogical level (though of course there is no systematic exploitation of these various exegetical levels in Prudentius's poem), this world altogether is a place of sin, a general darkness, which will end only at the Second Coming of Christ.

6

inde est quod omnes credimus
illo quietis tempore
quo gallus exultans canit
Christum redisse ex inferis.

tunc mortis oppressus vigor,
tunc lex subacta est Tartari,
tunc vis diei fortior
noctem coegit cedere.

That is why we all believe that in that quiet time when the exultant cock sings, Christ returned from hell.

Then the strength of death was suppressed, then the law of hell was conquered, then the stronger power of day forced the night to yield.

The symbolism of night, dawn, and day, is now referred to the historical events of the Passion and Resurrection. Literally, Christ is supposed to have been resurrected toward the hour of dawn. But the symbols also have allegorical meaning. With night are identified hell, death, and the damnation of all mankind which resulted from Adam's Fall and which ruled all history and all individual destinies during the period of the old dispensation. The sacrifice of Christ results in a new dispensation under which men can be saved from eternal death, and this new dispensation and the salvation it makes possible are both identified with day. At dawn Christ rose, as the sun rises, and He conquered the darkness of eternal damnation with the brightness of His saving power. This same movement from darkness to light, from night to day, is now possible for all men; and just as dawn symbolizes Christ's Resurrection, so too it symbolizes the salvation of the individual virtuous soul which the Resurrection guaranteed.

7

sunt nempe falsa et frivola
quae mundiali gloria,

ceu dormientes, egimus;
vigilemus, hic est veritas.

aurum, voluptas, gaudium,
opes, honores, prospera,
quaecumque nos inflant mala,
fit mane, nil sunt omnia.

They are indeed false and trivial, those things that we have
done, as if in our sleep, for worldly glory. Let us be wakeful;
this is truth.

Gold, pleasure, joy, riches, honors, successes, all those evil
things that puff us up—when morning comes, they are all
nothing.

Night, which is this world and all its uses, is also a symbol for
ignorance of true value, and for the reign of false and deceptive
values. The pleasures and achievements we enjoy in this world are
vain and worthless. It is only while we are in darkness, unable to
see true value, that we rejoice in such things. Morning, the word of
Christ, enables us to see true value, to judge things truly. Fortified
by Christ's word we can distinguish between what is of real value
and what is of false and trivial value. Moreover, the coming reign of
Christ, also symbolized by the dawn, will be a reign of truth, true
value, true reality, as against the deceptive appearances of the
present world (night).

This poem of Prudentius, it should be clear by now, is a kind of
unsystematic symbol dictionary—unsystematic because it constantly
shifts from one level of symbolism to another, thus gradually building up a large number of different (though closely related) signifi-
cations for each of the main symbols. Perhaps the only important
meaning of the three symbols we are considering that is not brought
out with perfect explicitness in this particular dawn-hymn is the
following: when the dawn symbolizes the Day of Judgment, it has
two contradictory feeling-tones—just as both day and night have,

from a naturalistic point of view. For the virtuous, this dawn is a time to be longed for, for it will result in their eternal bliss. For the wicked, those who have spent their lives in the vain pleasures of this world and who have not heeded the word of Christ, the Day of Judgment is a day to be feared and hated, because it will result in their eternal damnation.

To sum up the symbolism in these early Christian dawn-hymns: night is equated with death, sin, hell, devils, damnation, the old dispensation, spiritual torpor, ignorance of true value, worthless bodily pleasures and satisfactions, this world altogether, danger, and horror. Day is equated with eternal life, virtue, heaven, Christ, salvation, the new dispensation, spiritual awakening, knowledge of true value, spiritual joy, the world of God, and bliss. Dawn, in so far as its symbolism can be distinguished from that of day, represents Christ's Resurrection, our salvation, and the Day of Judgment. Everything about night is bad and to be shunned and feared; everything about day and dawn is good and to be desired—with the single exception of dawn in its meaning of the Day of Judgment, in which case it is to be feared by the wicked and desired by the virtuous. With this one exception, all of the values attributed to these symbols are represented as universal and objective; only the value of dawn as the Day of Judgment is variable and subjective, since whether the Day of Judgment is seen as desirable or not depends on the attitude, the personal set of values, and the style of life, so to speak, of the individual.

Dawn-hymns of this sort, with no significant changes in the symbolism, continued to be written up through the ninth and tenth centuries. Many of the older ones remained in use and were included in hymnals prepared during this later period. A good proportion of them eventually found their way into the Roman breviary (they were sung during the morning offices). The total number of extant dawn-hymns is quite considerable.[30] The same symbolism is found in many other hymns, of course, especially in those used for the evening and night offices. In the thirteenth century we find a fairly large number of vernacular (Provençal and German) dawn-hymns, which a number of scholars have seen as religious versions of the erotic *alba*,[31] but which in fact usually have nothing in common with the erotic *alba* except the use of the world "alba" (or "tac") in a refrain. There are no lovers and no separation, only the call to sinners to awaken from their night of sin to the light of God, all of which we have seen in the Latin dawn-hymns of the earlier Middle Ages. The writers of these poems may have been intentionally turning the erotic *alba* to Christian use, but the result of their efforts is merely a repetition of the familiar Christian symbolism, which they could have known either from the Latin dawn-hymns themselves or from any of countless other religious works of the Middle Ages.

Indeed, this symbolism of night, dawn, and day, with its firm roots in Biblical texts, may be said to be universal in medieval Christian thought, far beyond the boundaries of the dawn-hymns we have been speaking of. Let us look, for example, at one of the symbol dictionaries of the High Middle Ages, made for the use of preachers.[32] Night, we are told, may represent the blindness of matter, spiritual blindness, ignorance, guilt, misfortune, the period before the coming of Christ, the Old Testament, temporal death, the present life, the misery of time, the devil, captivity, and a sinner— among others.[33] Day may represent the time of grace, the time of judgment, the light of grace, eternal life, good fortune, the human intellect, the Jews converted to the faith, a spiritual teacher, the souls of the elect, the length of eternity, and the nature of angels— among others.[34] The sun may represent Christ, a saint, the brightness of a good work, the light of truth, the brilliance of preachers, a manifestation, the gift of wisdom, and the divine nature of Christ— among others.[35]

Alas for those who wish to use these symbol dictionaries as the infallible key to the meaning of medieval literature, the "others" we have omitted are often unrelated or in direct contradiction to the meanings we have quoted. Thus, night is also the hour when Christ will come in judgment, and, in another realm altogether, a preacher who preaches to the lower classes. Day is also the time of the present life, a wicked conscience, the misery of time, and the enjoyment of sin; and the sun is also tribulation, temptation, and Antichrist![36]

Almost all these symbolic definitions are based on a Biblical text, most of them directly on metaphors used in the Bible. Consequently, we cannot exclude any of them as being arbitrary allegorizations on Alanus's part: all the definitions are more or less living parts of medieval symbolical language. It follows that we cannot fix the symbols of night and day in medieval Christian literature as having any single, invariable meaning; we cannot even say that they have an invariable feeling-tone. Night sometimes signifies something good; day sometimes signifies something bad. We noted the same kind of ambiguity when we were discussing the kinds of meaning that proceed from a purely naturalistic attitude toward these natural phenomena. What we can say, however, is that the majority of Alanus's definitions for the day are good and the majority for the night are bad. Furthermore, whenever he mentions day and night together, whenever he contrasts their symbolical meaning, day is invariably the good or superior member of the pair and night is invariably the bad or inferior one. This is of much more importance for our purposes than the variable meanings of an occasional, isolated image of day or night or dawn. There is no question here of picking out symbols from the *alba* and interpreting them mechanically with the aid of Christian symbol dictionaries. What we are interested in is how the *alba* on the one hand and Christian thought on the other treat the symbols of night and day when they are both present and explicitly in contrast with each other.

From this point of view we may accept the symbolism in Prudentius's dawn-hymn, and the definitions in Alanus that conform with it, as constituting the general medieval Christian attitude toward the meaning of night and day; and it is with this set of meanings that the *alba* and its meanings are to be compared. Let us cite an example, taken more or less at random, of the way Christian night and day symbolism is used in a work not expressly devoted, as are the dawn-hymns, to the manipulation of these particular symbols. Here is an incident from the life of Saint Guthlac, an English hermit who died in 714 and whose feast is celebrated on April 11. Guthlac, like the desert fathers of several centuries before, is frequently subjected to temptations and tortures by graphically described devils. One night, a particularly unpleasant group of these demons emerges from the blackness; they torment the hermit in terrible ways, and when he continues to resist them they seize him, take him with them to hell, and are about to hurl him into the abyss, when

> ... ecce, S. Bartholomaeus, cum immenso caelestis lucis splendore, medias furvae noctis insuso lumine interrumpens tenebras, sese ab aethereis sedibus radiantis olympi coram illis, aureo fulgore amictus, obtulit. Maligni vero spiritus, non sustinentes caelestis splendoris fulgorem, frendere, tremere, fugere, timere coeperunt.... Imminente ergo aurora, cum sol nocturnas caelo demoverat umbras, praefatus Christi athleta, adepto de hostibus triumpho, in eodem statu à quo prius translatus est, grates Christo persolvens, constitit.
>
> ... lo, Saint Bartholomew, with an immense splendor of heavenly light, breaking upwards through the intervening darkness of the black night in a flash of light, coming from the ethereal seat of radiant Olympus, enveloped in golden brightness, presented himself before them. The evil spirits, unable to bear the brightness of that heavenly splendor, began to gnash their teeth, to tremble, to flee, to fear.... With the dawn about to appear, and as the sun drove the shades of night from the sky, the athlete of Christ of whom we have been speaking, having obtained victory over his enemies, stood firm in the same state of mind from which he had earlier been carried away, and rendered thanks to Christ.[37]

Night in this passage has many of the associations we have seen in Prudentius: it is the time of evil, of demons, of pain and torment, of temptation to sin, of damnation, of hell. Bartholomew, who is the instrument and symbol of God's saving grace, is described exclusively in images of light. At the end of the incident, the dramatic relationship of the moral symbols—the powers of darkness giving way before the light of Heaven, that is, sin and the danger of damnation being conquered by God's grace—is repeated on a literal level: the literal night gives way to a literal dawn. Just as Bartholomew, in his cloak of brightness, swept the nocturnal demons away, so now the natural phenomenon of the sunrise sweeps the nocturnal shadows away. But this rising sun also carries with it its conventional symbolic meaning of Christ, the source of all light and the destroyer of all darkness. All of these associations are perfectly conventional, and the same complex of symbols with the same complex of meanings could be found in great numbers of medieval literary works written under the influence of Christian symbolism.

Before we turn to night and day in the *alba*, there is one more use of the notion of God as light that ought to be mentioned. This particular symbolic structure brings together the conventional sun and light symbolism we have just been speaking of with the symbolism of windows and *breaking through* which we spoke of earlier. Both window symbolism and light symbolism are frequent in Flemish painting of the fifteenth century, particularly in the work of Jan van Eyck.[38] We spoke before of windows having two functions, to let persons inside see into the world outside, and to let forces from the outside, mainly light, enter into the inside. Windows serve both functions in van Eyck's paintings. They almost always let light in—a purely realistic light for which they serve a purely realistic function, for van Eyck was greatly interested in the actual effects of light on physical objects. They also serve symbolic functions. One of the most characteristic structures of van Eyck's paintings (and of the paintings of his contemporaries and followers) is an interior, domestic or ecclesiastical, with windows or equivalent openings in the rear giving on a minutely rendered cityscape. Inside the room or hall we find the Virgin, often in the company of saints or contemporary patrons of the painter. The town outside presents various kinds of medieval architecture, chosen for their representational and symbolic value. In van Eyck's *Rolin Madonna* (in the Louvre), for example, we see the painting's donor, Chancellor Rolin, together with the Virgin and Child, in a palatial chamber; and through the arched openings at the back we see sections of a splendid medieval city, with its surrounding landscape. In the London National Gallery's painting of the Virgin and Child by the so-called Master of Flémalle, a painting which preceded van Eyck's *Rolin*

Madonna by some ten years (it is dated c. 1425), the Virgin is found in a contemporary domestic room, while through the window we see a charming Flemish town, with its houses, streets, and inhabitants. The kind of reality depicted in the two paintings is quite different. Jan van Eyck shows us an elegant, royal, enthroned Madonna, in a room of a richly appointed romanesque and gothic palace, with the greater part of the city that is seen through the windows a magnificent collection of monumental architecture: churches, towers, and palaces. This is Mary as the queen of heaven, and numerous symbolical details in the cityscape suggest that at least the right half of the city is intended to represent the heavenly Jerusalem. In the painting by the Master of Flémalle, the Virgin is a large, homely, middle-class Flemish lady, sitting on the floor or on a low bench, in an ordinary domestic room, and with a perfectly commonplace Flemish town seen through the window. This is the madonna of humility, the Virgin seen as an ordinary human being, easily accessible to other human beings, and living right in the midst of the contemporary world. The paintings are alike, however, in that both show the Virgin Mary in juxtaposition with a city; and in both it is windows that provide the connection. Jan van Eyck's painting shows us the queen of heaven, who is the intercessor for all mankind, and in juxtaposition with her the community of the blessed in heaven, a community whose very existence is due to the child Mary bore. The Master of Flémalle's painting shows us Mary, the human mother of Christ, and in juxtaposition with her the community of men of the present day and in the present world who look to her and her son for the salvation they are seeking. In both cases we see in the foreground the single, historical individual who brought Christ into the world; and in both cases we look beyond her, through the window, at the great community of mankind (represented, as usual in the Middle Ages, by a city), whose lives both in this world and in the next have been so radically transformed by her motherhood.

In Jan van Eyck's painting of the Annunciation, in the National Gallery in Washington, one of the windows serves this same function, enabling us to look out into the world of mankind which is to be transformed by the event taking place in the inner world. The

Annunciation takes place in the enclosed space of a church, and through one of the many windows we see a contemporary Flemish city, symbolic of this world and the community of mankind that will be saved because of the Incarnation of Christ. Higher on the church wall (and its height is symbolic, of course) there is another window with a different sort of function, the second function of symbolic windows that we have already spoken of. This window does not serve to let us look out; it serves to let the power of light come in. The light in the present case is not the natural light of day, which comes in through other windows and from the opposite direction. It is the symbolic light of God, by which, in traditional representations of the event, the Incarnation was effected. Seven rays of light stream in through the window, one of them bearing the bird of the Holy Spirit, who is flying on a direct line for the Virgin's ear where the impregnating power of God was traditionally believed to have entered the Virgin's body.

The source of this iconographic representation, along with the explanation of its symbolic meaning, is found in a passage from Saint Bernard:

> *Sicut splendor solis vitrum absque laesione perfundit et pene-trat eiusque soliditatem insensibili subtilitate pertraicit nec cum ingreditur, violat nec, cum egreditur, dissipat: sic Dei verbum, splendor Patris, virginum habitaculum adiit et inde clauso utero prodiit.*

> Just as the brilliance of the sun fills and penetrates a glass window without damaging it, and pierces its solid form with imperceptible subtlety, neither hurting it when entering nor destroying it when emerging: thus the word of God, the splendor of the Father, entered the virgin chamber and then came forth from the closed womb.[39]

The theological mystery of the Virgin's being able to conceive and yet remain *virgo intacta* is here likened to the natural phenomenon, itself sufficiently mysterious, of light's passing through glass without breaking it. Jan van Eyck's painting thus shows us two representations of the Incarnation: what was believed to be a literal representation, namely the entering of the Holy Spirit into the Virgin's ear, along with a symbolic representation of the same event, that is, the rays of light passing in through the glass window. God's power is represented as light; that light comes from an external, higher, heavenly world, and passes through a window into the inner world of the church in which the Virgin is enclosed. In the same way, the Son of God comes from the outer, heavenly world, and passes in through the Virgin's ear into the enclosed space of her womb, which is at the same time a symbol of the enclosed earthly world of the flesh that God has now entered into.[40]

We have here, in a quite different context, many of the same symbols and many of the same structural principles we have seen in the *alba*. The inside-outside structure, the light streaming in through a window, the fact that what is taking place in the inner world is in both cases essentially a sexual act—these similarities bring the *alba* closer to this representation of the Annunciation than to any of the other analogues we have already pointed out (in Chapter One). Many of the earlier analogues are, so to speak, subsumed in this one: the notion of the Virgin as a *hortus conclusus*, the church building as an inside of differing value from the outside surrounding it, the analogue of the womb. What Jan van Eyck's painting has that none of the other analogues does is the motif of light breaking in through a window.

But does this motif in the *alba* carry with it any suggestion of the *symbolical* meaning the painting gives it? We have already noted the image of the sun penetrating in through the windows in Wolfram's "Sîne klâwen" and "Den morgenblic bî wahters sange erkôs." Certainly, on the literal level this sunlight is nothing more than natural sunlight, a great natural force which the lovers feel is opposed to them. But elsewhere in Wolfram's poetry we find instances of the conventional symbolic identification of light and God, such as we have seen it in the Bible, Prudentius, medieval dawn-hymns, medieval symbol dictionaries, and Jan van Eyck's *Annunciation*. For example:

Von dem wâren minnaere
sagent disiu süezen maere.
der ist ein durchliuhtec lieht,
und wenket sîner minne nieht.

These sweet stories tell
of the true lover [i.e. God].
He is a light that shines through [everything],
and He does not waver in His love.[41]

In addition to the symbolism of God as light, the word "durch-liuhtec" in this passage suggests that this light is not merely a glow but a force that penetrates through something. The word "every-thing" in my translation is not strictly justified by the construction in German, although it is suggested by it. But that this is precisely what Wolfram means is made clear by some later lines in the same passage, where the image of the universal penetrating power of God's vision (metaphorized as light) is made specific:

die treit der durch gedanke vert.
gedanc sich sunnen blickes wert:
gedanc ist âne slôz bespart,
von aller crêatiure bewart:
gedanc ist vinster âne schîn.
diu gotheit kan lûter sîn,
si glestet durch der vinster want . . . .
ez ist dechein gedanc sô snel,
ê er vom herzen für dez vel
küm, ern sî versuochet:
des kiuschen got geruochet.
sît got gedanke speht sô wol,
ôwê der broeden werke dol! . . .
war hât diu arme sêle fluht?

This [grace] comes from Him who moves through thoughts.
Thought defends itself from the sun's glance.
Thought is locked away without a lock,
protected from all creatures.

Thought is dark without brightness.
The Godhead can be pure;
it shines through the wall of darkness . . . .
There is no thought so swift
that before it gets from the heart out through the skin
He has not already examined it.
The virtuous thought God approves of.
Since God sees into our thoughts so well,
alas for him who indulges his own morally weak acts! . . .
Where can the poor soul flee to?[42]

The picture here is of man's thoughts locked away in a dark chamber, and of God's pure understanding enabling Him to pierce through the walls of that chamber and see man's thoughts just as they are. Not only does God see our hidden thoughts; He judges them on moral grounds; and if He disapproves of them there is no place that the condemned soul can flee to so as to be beyond the reach of God's sight and His power.[43]

Let us consider the various *albas* we have spoken of from the point of view of this symbolism. We have said that the violent bursting through of the wall barrier by the sunlight is at the same time felt as an act of peering, spying. It is the sun's *eyes* that Troilus sees in every chink. In Wolfram's "Sîne klâwen," the sun is sending "blicken" through the window. These glances of the sun see into the hidden world of love, expose the acts that have taken place under the cover of darkness. Our passage from *Parzival* affirms that the sun's glances are not powerful enough to see into men's thoughts; only God can pierce the blackness in which thoughts are hidden. But the structure of the two images—the penetrating, inquisitive light of the sun and the penetrating, inquisitive insight of God—is identical. Indeed, when Wolfram speaks of the Godhead shining through a wall of darkness and exposing the thoughts locked within, he is using as a metaphor the exact same situation which we see *literally* depicted in his *albas*; it is the conventional equation of God and light that provides the fundamental connection.

Furthermore, let us remember that in "Den morgenblic bî wahters sange erkôs" the lovers, in dread of the sun, try to lock it out, but to no avail. Even the most intense of loves cannot escape from the great processes of nature. In the passage from *Parzival* we are told that thoughts are hidden from all creatures' eyes without the necessity of a lock; but that no matter how we may try to hide our thoughts from God, He sees into them and judges them. Again the *Parzival* passage is using as metaphor an action that appears as a literal event in the *alba*. The lovers try to lock the sun out, but cannot; men try to hide their thoughts from God, but cannot. More precisely, it is men's evil thoughts that they try to hide from God. And while there is no hint in Wolfram's *albas* of the love affair's being considered evil, it is clear that the secret love-tryst is opposed to everything symbolized by the sun and that the sun exposes that tryst and condemns it to destruction, just as evil thoughts are opposed to God and His law and just as God exposes those evil thoughts, condemns them, and punishes them. In addition, the notion of evil thoughts fearing and shunning God's light, which comes upon them anyway and judges and condemns them, is a small-scale version of the attitude of sinners toward the Last Judgment which we noted earlier. In both cases the arrival of the light is feared; in both cases the arrival is inevitable; and in both cases God judges and condemns.

It does not follow from this that Wolfram intended the sun in his *albas* to symbolize God, or the acts of the lovers to symbolize sins or hidden wicked thoughts. On the other hand, there is no doubt that the structure of images in the *Parzival* passage and the structure of events in the *alba* are very much the same, and that consequently the ideas expressed by the images in the *Parzival* passage are analogous to the experiences depicted in the *alba*.

This is not a matter of Wolfram's subconscious associations. Chaucer cannot have known Wolfram's *albas* or his *Parzival*, but he knew that the sun has eyes that peer into the shadows, and he must have known that according to Christian thought God sees into all secrets and according to Christian symbolism God is often represented as light. Is it likely, after all, that Chaucer was ignorant of what must have been the ultimate source of Wolfram's passage?

Domine, probasti me, et cognovisti me:

Tu cognovisti sessionem meam, et resurrectionem meam:

Intellexisti cogitationes meas de longe: semitam meam, et funiculum meum investigasti. . . .

Quo ibo a spiritu tuo? et quo a facie tua fugiam?

Et dixi: Forsitan tenebrae conculcabunt me: et nox illuminatio mea in deliciis meis.

Quia tenebrae non obscurabuntur a te, et nox sicut dies illuminabitur: sicut tenebrae ejus, ita et lumen ejus. . . .

Proba me, Deus, et scito cor meum: interroga me, et cognosce semitas meas.

Et vide, si via iniquitatis in me est: et deduc me in via aeterna.

Lord, thou hast proved me, and known me:

thou hast known my sitting down, and my rising up.

Thou hast understood my thought afar off: my path and my line thou hast searched out. . . .

Whither shall I go from thy spirit? or whither shall I flee from thy face?

And I said: Perhaps darkness shall cover me: and night shall be my light in my pleasures.

But darkness shall not be dark to thee, and night shall be as the day: the darkness thereof, and the light thereof are alike to thee. . . .

Prove me, O God, and know my heart: examine me, and know my paths.

And see if there be in me the way of iniquity: and lead me in the eternal way. (Psalm cxxxviii)

The notion of God seeing into secrets is thus just as pertinent to the *alba* in *Troilus* as it is to the *albas* Wolfram wrote, and it may very well be that both Chaucer's and Wolfram's audiences were aware of the analogy and that it added something to their experience of the *alba*.

Of course we cannot really know very much about what audiences six or seven hundred years dead may have thought while listening to these poems. But we do know that they tended to think according to certain structures of thought, that they must have been aware of certain conventional symbolic identifications, and that they were acute about seeing analogies. As to the analogies we have pointed out between Wolfram's *albas* and the *Annunciation* of Jan van Eyck, we need not suppose any direct connection between them in order to accept the fact of their similarity in structure and symbolism. Although they are in different media, have different purposes, and are separated by some two centuries, they both spring from a common background of medieval patterns of thought and medieval symbolism. Our comparison of the *albas* with the metaphorical passage in *Parzival* has shown us that even the idea of sunlight as God, which is crucial to the iconography of the painting, is not foreign to Wolfram's imagination and may in fact enter to some extent into the meaning of the *albas*.

It is important, however, to point out some very profound differences between the *alba* and the van Eyck painting. The *alba*, for one thing, shows us two worlds in conflict, an interior world which contains all that is good and valuable pitted against an exterior world felt to be morally inferior. This is not the case in the *Annunciation* at all. Here the inner world is a holy place, a church, and the actors in it are an angel and the mother of God. The outer world, which is penetrating into the inner world, is the world of God himself. There is no contrast between a good world and a bad world; the only contrast is between the goodness of all that is best in the world of earth and the higher goodness of heaven. And these two worlds are not in conflict, but rather in the most perfect harmony.

In both the poem and the painting, to point out another vital difference, sunlight enters into the inner world, but the attitude of those inside toward this sunlight is radically different in the *alba* and in the *Annunciation*. The lovers shun and fear the sun, and try to lock it out; the Virgin, slightly fearful of the mysterious event, nevertheless accepts it with humility: "Ecce ancilla Domini." And, of course, each of these attitudes is the inevitable response to the event that is calling it forth. In the *alba* the sunlight results in the ending of something valued, in separation, in destruction; the reaction of the lovers is, quite naturally, one of fear, anger, and grief.

In the *Annunciation*, the entry of the divine sunlight results in the creation of a child and the beginning of His earthly life; this is not separation but union, a fruitful sexual union which is at the same time the union of God and man, of heaven and earth, of divine spirit and human flesh.

Nor, in detailing these differences, must we forget the other window in van Eyck's painting, the lower window that shows us a section of a Flemish town. The meaning of the joyous event taking place in the church is that the community of mankind, represented by the town outside, is going to have the possibility of achieving eternal salvation. What is happening to one individual, the Virgin Mary, is the most important event in the lives of all human beings, for all time to come. In the *alba*, on the contrary, the night of love and the grief-filled parting are events of importance to the lovers only. They are experiences of the individual soul divorced from society, indeed in opposition to society, as we have noted. The Virgin is one with all the Christian community, present, future, on earth, and in heaven. The lovers are in solitude, against all the world.

Thus, the *alba* and van Eyck's *Annunciation* present us with the same symbols and a strikingly similar structure, but the values and feelings attributed to the symbols and structure are virtually opposite in the poem and the painting. In one case, an inside and outside in conflict; in the other, an inside and outside in harmony. In one case, an event in the interior world that has meaning only for its actors; in the other, an event meaningful for all mankind. Above all, a difference in the attitude toward the light. This, indeed, is what we see in the whole treatment of the symbols of light and darkness in the *alba*, as over against the Christian tradition we have been discussing. The essentially dualistic nature of the Christian symbolism of day and night appears with equal intensity in the *alba*, but the symbols are valued in the opposite way. In the *alba*, the night, the time of love, union, and the satisfaction of desire, is a symbol of the good; the day, the time of separation and of the denial of desire, is a symbol of the bad. The sun is a powerful enemy, to be hated, reproached, and even cursed.

This reversal of Christian sun-symbolism can perhaps be seen at its most extreme in a version of the *alba* written long after the Middle Ages, John Donne's "The Sunne Rising."[44]

> Busie old fool, unruly Sunne,
> Why dost thou thus,
> Through windowes, and through curtaines call on us?
> Must to thy motions lovers seasons run?
> Sawcy pedantique wretch . . . .

The sun, the great inimical force which in medieval *albas* comes bursting violently through the window, has here been reduced to an elderly busybody who insists on paying calls where he is not wanted and who has so lost sight of courteous usages that he makes his entry through the window instead of by the normal means. This represents something of a comedown for what, in other contexts, had symbolized the divine creator of the universe. Moreover, the poem goes on to speak of the sun as a sort of old servant whose "duties bee / To warme the world"; that world, with all that is valuable in it, has been contracted into the room where the lovers are making love; and thus the sun has become a servant of the lovers, of importance only in his service to them. It is the lovers, not the sun, who set the standard of what is valuable and real in the world.

The reversal of the values of night and day which we find in the *alba* thus indicates a concept of the good and the true quite different from that of Christianity. The symbol of salvation and resurrection becomes a hated adversary, eventually treated with contempt. And the time of sin and spiritual sluggishness, symbolic of eternal death according to accepted Christian symbolism, here becomes a symbol for the most real, exciting, meaningful thing in the universe: the love of a man and a woman. Day symbolizes a limited and imperfect existence. Night symbolizes the enjoyment of perfection, the full self-realization of the lover, the experience of a total, limitless reality.[45] "*Hic* est veritas," the *alba* would say in reply to Prudentius. In the *alba*, the lovers are full of grief when the night, symbol of all that is good, comes to an end. And in a somewhat playful variation on the theme of the *alba* called the *serena*, the lover spends the whole day in anguish as he longs for the night to arrive, at which time he will be able to meet with his lady.[46] What Christianity had seen as the epitome of all negative values is now raised to the height of desirability.

But while changing the *value* of the symbols, as they are treated in the Christian scheme, the *alba* takes over many of their essential *meanings* virtually unaltered. In Christian symbolism the sun, as God, is a great and good force that cannot be escaped or resisted. In the *alba* the sun remains a great force that cannot be escaped or resisted, although from the point of view of the lovers it is a force for evil, not for good. Similarly, Christian symbolism condemns the night as the time of the pleasures of the world and the flesh: "aurum, voluptas, gaudium." The *alba* retains this symbolism (though narrowing it to the pleasures and joy of love: gold and worldly honors play no part in the *alba*.) But what Christianity condemns, the *alba* exalts.

THE LOVERS VERSUS CHRISTIAN VALUES: THE KULTURPROBLEM DES MINNESANGS

The question naturally arises as to what the real intentions of the *alba* writers were. In speaking of their "reversal" of Christian symbolism I am afraid I may have given the impression of having prejudged this issue. Surely no influence of Christian values, negative or otherwise, is required for a poet to praise love or for love to be associated with night. Ancient Chinese and Sanskrit poetry, in which no trace of Christian influence is to be suspected, make this perfectly natural association. Nevertheless, the meaning of a literary symbol is not a fixed quantity; it varies, often radically, according to the culture in which it appears. The symbolism of night as a time of evil is pervasive in Christian thought, and it is Christianity that constituted the chief intellectual environment of the European Middle Ages. When the notion of night as the time of all that is good and meaningful is introduced into such a context, it must take on some reverberations of meaning from the dominant thought patterns that surround it. As Leo Spitzer observes: "... il faut concevoir le développement de certaines formes d'art et de certaines littératures *à partir d'un climat de civilisation*—qui pour le moyen âge chrétien sera avant tout chrétien."[47] This does not mean that every dawn that appears in medieval secular literature is a direct or ironic reference to the Last Judgment, but it does mean that when we find a complex of symbols in a medieval secular work which closely corresponds to a similar complex of symbols in religious thought (even though the symbols may be used for radically different ends), we must take the religious analogies into account in any investigation of the meaning of the secular work. This is especially so in troubadour love poetry, which makes such frequent use of explicitly Christian imagery and ideas.[48]

But if the writers of erotic *albas* were reversing the accepted Christian symbolism for night and day, were they aware of the moral implications of such a reversal? Was it simply a matter of naturally thinking in terms of Christian symbolism and more or less casually adapting that symbolism to the demands of the *alba*'s plot? Or are we dealing here with a conscious, intentional use of Christian symbols, turned upside down, so to speak, in order to show that the values of erotic experience were in rivalry with those of Christianity, and perhaps even superior to them?

Let us reserve judgment for the moment on the larger aspects of this problem, and look in more detail at an *alba* that reverses Christian light symbolism in a particularly striking way. This is the *alba* by Giraut de Bornelh, the first strophe of which, spoken by the lover's friend, runs as follows:

I

Reis glorios, verais lums e clartatz,
Deus poderos, Senher, si a vos platz,
Al meu companh siatz fizels aiuda;
Qu'eu no lo vi, pos la nochs fo venguda,
    Et ades sera l'alba.

Glorious king, true light and brightness,
powerful God, Lord, if it please you

be a faithful help to my comrade,
for I have not seen him since night came,
and in a moment it will be dawn.*

One critic, in referring to this opening, has spoken of "il tono solenne e paganeggiante dei primi versi,"[49] but so far as the imagery goes there is nothing pagan or paganizing about these first lines. The imagery is conventional and Christian, and the very language it is expressed in finds frequent echoes in Provençal references to God:

> . . . *rey glorios* . . .[50]
>
> *Senher Dieus glorios* . . .[51]
>
> . . . *verai soleilh de drechura* . . .[52]
>
> . . . *Dieus, qu'es clardatz e rays* . . .[53]
>
> *Senher verais Jhesus, cui son acclis,*
> *Lums dreituriers de vera resplandor* . . .[54]

Giraut de Bornelh himself uses this imagery in poems written from a perfectly orthodox Christian point of view. For example:

> *Senher Deus drechurers, chars,*
> *Umils, resplandens e clars,*
> *Entre mos nescis pensars*
> *Sui endevengutz liars!*
> *Mas er conosc que l'amars*
> *D'aquest segle s'es amars;*
> *C'om n'es fols e tan avars,*
> *Per que n'a pois dol e pena.*

> Lord God, just, beloved,
> humble, shining and bright,
> among my foolish thoughts
> I have become gray.
> But now I recognize that the love
> of this world is bitter;

---

* Ed. Kolsen, I, 342. For the complete text and translation, see below, pp. 200–3.

for a man is mad and so greedy for it
that afterwards he gets pain and suffering from it.[55]

In its invocation, this strophe resembles Giraut's *alba* and also recalls Christian hymnody, while in the subsequent lines it expresses
Christian commonplaces—the vanity of the world and its pleasures,
the painfulness of man's unceasing appetite for the world—of the
sort we have seen in Prudentius's dawn-hymn. The language both
here and in the opening of Giraut's *alba* is perfectly in consonance
with the ordinary Christian symbolism of God as light which we
have seen in numerous examples.[56]

A further connection between Giraut's *alba* and Christian tradition appears in the fact that the melody the poem was written to
was that of an older Provençal hymn to the Virgin:

> *O Maria, Deu maire,*
> *Deu t'es e filh e paire;*
> *Domna, preira per nos,*
> *To fil lo glorios.*

> O Mary, mother of God,
> God is son and father to you.
> Lady, supplicate for us
> your son the glorious one.[57]

These connections have inclined a number of scholars to see the
Latin religious dawn-hymns as the "origin," or at least one of the
origins, of Giraut's *alba*, and, by extension, of the erotic *alba* in
general.[58] There are certainly points of resemblance between Giraut's
alba and the dawn-hymns. What is important for an understanding
of his poem, however, is the use it makes of the common store of
medieval Christian symbolism, not any supposed genetic relation it
may have had to some single genre of Christian poetry. Whether or
not the opening lines of the poem are based on Christian dawn-
hymns, it is certain that they are employing the language and the
symbolism of medieval Christianity.

But toward what end does Giraut's *alba* employ this language
and symbolism? That, of course, is the crucial point. God is invoked

here, not to listen to the poet's confession of his worldly vanities, as in "Be vei e conosc e sai," which we quoted earlier, but to aid the speaker's friend in the safe achievement of an adulterous sexual union! And let us note the implications of the treatment of light imagery in this strophe. God is invoked to aid the doings of night, and He is addressed in the light imagery that traditionally associates Him with the sun. A tension between what God is and what He is asked to do is thus immediately established. Furthermore, the refrain to the first strophe (as to the five strophes following) indicates that the imminent dawn is something to be feared, as it brings with it the danger of discovery and the necessity for separation. Dawn, of course, is light, just as God is (although God is light only metaphorically, while the dawn is the literal rising of the sun). But the dawn's light carries with it a feeling tone quite different from that attributed to the light of God in this poem; in fact, the literal dawn functions here in the same way as does the dawn of the Day of Judgment, seen from the point of view of sinners, in the tradition of Christian symbolism: it is superhuman, inevitable, and dreaded. The first strophe thus gives us two kinds of light, with contradictory meanings. God is light, and the sun, and good, and is begged for help in preserving the love union. The dawn is light, and the sun, and bad, and is feared because it will destroy the love union.

In interpreting this strophe we are faced with what many scholars of medieval literature would consider a difficult choice. If we assume that Giraut de Bornelh knew what he was doing, then we must assume that this conjunction of two kinds of light conveying contradictory meanings was intentionally designed to express a paradoxical idea or experience, an idea or experience which plays a fundamental part in the meaning of the poem as a whole. The alternative is to suppose that Giraut did not realize that he was using light imagery in a contradictory way, or that if he did realize it he nevertheless intended nothing by it.[59] In the absence of letters or journals of Giraut explaining his poetic procedures and intentions, this is not a problem that can be resolved on the basis of documentary evidence. To suppose that a writer of whom we know virtually nothing aside from his actual writings had a real poetic intelligence and subtlety is a matter of faith. It is a faith which modern criticism accords without hesitation to writers such as Vergil or Shakespeare. But of medieval writers the only one who has been consistently suspected of knowing what he was doing has been Dante, and even Dante has been criticized for poetical naivety (by Croce, for example). As for the troubadours, it takes some temerity to suggest that at least a few of them were capable of subtle thought and complex meaning, especially when the standard judgment on them remains that of Jeanroy to the effect that they were not much more than skilled versifiers of rather absurd conventional situations.

Nevertheless, I propose to take it for granted, here and at later points in this study, that the poets I am dealing with were not mere scribblers, but that in fact they were quite aware of what they were doing. This simply means that when a text presents us with a complex or problematic effect we ought to accept the fact that the effect *is* there and attempt to explain it on the assumption that good medieval poetry, like good modern poetry, is not based on a series of accidents.

In the present instance, therefore, I would like to suggest that the paradoxical effect of the two kinds of light imagery is meaningful, and, indeed, constitutes one of the central meanings of Giraut's *alba*. The proximity of God and the dawn, both images of light, results in an interplay of meaning between the two. The sense of power and greatness in the invocation to God transfers itself, to some extent, to the dawn, which is conceived of as a great natural force, hostile to love. Similarly, the sense of danger and hostility in the swiftly approaching dawn contributes something to the notion of God that the strophe conveys: He is a great good force that can be asked for help, but at the same time he is a danger to the lovers and to the non-Christian ethical system they seem to be operating under. The suggestion of a symbolic identity between the God who is prayed to and the dawn that is feared leads to the inference that the friend is praying to God, the origin of the Christian moral code, to help the lovers by *not* being imminent, as the dawn is—that is, by effacing Himself and His moral judgments.

All of this is most suggestive, but it would be improper not to admit that the symbolic identification of the dawn with God that is so important for this analysis is not given to us specifically. We are compelled to deduce it from the context and from what we know about medieval dawn symbolism. Consequently, as a critical fact it has less reality than, for example, the identification of God with light in the opening lines, which is perfectly explicit. If we look at the last strophe of the poem, however, we will see that it is not vitally necessary for us to read the dawn as a symbol for God; the paradoxical nature of the poem's attitude toward God remains evident, even without such a symbolic reading.

> VII
>
> *Bel dous companh, tan sui en ric sojorn*
> *Qu'eu no volgra mais fos alba ni jorn,*
> *Car la gensor que anc nasques de maire*
> *Tenc et abras, per qu'eu non prezi gaire*
> > *Lo fol gilos ni l'alba.*

> Handsome sweet comrade, I am in such a precious resting-
> > place
> that I would not want there ever to be dawn nor day,
> for the most noble lady that ever was born of mother
> I hold and embrace; for which reason I do not care at all
> > about the foolish jealous one or the dawn.[60]

This strophe, spoken by the lover himself, rejects the dawn and the day as inferior in value to the lady and to the lover's experience in embracing her. If we accept the supposition that the dawn carries with it some symbolic reference to God, we may read the lover's rejection of the dawn directly as a rejection of God. If we are not convinced of the dawn symbolism, if we think of the dawn merely as a force of nature and a literal narrative fact, the lover's words nevertheless still constitute a rejection of God. The lover's friend has invoked God's aid in Strophe I, and indeed has been praying to Him all night long, as is indicated in Strophe V:

> V
>
> *Bel companho, pos me parti de vos,*
> *Eu no·m dormi ni·m moc de genolhos,*

Ans preiei Deu, lo filh Santa Maria,
Que·us me rendes per leial companhia,
     Et ades sera l'alba.

Handsome comrade, since I left you,
I have not slept nor risen from my knees;
on the contrary, I have prayed God, the son of Saint Mary,
that He might give you back to me for loyal companionship;
     and in a moment it will be dawn.

What, then, is the lover's reply, taken purely in terms of narrative? It amounts to something like this: "All your prayers to God are unnecessary, a waste of breath. I do not need to be protected. I do not need God's help, God's grace. I do not need God at all—because the reality and the excitement of my making love to this paragon of women is so intense that nothing else is real to me, nothing else matters." In his contempt for the *gilos* and the dawn (note the association of the two: the husband with his social values, inferior to those of illicit love, and the day with its natural splendors, inferior to those of the night) the lover is at the same time showing contempt for God, without whose aid, according to Christian dogma, we cannot achieve anything of our own. His scoffing at his friend's prayers declares him to be contemptuous of God's power, just as his adultery declares him contemptuous of God's moral law.

The notion of praying God to give aid in an adulterous love relationship, such as we find it in the first strophe of Giraut's *alba*, is by no means the unique invention of this poet. The same idea, though with a far less elaborate treatment, appears in many *albas*:

> *Plagues a Dieu ja la nueitz non falhis*
> *Ni·l mieus amics lonc de mi no·s partis*
> *Ni la gayta jorn ni alba no vis!*
> *Oy Dieus, oy Dieus, de l'alba! tan tost ve.*

> Might it please God that the night never end,
> nor that my friend ever go far away from me,
> nor that the watchman ever see day or dawn.
> O God, o God, the dawn! how soon it comes![61]

. . . got der lâze iu beiden iemer wol gelingen!

[The watchman:] . . . may God let you both always have
    good fortune![62]

. . . der ritter dô mit triuwen sprach
"nieman kan dich mir geleiden.
der himel segen sî dîn dach."

 . . . the knight then said sincerely [to the lady, as they were
    parting],
"No-one can make me cease to love you.
May the sign of heaven be your protection."[63]

Similar formulas appear in other genres of Provençal and Middle
High German love poetry, with much the same effect. These are
conventional formulas, of course, and we would be wrong to attribute too ponderous a meaning to them. Nevertheless, the fact that
medieval poets can use such formulas at all in such a context is
significant. From the point of view of Christian morality, the morality
we saw in Prudentius's dawn-hymn for example, what the poets are
saying is: "May God help me to enjoy the illicit pleasures of the
wicked, fallen, sinful, flesh-dominated world, and may He shower
his blessings on me and my acts!"—in short, "May God help me
to go to the Devil!" But in the first stanza of Giraut's *alba*, and in
most other poems where the formulas we are speaking of appear,
there is no hint of diabolism or willful blasphemy. It is taken for
granted that there is nothing outrageous in asking for God's help
in adultery or in associating God's beneficent government of the
universe with the successful achievement or repetition of a night of
sexual love.

 To explain this odd circumstance, a number of medievalists have
suggested that what is operating here, as in other cultural phenomena of the High Middle Ages, is a philosophical system known as
"gradualism."[64] This is a name given to the world-view of Saint
Thomas Aquinas, according to which each thing in the universe,

having been created by God, must be good, but with a particular measure of goodness defined by the particular level or "gradus" it occupies in the Great Chain of Being. The world of nature, although inferior to the world of spirit, has its own goodness and value; human institutions, life in this world, secular pleasures, are not in opposition to the divine plan but harmonious parts of it, although of course they are on a relatively low level of goodness. Gottfried Weber sees Wolfram's *Parzival* as a gradualistic poem, in which secular chivalry is shown as good and worthwhile, although it is inferior to the service of the grail and a life dedicated explicitly to God. And Friedrich Ranke points out something similar in certain of the *Minnesänger*. Friedrich von Hausen, for example, praises God for enabling him to love a worthy lady:

> *Ich lobe got der sîner güete,*
> *daz er mir ie verlêch die sinne*
> *daz ich si nam in mîn gemüete:*
> *wan si ist wol wert daz man si minne.*

> I praise God for His goodness,
> that He ever gave me the good sense
> to take her into my heart;
> for she is fully worthy of being loved.[65]

God and the lady are not opposite centers of value; she and the love she gives rise to in the poet are manifestations of God's grace, created by God's goodness, approved of by God and aided by God.

In this poem of Friedrich von Hausen, however, there is no indication that the lady is married. Furthermore, what Friedrich is praising God for is the ennobling feeling of loving a worthy lady; nothing is said of their going to bed with each other. What if the love of a lady leads to an act condemned by Christian morality as a sin? How can that love be enrolled into the harmonious, gradualistic scheme of goodness, presided over by God?

In answer, Ranke cites some lines of Albrecht von Johansdorf:

Swer minne minneclîche treit
gar âne valschen muot,
des sünde wirt vor gote niht geseit.
si tiuret unde ist guot.

A man who loves in a way proper to love,
without any falseness—
his sins will be overlooked by God.
Love ennobles and is good.[66]

The ennobling quality of love for a woman overshadows any sinfulness the lover may have (whether in the act of love or otherwise is
not specified), and God approves of this overshadowing. God Himself is on the side of lovers, not on the side of moralists and church-
men who condemn various kinds of earthly love as sinful. Earthly
love, love for a woman, is a positive good, which in the sight of
God cures and erases sin. It is, so to speak, a substitute for the
sacrament of penance and absolution. Thus even sinful love fits
harmoniously into God's universe.

   The advantage of the gradualistic explanation of troubadour
lyric and *Minnesang* is supposed to be that by it the odd moral
contradictions that are so striking in this poetry can be resolved
and rationalized. The universe of Thomism is a rational whole in
which every part fits perfectly and all relations are rationally ex-
plicable. There is much to be said for *Parzival* as a gradualistic
poem, but I cannot see that gradualism resolves any of the contradictions so apparent in the love poetry we have been speaking of.
What can it tell us that will harmonize, in a *rational* scheme, the
contradictory light symbolism in the first strophe of Giraut de
Bornelh's *alba*, for example? If adultery is taken as a relative good,
it is rational to suppose that God approves of it. But if adultery is
taken into the system, then the Church is thrown out of it. If Albrecht von Johansdorf is suggesting that God loves adulterers, then
he is also suggesting a conflict between the moral judgments of God
and the divine moral law as administered by the Church. The contradiction has been displaced, but it remains a contradiction. Let us

note how Albrecht's poem continues. He declares that if he can find the right kind of women,

> ... *für die wil ich ze helle varn.*
> *die aber mit valschen listen wellent sîn,*
> *für die wil ich niht vallen.*

> ... for them I will go to hell.
> But those whose being is based on false cunning—
> for them I don't intend to be damned.

If God ignores all sins for the sake of a man's love for a woman, why need Albrecht worry about risking hell?

On the other hand, we have seen that Giraut, in his first strophe, does make God an ally of adultery. There is indeed a tension between the two moral systems, a tension suggested by the two kinds of light imagery, but this tension does not lead to rupture. If gradualism does not provide a rational connection between the two, where are we to seek for such a rational connection? I suggest that there is no rational connection at all. We are dealing, in this first strophe of Giraut's *alba*, with an artful poetic representation of that kind of nonrational compromise between the world and God that is characteristic of much of high medieval civilization in general. The demands of God for absolute and total allegiance, as we find them in the Gospels, in Paul, and in the Fathers, are attenuated and reconciled with the pleasures of the world; and the deep contradictions in such an apparent reconciliation are simply accepted and passed over. The elegance and richness of courtly manners and life, treated as ends in themselves and yet not in conflict with the demands of God and the teachings of Christ, constitute a salient example of this courtly compromise. Indeed, the very existence of a secular literature—of romances, lyrics, fabliaux, and so forth, which make their subject the life of love or sex or chivalric prowess or personal development, without considering God at all, and yet without any implication of an *anti*-Christian attitude—is a sign of this nonrational compromise.

Felix Schlösser, in an interesting book on the twelfth-century codifier of "courtly love," Andreas Capellanus, sees the puzzling structure of Andreas's book, *De arte honeste amandi*, as an exceptionally clear expression of this very attitude.[67] Books One and Two of Andreas's treatise, according to Schlösser, depict a cult of love, "eine höfische Heilsordnung," which imitates the forms of the Christian religion: the God-like lady is the object of adoration, the source of value, the dispenser of grace, the means of salvation. Book Three, in contrast, is a straight exposition of orthodox Christian doctrine on love, condemning not only adultery and fornication but also any kind of amorous passion, and attacking women as the source of all evil. The two world-views are not shown to be harmoniously related in a gradualistic scheme. Nor are they shown to be opponents: secular love, with all its cultic observances, is not anti-Christian but merely non-Christian. There are no logical relations whatever between the first two books and the third. The two world-views are simply placed side by side.[68]

But what kind of mentality lies behind this ability to dispense with logical relationships between moral categories that we would consider to be mutually contradictory? Schlösser points to the equally contradictory moral attitudes of many Southern European Catholics today, who find no difficulty in believing in the moral tenets of the Church while at the same time following their proclivities toward sexual relationships condemned by that very Church. The considerable number of sincerely faithful Italian Catholics who vote for the Communist Party might be added as another example of this mentality.[69] In contrast to the logical type of mentality that feels compelled to exclude paradoxes and contradictions—what Schlösser aptly calls the "Entweder-Oder" ("Either-Or") mentality —these Southern Europeans possess a "Sowohl-als-Auch" ("Both-And") mentality.[70] And this is precisely the kind of mentality that could create and accept the odd contradictions between erotic love and Christianity that we find in the first strophe of Giraut's *alba* and in the other examples of the "God-aid-me-in-adultery" formula we have mentioned. The breadth of the high medieval acceptance of this "Sowohl-als-Auch" compromise is perhaps demonstrated even more clearly in these conventional formulas than in such elaborate structures as *De arte honeste amandi*. The fact that we find such formulas in lyrics that give us no sign of making formal philosophical statements about the relations of God and the world—indeed, the very fact that such a paradoxical attitude has been reduced to a formula—indicates an acceptance of the compromise so widespread and unselfconscious that we really seem justified in speaking of a particular (and, to us, rather alien) "mentality" at work in this poetry.

On the other hand, neither gradualism, which sees God and the world harmoniously joined, nor the "Sowohl-als-Auch" mentality, which sees God and the world as contradictory, yet ignores the contradictions, can account for all the kinds of relationship between God and the world that we find in medieval literature. There is a strong strain of medieval thought which thinks of God and the world as irreconcilable opponents, and which, in the conflict between the two, resolutely takes the side of God. This is the tradition of Christian asceticism and hatred of the world that we find so prominent in Saint Jerome, Saint Augustine, and other apologists of the early Church; it is the tradition of treatises "de contemptu mundi," a tradition perfectly alive at the height of the High Middle Ages. The mentality at work here is acutely of the "Entweder-Oder" type, and the world-view it holds is a thoroughgoing dualism, with God and the spiritual held to be all good and the only good, and the world and the fleshly treated as beneath contempt. Prudentius's dawn-hymn reflects this mentality and this world-view, and it makes them concrete in the literally black and white distinctions it draws between the good light and the evil darkness, the desirable day and the abominable night.

Another literary tradition in the Middle Ages, the obverse of the Christian dualistic world-view, acknowledges the irreconcilable conflict between the ethics of erotic love and the ethics of Christianity, but comes out on the side of love. Or perhaps it would be better to say that certain scholars assert the existence of such a literary tradition; for it is a matter of controversy whether the texts in question are legitimately to be interpreted as anti-Christian. The classic statement of this theory in regard to troubadour poetry is that of Eduard

Wechssler in his influential book, *Das Kulturproblem des Minne-sangs* (1909):

It was just at that time that the troubadours, as spokesmen for courtly society, had attained a new view of life. A transvaluation of values had taken place, a new *Weltanschauung* had been proclaimed, in open opposition to the Church. . . . Instead of asceticism, it was the joy of life that was represented not only as a right but as the primary duty of cultivated men and women. . . . Then, for the first time, sexual love recovered its rights and reviled Nature was permitted to return to her place. . . . Formerly, fleshly concupiscence had appeared to the Fathers of the Church as a stigma of man's corrupted nature; now, from merry Provence, a new gospel of salvation rang out, according to which a noble love between man and woman was the source and origin of everything good.[71]

For Wechssler, troubadour love poetry was consciously anti-Christian. It elevated what the Church considered base sin to the acme of all human experience. It set up a religion of love in competition with Christianity and showed the demands of erotic love as more urgent and more important than the demands of Christ.

Opinions similar to those of Wechssler were later voiced by other scholars in regard to the interpretation of the quintessential medieval romance of adultery, the *Tristan* of Gottfried von Strassburg: Schwietering,[72] Ranke,[73] and especially Gottfried Weber, who asserted without qualification that *Tristan* is anti-Christian, an "inhaltlich zweifelsohne antichristliches Werk."[74] All of these interpretations have met with criticism of various kinds,[75] so that the problem of the putative anti-Christian philosophy of *Tristan*, of troubadour lyric, and of the vast field of *Minnesang*, has grown extremely complex. It is far beyond the ambitions of the present work to attempt to resolve so large a problem in regard to so many different poems; but I should like to contribute a few words to the discussion insofar as it is relevant to the *alba*.

We have seen that the *alba* is constructed in terms of dualistic oppositions: so far we have spoken of the inside-outside opposition and the night-day opposition, and we will point out others in later sections of this study. They are oppositions of worlds of reality and of worlds of value, and, as we have noted, they have a particular analogical relationship to the same categories of oppositions in various forms of Christian thought. In each case there is a close parallel to the structure of Christian thought, and at the same time a reversal of Christian values and Christian symbols. The dualism of the worlds of value in the *alba*, and the reversal of the values Christianity attributes to those worlds, indicate, at least to a certain extent, the kind of anti-Christian world-view, modeled on Christian forms, that Weber has seen in *Tristan* and Wechssler has seen in all troubadour poetry and *Minnesang*. When Albrecht von Johansdorf, in the poem (not an *alba*) quoted earlier, says that a lady who meets his qualifications is worth being damned for, he is clearly—if only playfully—setting up an irreconcilable opposition between loving a lady and obeying God. In quite the same way, the lover who speaks in the last strophe of Giraut de Bornelh's *alba* is setting himself up in opposition to God, in terms of the narrative and perhaps in terms of the light symbolism as well. His inner world, dominated by the lady and her love, is not merely placed in "Sowohl-als-Auch" juxtaposition with the God his friend has been praying to; it is declared to be superior to God's grace and perhaps to God Himself.

Thus, the seven strophes of Giraut's *alba* (whether we take them to be all by Giraut or to result from a collaboration between Giraut and another poet—see Appendix B) present us, in their narrative and perhaps in their light imagery, with two different concepts of the relationship between erotic love and God. The first six strophes, spoken by the friend who is taking the role of watchman, show us the "Sowohl-als-Auch" mentality Felix Schlösser posited as the basis of Andreas Capellanus's treatise on love: the essential ideological incompatibility between adulterous love and the Christian God is blithely ignored. In the last strophe, spoken by the lover, the author presents us with the notion of a religion of love, modeled on Christianity and in opposition to it, that Wechssler, Schwietering, Ranke, and Weber have spoken of in other connections. This little poem thus gives us two ("Sowohl-als-Auch" and anti-Christian dualism) of the four attitudes toward the relationship between God and the world which we noted earlier. We also encounter the other two (gradualism and Christian dualism) in certain *albas*, although they are scarcely present in this one. Wolfram's "Sîne klâwen," as we shall see, attempts to resolve its dualism by some form of gradualistic thought; and the Christian dualism we saw in Prudentius reappears in the later Christian versions of the erotic *alba*.

We shall consider in the concluding chapter the crucial question as to whether the meanings we have pointed out in the structure and imagery of Giraut's *alba* really deserve to be called world-views —or, in a more general way, whether the ideas we find in medieval love lyrics can be said to represent real attitudes and to constitute a real philosophy. For the present, it will be sufficient to say that— with the various qualifications and complexities we have noted—the structural opposition between the two worlds of value in the *alba* symbolizes three different kinds of ideological opposition: erotic love versus society and erotic love versus nature—as we showed earlier in this chapter—and, finally, erotic love versus Christianity.

LATER DEVELOPMENTS OF NIGHT AND DAY SYMBOLISM

Before we leave the subject of light symbolism, I should like to add a few words about some post-medieval developments of the set of symbols we have been speaking of. It is not my purpose here to attempt a thoroughgoing history of night and day imagery, or even a general survey of these images as they appear in later versions of the *alba*.* But I do want to mention a curious conflation of the different concepts of night and day we have noted in the Middle Ages, a conflation that appears in its full bloom in the Romantic period. I mention this not only for its own interest but also for the interesting perspective it gives us on the medieval poems and systems of thought we are mainly concerned with in this study.

We have noted that in medieval Christian symbolism night symbolizes sin, death, damnation, and all the iniquitous pleasures of

---

* I omit, for example, *Romeo and Juliet*, a work in which *albas* and *alba*-like situations play a prominent part, and which has frequently been analyzed from the point of view of light imagery.

this world, including sexual pleasure, while day symbolizes the reward of virtue, heavenly bliss, and the true reality of God. The erotic *alba* reverses the values of these symbols. Night comes to signify true reality and true bliss, which consists in sexual union; day comes to signify separation, grief, and the lower-grade values of society, nature, and Christian morality. By the time of the Romantics, these two antithetical symbol systems have been combined and fused in a singular way. Night, in the tradition of the *alba*, remains the time of superior value, but it now contains not only love and sexuality but death (as in Christian tradition) as well—and both valued together as the utmost good. In this symbolic night, love and death become one. A death-wish, conceived in erotic terms, takes the place of the union of lovers as we saw it in the *alba*; or when actual lovers do appear, their sexual union is portrayed as a mystical or literal death. Here is Keats, for example:

> *Darkling I listen; and for many a time*
> *I have been half in love with easeful Death,*
> *Called him soft names in many a musèd rhyme,*
> *To take into the air my quiet breath;*
> *Now more than ever seems it rich to die,*
> *To cease upon the midnight with no pain . . . .*[76]

Night is the time of highest reality, associated with the ecstatic song of the nightingale. Personified death becomes the object of a metaphoric erotic yearning. The aim of *eros* becomes nonbeing, conceived of as the highest state of being. And the achievement of this erotic union with death is to take place in the blackness of midnight, portrayed with all the dense sensuality of language Keats could command.

The second act of Richard Wagner's *Tristan und Isolde* may be taken as a vastly expanded *alba*. First the preparations for Tristan's night visit; then his arrival; the passionate dialog of the lovers; the warnings as to the approach of dawn, sung by Brangäne from the ramparts ("von der Zinne her") in the manner of so many medieval-*alba* watchmen; the lovers' refusal to listen—all these belong to the plot of the *alba*, in its various medieval forms. (Only the arrival of

Marke, the injured husband, is foreign to the *alba*; such an arrival
is the ever-present danger that constitutes the emotional frame of
the poem, but in the *alba* the husband never arrives.) The sentiments
of the lovers ultimately derive from Wagner's source, the *Tristan* of
Gottfried von Strassburg, in which the painful ecstasy of love, the
opposition of the lovers to the values of the rest of the world, and
even the association of mystical erotic union with death, are all to
be found. To these elements Wagner added a full panoply of night
and day symbolism (not found in Gottfried), which, whatever its
immediate source, may be seen as a fusion of the kind of symbolism
we have found in the erotic *alba* and the kind we analyzed in Prudentius.[77] Day is cursed as the time of illusion, unreality, superficial
values; night is the true reality of love and the true reality of death;
and love *is* death, to be sought after above all things, a "sehnend
verlangter Liebestod":

> *O nun waren wir*
> *Nachtgeweihte!*
> *Der tückische Tag,*
> *der Neidbereite,*
> *trennen konnt uns sein Trug,*
> *doch nicht mehr täuschen sein Lug!*
> *Seine eitle Pracht,*
> *seinen prahlenden Schein*
> *verlacht, wem die Nacht*
> *den Blick geweiht:*
> *seines flackerndern Lichtes*
> *flüchtige Blitze*
> *blenden uns nicht mehr.*
> *Wer des Todes Nacht*
> *liebend erschaut,*
> *wem sie ihr tief*
> *Geheimnis vertraut:*
> *des Tages Lügen,*
> *Ruhm und Ehr',*
> *Macht und Gewinn,*

so schimmernd hehr,
wie eitler Staub der Sonnen
sind sie vor dem zersponnen!
In des Tages eitlem Wähnen
bleibt ihm ein einzig Sehnen,—
das Sehnen hin
zur heil'gen Nacht,
wo urewig,
einzig wahr
Liebeswonne ihm lacht!

O now we were
consecrated to night!
The spiteful day,
capable of all envy—
his illusion could separate us,
but his lie could no longer deceive us!
His vain splendor,
his gaudy brightness,
he laughs at, he to whom night
has dedicated her gaze.
The fleeting lightning-flashes
of his flickering light
no longer blind us.
He who looks lovingly
on death's night,
he to whom she entrusts
her deep secret—
the day's lies,
fame and honor,
power and profit,
so gleamingly exalted,
they whirl away before him
like insubstantial dust before the sun!
In the day's vain illusions
there remains to him a single yearning:

the yearning thither
to the holy night,
where from all eternity,
alone true,
the joy of love smilingly greets him![78]

Compare Prudentius:

aurum, voluptas, gaudium,
opes, honores, prospera,
quaecumque nos inflant mala,
fit mane, nil sunt omnia.

Gold, pleasure, joy, riches, honors, successes, all those evil
things that puff us up—when morning comes, they are all
nothing.

But the worldly profit and honor that Prudentius associated with
false value, death, and night are associated by Wagner's Tristan
with the false values of day. The "voluptas" and "gaudium" of
sexual love still belong to night, and so does eternal death; but in
Wagner sexual love and eternal death, both still symbolized by the
night, have become the ultimate of desirability, Romantic substi-
tutes for the divine love and eternal life Prudentius symbolized by
the day.

A final example of the Romantic manipulation of night and day
symbolism—Baudelaire's "Recueillement":

Sois sage, ô ma Douleur, et tiens-toi plus tranquille.
Tu réclamais le Soir; il descend; le voici:
Une atmosphère obscure enveloppe la ville,
Aux uns portant la paix, aux autres le souci.

Pendant que des mortels la multitude vile,
Sous le fouet du Plaisir, ce bourreau sans merci,
Va cueillir des remords dans la fête servile,
Ma Douleur, donne-moi la main; viens par ici,

Loin d'eux. Vois se pencher les défuntes Années,
Sur les balcons du ciel, en robes surannées;
Surgir du fond des eaux le Regret souriant;

Le Soleil moribond s'endormir sous une arche,
Et, comme un long linceul traînant à l'Orient,
Entends, ma chère, entends la douce Nuit qui marche.

Be wise, o my Suffering, and be calmer.
You asked for the evening; it is coming down; it is here:
A dark air is wrapping round the city
Bringing peace to some, and care to others.

While men of the vulgar crowd,
Beneath the whip of Pleasure, merciless tormentor,
Go gathering remorse from their slavish merriment,
My Suffering, give me your hand; come this way,

Far from them. See how the dead Years are bending
Over the sky's parapet, in the dress of a time long past;
How Sorrow, smiling, is rising from the water's bottom;

How the dying sun is going to sleep under an arch;
And, like a long shroud trailing Eastward,
Listen, my dear, listen to the steps of the peaceful Night.[79]

With a movement like that of the *serena*, the variant of the *alba* we mentioned before, Baudelaire's poem longs for night to come. It is a night with many meanings, all of which we have seen before in this chapter. Just as the dawn of the Day of Judgment, in Christian symbolism, took its value-tone from the attitudes toward it of the various kinds of people it came upon (for sinners it was fearful and for the virtuous it was full of joy), so this night brings peace to some and care to others. (The night in the passage we quoted from Vergil had much the same kind of dual effect: for the beasts and birds night brought peace, which is the meaning of night from a naturalistic point of view; but not so the Phoenician queen, set apart from nature by her erotic passion.) The city crowd—the faceless nineteenth-century mob in its oppressive, imprisoning, Romantic city—goes in pursuit of the "voluptas" and "gaudium" Prudentius condemned, the false goods of the flesh. The tormenting "Plaisir" who pursues them with his whip is at once a personification of their sins, of the sort any medieval Christian moralist might have invented; a demon of the darkness, of the sort we have spoken of in connection with the popular superstitious evaluation of night; and a punishing devil in hell—for the Romantic city is the secularized version of the Christian hell.

Night is thus a symbol of peace, as it is in nature; of demonic spirits, as it is to the superstitious mind; and of care, fleshly pleasures, sin, torture, and hell, as it is in Christian symbolism. Night is also death—the dead years, the dead fashions of the past, the dying sun, the long trailing shroud, a world in which nothing is capable of resurrection but Sorrow. But this is death seen as a great good, as peace, calmness, and an end to all suffering; not the death the Christian seeks to avoid, but the death the Romantic seeks to embrace.

And the night is also a setting for erotic love, as in the *alba*; for this *serena* is a love poem, with the poet's personified Suffering as his beloved, retiring with him to a solitary place far from the contemptible world of society and its superficial values, and enjoying with him the highest experience men and women are capable of—the experience of Night.

THREE

HE WATCHMAN AND THE LADY

THE MAIN ACTIVE characters of most erotic *albas* are the watchman and the lady; in a majority of the *albas* the lover plays a more passive, and frequently a silent, role. Scholars of medieval literature, so often inclined to see medieval poems as amalgams of independent traditions, each with its own distinct origin, have seized upon the prominence of the watchman and the lady in the *alba* as evidence that each of these personages must derive from a genre in which he or she at one time figured alone. Some have insisted that the watchman's song came first, and that the lady and her love affair were subsequently added to this core.[1] Others have maintained that the *alba* was originally a branch of the genre of women's laments (*Frauenstrophen*), ultimately of folk origin, and that the watchman was a later addition.[2] And others, more circumspect in matters of chronology, have suggested only that the *alba* is a combination of genres, without insisting on precedence.[3]

In fact, however, these theories as to separate genres bear only on the hypothetical prehistory of the *alba*, and are of no use whatever in the critical analysis of the texts we have. In no *alba* in which both the lady and the watchman appear is there the slightest evidence that either was pasted onto the genre of the other. They are both characters in a conventional, coherent dramatic situation, and in their fictional world they quite satisfactorily belong together.

Let us look at an *alba* consisting entirely of speeches by the lady and the watchman, one which more than any other has given impetus to the notion that the *alba* combines two originally distinct lyric genres.

I

" S'anc fui belha ni prezada,
ar sui d'aut en bas tornada,
qu'a un vilan sui donada
tot per sa gran manentia;
e murria
s'ieu fin amic non avia
cuy disses mo marrimen
e guaita plazen
que mi fes son d'alba."

II

" Eu sui tan corteza guaita
que no vuelh sia desfaita
leials amors a dreit faita,
per que·m don guarda del dia,
si venria,
e drutz que jai ab s'amia
prenda comjat francamen,
baizan e tenen,
qu'ieu crit, quan vei l'alba.

III

" *S'ieu e nulh castelh guaitava*
ni fals' amors y renhava,
fals si' ieu, si no celava
lo jorn aitan quan poiria;
car volria
partir falsa drudaria,
et entre la leial gen
guait ieu leialmen
e crit, quan vei l'alba.

IV

" *Be·m plai longua nueg escura*
el temps d'ivern, on plus dura,
e no·m lais ges per freidura
qu'ieu leials guaita no sia
tota via,
per tal que segurs estia
fins drutz, quan pren jauzimen
de domna valen,
et crit quan vei l'alba."

V

" *Ja per guap ni per menassa*
que mos mals maritz me fassa,
no mudarai qu'ieu non jassa
ab mon amic tro al dia,
quar seria
desconoissens vilania
qui partia malamen
son amic valen
de si, tro en l'alba."

VI

" *Anc no vi jauzen*
drut que·l plagues l'alba.

VII

"*Per so no m'es gen
ni·m plai quan vei l'alba.*"

I

"If ever I was beautiful or renowned,
now I am changed from high to low,
for I am given to a boor
all for his great wealth;
    and I would die
if I did not have a true lover
to whom I could tell my sorrow,
  and a complaisant watchman
  who could warn me of the dawn."

II

"I am such a fine-hearted watchman
that I do not want a faithful and justly established
    love affair
to be undone;
for which reason I am attentive
    lest the day should come,
in order that a lover who is lying with his lady
may freely take his leave,
  kissing and embracing,
  because I cry out when I see the dawn.

III

"If I were on watch in some castle
and false love ruled there,
I would be false myself if I did not hide
the day as much as I could;
    for I would want
to break up false love-making;
but among faithful people
  I watch faithfully,
  and cry out when I see the dawn.

IV

"I like the long dark night
in the wintertime, when it is longest,
and not for the cold will I cease the least bit
to be a faithful watchman
      always,
so that a true lover
may be safe when he is taking enjoyment
  of a worthy lady;
    and I cry out when I see the dawn."

V

"Not for any jibe or threat
that my wicked husband may offer me
will I refrain from lying
with my lover till daylight,
    for it would be
ignorant boorishness
to rudely separate
  one's worthy lover
    from oneself, until the dawn."

VI

"I never saw a lover rejoicing
because he liked the dawn.

VII

"For that reason it does not suit me,
nor do I like it, when I see the dawn."[4]

It will be noted that Strophes I and V of this poem by the
troubadour Cadenet (as it appears in the standard edition by Appel)
are spoken by the lady, while II, III, and IV are spoken by the
watchman. It is not clear who speaks VI and VII—the *tornadas*, as
they are called. The exact arrangement of the strophes poses a difficult
editorial problem—a problem which, by its very existence, tells us
something of considerable importance about what the poet was trying

to do. The fact to be explained is that the number and arrangement of the strophes varies so radically from manuscript to manuscript.[5] All of the manuscripts but three give us different arrangements of the speeches of the lady and the watchman: lady–watchman–lady; watchman–lady–watchman; lady–watchman. One manuscript contains only one of the strophes, and so may be discounted for purposes of ascertaining the correct arrangement. Two manuscripts contain the watchman's strophes only—along with the two *tornadas*, which these manuscripts evidently assign to him. The varied arrangements of the strophes in the manuscripts show us—but of course this is already evident from the text itself—that there is no story being told that would have suggested some kind of chronological narrative ordering of the strophes, and that there is no interaction between the watchman and the lady that might also have served in establishing an order. The existence, in MSS. A and D, of a version composed solely of the watchman's strophes shows us—and again this is evident from the text of the poem—that the watchman's part forms a coherent whole in itself, easily isolable from the rest. It is also evident that the lady's strophes are equally isolable and could form an independent poem.

All of this led Stengel ("Entwicklungsgang") and Appel, the editor of Cadenet's works, to conclude that the poem is a combination of two genres. For Stengel the two genres were the *watchman's song* and the *chanson de la mal mariée*, a traditional form of female lament in which the lady complains of her incompatibility with her boorish, wicked, or emotionally inadequate husband. Appel agreed as to the lady's strophes, but suggested that the watchman's strophes would better be thought of as constituting, in themselves, an *alba*.

I would submit, however, that the real reason for the chaotic disagreements among the manuscripts lies in the very nature of Cadenet's poem. We are dealing here not with two poems but with one, as should be evident merely from the unity imposed by the metrical scheme and the rhymes. It is true that we do not have any dramatic action, leading from one event to another; and that the two speakers do not interact with each other, or even speak to each other. But that is because what Cadenet wished to give us was a formal exposition of the characters involved in a drama that had already become perfectly conventional and perfectly familiar (the poem may have been written as late as the 1230s). He does not present a dramatic scene taking place at a dramatic moment—the moment of separation which forms the emotional focal point of most *albas*. Instead, he characterizes, through their first-person dramatic monologues, the well-known conventional characters of the *alba*, and in doing so he makes these characters ideal and timeless. The lady is beautiful, grief-stricken, passionate, and in love: she is a pure distillation of the characteristics demanded of her by the conventional situation she finds herself in. Anna Karenina and Emma Bovary, those later *mal mariées*, are, so to speak, this same ideal lady clothed in a great number of psychological and social particularities; the situations they are involved in are more complicated and "realistic" than hers, but their realistic situations diverge from her archetypal situation only in details. The watchman, too, is an ideal. He is perfectly "corteza" and "leials"; he has perfect sympathy with the lovers; he is perfectly attentive to the time of night; he is a perfect upholder of "leials amors" and a perfect condemner of "falsa drudaria." In short, he is all that an *alba* could ask for, and that is exactly what he is intended to be: an ideal and almost abstract combination of all the qualities watchmen are compelled to have by their function in the *alba*-situation.

What we have here, then, is not a combination of different poems or different genres, but a kind of animated dramatis personae of a single genre, the *alba*. The type of theoretical dramatic monologue or self-presentation of an ideal character that we find in both the watchman's and the lady's strophes is by no means unusual in medieval literature. It is one of the common techniques of allegory. At the beginning of *The Castle of Perseverance*, for example, three of the main characters in the conventional and well-known dramatic situation of temptation and sin, the World ("Mundus"), the Flesh ("Caro"), and the Devil ("Belyal"), describe themselves in quite the same theoretical, abstract, and ideal manner we have noted in the speeches of Cadenet's watchman and lady.[6] Here is what Caro has to say for himself:

I byde, as a brod brustun gutte, a-bouyn on these touris!
Euery body is the beter that to myn byddynge is bent.
I am Mankyndis fayre Flesch, florchyd in flowris;
My lyfe is with lustys and lykynge i-lent;
With tapytys of tafata I tymbyr my towris;
In myrthe and in melodye my mende is i-ment . . . .

He is a perfect distillation of all the qualities of overvalued physical pleasures as such pleasures function in the story of each Christian's moral life, just as Cadenet's watchman is a perfect distillation of all the qualities of trusty watchmen as such watchmen function in the plot of most *albas*. We should notice, too, that each of these three allegorical personages in *The Castle of Perseverance* simply stands up on his tower and speaks his piece; there is no interaction among them, indeed no action of any kind in this part of the play. Furthermore, there is nothing in any of the speeches to indicate some necessary order in which the three "persons" must speak; the speeches could easily be rearranged, without any damage to the drama. But it has not been suggested that what we have here is a conflation of a Mundus genre, a Belyal genre, and a Caro genre. Although the three do not interact, they clearly belong together, just as the trusty watchman and the lady-married-to-a-boor belong together in Cadenet's *alba*; for whatever the prehistory of the latter two figures may have been, by the time the *alba* plot had become established both of them were firmly (although not indissolubly) part of it.

Let us try to find out something more about these two prominent actors in the drama of the *alba*. What part do they play in the dramatic action? How do they relate to each other, to the knight, and to the structure of the *alba* world? What meanings do they and their relationships convey?

THE WATCHMAN

We will begin with the watchman. We have already seen him in his ideal character, a character which owes its nature to the role assigned the watchman in the *alba* plot. The question presents itself, as in all studies of medieval literature, as to how much true social history we can discern behind this idealized fictional personage. To what extent may the portrait of the watchman given us in *albas* such as Cadenet's or Wolfram's "Sîne klâwen" be said to constitute a portrait of real historical watchmen behaving as real watchmen did behave? And this, of course, is part of the larger question as to the historical and social reality of the *alba* story in its entirety.

An older school of criticism, now largely discredited, took the *alba* (and medieval poetry in general) as a more or less accurate portrayal of real events, and, therefore, as a legitimate source for social history. The more conservative members of this school, while believing that the *alba* plot must have had its origin in a real experience, were nevertheless willing to admit that in its later history the genre had become conventional and merely literary.[7] More thorough-going "realists" (such as Alwin Schultz) have taken the *albas* as actual historical and biographical records of individual events: each *alba* narrates a real night of love, and a real separation at dawn engineered by a real watchman, with the knight of the story representing the poet himself.[8] A more sophisticated branch of this school takes the position that, while the *albas* are only fictions, they represent wish-fulfilment fantasies on the part of poets really in love with inaccessible married women. The *alba* would thus be a psychological symptom of an actual biographical frustration. Furthermore, it would have been directed by the poet at an actual lady, to tell her what sort of fantasies the frustrated poet was having about her.[9]

Later criticism has discarded most of these judgments as historically unjustifiable or logically absurd. Courtly lyric, along with other vernacular literary forms in the Middle Ages, was fictional, not reportorial. We know virtually nothing about the actual customs of courtly society in regard to the relations of men and women in love. Most of our information on this subject comes from literary works, and we are not justified in taking literary fictions as actual social history. Nor are we justified in taking love-lyrics as depictions of the real love-affairs and real amorous feelings of the poets—not even of their frustrated fantasies. A poet who professed himself, before a courtly audience, as violently in love with the wife of his

liege-lord was not baring his heart in the manner of an autobio-
grapher; he was singing a dramatic aria, acting out a fictional role,
and his audience must have been perfectly aware of this. Furthermore, the fact that troubadour lyrics—and *albas* especially—repeat
the same dramatic situation again and again, with only minor variations, should give prima-facie evidence that these poems are theoretical and conventional, not autobiographical. A poet wrote *albas*,
not because he had experienced the situation depicted by the *alba*,
and not even because he fancied himself experiencing it with a
particular woman he was in love with, but simply because it was one
of the current literary genres. The watchman's role, in particular,
was not drawn from life, but was simply a fixed part of the convention.[10]

If the watchman's role in the *alba* was strictly literary and conventional, it might be plausibly supposed that this role derived from a
literary source antedating the first Provençal *albas*. The source that
has most frequently been suggested is Leander's letter to Hero, in
Ovid (*Heroides* xviii).[11] Leander narrates the night he spent together
with Hero in her tower, the arrival of the dawn, their complaints
at the brevity of the night and their hasty farewell kisses, the bitter
warnings of Hero's nurse ("monitu nutricis amaro") that they must
part, and their tearful parting ("digredimur flentes").[12]

There can be no doubt that, in its broad outlines, the moment of
parting in Ovid's poem resembles the plot of the *alba*. In addition,
the role the nurse plays in Ovid is similar to the role of the *alba*'s
watchman. There are, indeed, some *albas* (mostly late) in which the
love is not adulterous, as it is not in Ovid, and also some in which
the watchman's part is taken by a maidservant of the lady. *Romeo
and Juliet* gives us both of these motifs. But in the great majority of
the *albas* written during the High Middle Ages the love affair *is*
adulterous, with considerable effect on the structure and meaning of
the *alba*, as we indicated in Chapter Two. It is, therefore, not enough
to say (and in any case no real proof can ever be offered for such an
assertion) that the Leander letter is the source of the *alba*; it is
necessary to differentiate between the two kinds of love, adulterous
and nonadulterous, and to show the function each kind of love

plays in the work it appears in. Very much the same thing is true of the watchman. Hero's nurse and the *alba*'s watchman both urge the lover to leave at dawn. The watchman may perhaps "derive" from the nurse; but if so, why did he not remain a nurse? The *alba* does not limit its references to the watchman to a one-line indication that he urges the lover to leave. There is great emphasis laid on this figure and the part he plays in the story, and there is great emphasis laid on the fact that he is a watchman. Replace him by a nurse and you have a very different poem indeed.

In short, we must recognise that a watchman in medieval literature carries with him certain meanings and associations, and that the very fact that he is a watchman (and not a nurse or a serving-maid) is of considerable significance for the nature of his role in the poem. To understand that role we must look, not at Ovid's nurse, but at other watchmen and watchmen-like figures in medieval literature—or, to be more accurate, in the literature that the Middle Ages thought of as its own.

This last qualification is necessary because some (and not the least important) of the literary watchmen we are going to look at are Biblical, rather than strictly medieval. One of these is God Himself:

> *Ecce non dormitabit neque dormiet, qui custodit Israel.*
> *Dominus custodit te, Dominus protectio tua, super manum dexteram tuam.*
> *Per diem sol non uret te: neque luna per noctem.*
> *Dominus custodit te ab omni malo: custodiat animam tuam Dominus.*

> Behold he shall neither slumber nor sleep, that keepeth Israel.
> The Lord is thy keeper, the Lord is thy protection upon thy right hand.
> The sun shall not burn thee by day: nor the moon by night.
> The lord keepeth thee from all evil: may the Lord keep thy soul. (Psalm cxx.4–7)

God is the keeper or watchman of Israel and of the individual believer under His protection. The metaphor here, carried out only vaguely, is of Israel (and the individual believer and the believer's soul) as a city, with God as its watchman. In this capacity, God's most salient characteristic is His wakefulness: He does not sleep, even at nighttime when everyone else does. He is thus superior to the cycles of time that dominate human life. Whether evil comes during the day or during the night, the unsleeping God will immediately see it and be able to ward it off. That He is unsleeping, then, means that both His knowledge and His power are continuous, unlike the knowledge and the power of men, which are cut off periodically for sleep.

God is also figured as a sunshade or covering on the believer's right hand. This protects the believer from being burned by the heavenly bodies; it separates him, by covering him over, from the great destructive forces of nature. This protection, too, is independent of time. At night God protects us from the dangers peculiar to night, and during the day against the dangers peculiar to day.

Another significant Biblical passage figuring God as a watchman is the following:

> *Nisi Dominus aedificaverit domum, in vanum laboraverunt qui aedificant eam. Nisi Dominus custodierit civitatem, frustra vigilat qui custodit eam.*
>
> Unless the Lord build the house, they labour in vain that build it. Unless the Lord keep the city, he watcheth in vain that keepeth it. (Psalm cxxvi.1)

The meaning of this passage is that human works, without God's help, are futile. A city has two kinds of guardians or watchmen: those human beings who are assigned to the task, and God. A city, which is a center of civilization, must be guarded from the destructive human forces without. God, as usual in the Old Testament, takes the part of His people, His city, against those enemies who lie outside it and may attack it.

The metaphor of God as watchman does not exhaust the metaphorical use in the Bible of watchmen and watchmen-like persons.

In the following passage, it is the prophet Ezekiel who is a watch-man—or perhaps "scout" would be a better translation:

Cum autem pertransissent septem dies, factum est verbum Domini ad me, dicens:
Fili hominis, speculatorem dedi te domui Israel: et audies de ore meo verbum, et annunciabis eis ex me.
Si dicente me ad impium: Morte morieris: non annunciaveris ei, neque locutus fueris ut avertatur a via sua impia, et vivat: ipse impius in iniquitate sua morietur, sanguinem autem ejus de manu tua requiram.
Si autem tu annunciaveris impio, et ille non fuerit conversus ab impietate sua, et a via sua impia: ipse quidem in iniquitate sua morietur, tu autem animam tuam liberasti.

And at the end of seven days the word of the Lord came to me, saying:
Son of man, I have made thee a watchman to the house of Israel: and thou shalt hear the word out of my mouth, and shalt tell it them from me.
If, when I say to the wicked, Thou shalt surely die: thou declare it not to him, nor speak to him, that he may be converted from his wicked way, and live: the same wicked man shall die in his iniquity, but I will require his blood at thy hand.
But if thou give warning to the wicked, and he be not converted from his wickedness, and from his evil way: he indeed shall die in his iniquity, but thou hast delivered thy soul. (Ezekiel iii.16–19)[13]

In the previous two quotations the idea of "watchman" appeared in the forms of the verb *custodire*. This verb means, essentially, 'to guard', but since guarding necessitates looking out for danger, *custodire* could also be used in the sense of 'to observe, look at'. The Romance languages, in a series of words deriving from a Germanic root *wardôn*, also associate the two ideas: cf. Italian *guardia* 'guard' and *guardare* 'to look at'.[14] The two functions of God as watchman, then, are to protect and to see. He sees the dangers and He protects the threatened city against them by using His power. The prophet as watchman, in the passage from Ezekiel we have just quoted, is not a *custos* but a *speculator*, that is, one who spies out the land, who observes, examines, sees. This is the watchman purely in his function of seeing and knowing. The *speculator*, having perceived the imminence of danger, does not then take on the function of fighting against it, as God, the *custos* of the city, does. His job is to pass his knowledge along to those who can make use of it. The *speculator* as a military scout is thus a connecting link between the enemy army, to whom he is related by the fact that he sees them, and his own army, whom he rouses to action; he is a mediator between knowledge and action. In the same way, the prophet is a mediator between the word of God and the actions of men. He perceives (the sense here is hearing, rather than sight) the moral laws of God, he transmits them to men, and it is then up to those who have heard him to act on what he has told them. The prophet does not speak his own thought, but gives voice to the thoughts of a higher power, God. Furthermore, the message that God gives to him (and to all Biblical prophets) to transmit is a message about the necessity for a certain kind of action, namely, repentance, a change of heart, a turning of one's life from the wrong path to the right path.

The *speculator* also appears in Christian dawn-hymns. In Prudentius, for example, we find:

> *Speculator astat desuper,*
> *Qui nos diebus omnibus*
> *Actusque nostros prospicit*
> *A luce prima in vesperum.*

> A watchman [or scout] stands above, who every day looks out upon us and our deeds from the first light until evening.[15]

This watchman is probably Christ, viewing the acts of men from a high position, which is literally heaven and metaphorically—as is suggested by the *speculator* metaphor—a *specula* ("watch-tower"), the high tower from which a watchman looks out. We have noted that a *speculator*'s function is to transmit knowledge of what he has seen to others who will take action on that knowledge. The implication of the metaphor here—only suggested, however, rather than explicitly stated—is that the *speculator* (Christ?) transmits what he has seen of the acts of men to someone else (God the Father?) who will take action on it, rewarding or punishing as the case requires. The exact identification of the *speculator* and of whoever stands behind him is not possible on the basis of what is given us in the poem, and we may suppose that Prudentius did not intend the metaphor to be carried through to a precise allegory. We should note, however, that the relation of this *speculator* to mankind is the opposite of the relation of the prophet-as-*speculator* to mankind. This heavenly watchman perceives the acts of men and transmits His knowledge upward; the prophet perceives the word of God and transmits his knowledge downward, to be acted upon by men. Ezekiel in his watchman role resembles the watchman of the erotic *alba*, in that they both transmit knowledge of a heavenly force (the word of God, or the rising of the sun) to a human being (the sinner, or the lover) in order to impel him to action (the sinner is to turn from the world of sin to the world of virtue, the knight is to leave the inner world of love and go out into the world of society). If we were to seek an analogy in troubadour lyric for the *speculator* in Prudentius's poem, we would find such an analogy not in the watchman of the *alba* but rather in the *lauzengier* (Old French *losengier*), the traditional figure—so prominent in the *chanson*—whose role is to spy on the lovers and to bear tales back to the husband: "the all-seeing eye which springs into being the moment something is concealed." [16]

However, in the other dawn-hymn of Prudentius, "Ales diei nuntius," which we studied in detail in Chapter Two, we find a suggestion of Christ as a metaphorical watchman playing the role of prophet rather than spy. The relevant lines, also quoted in the earlier chapter, are these:

> *sed vox ab alto culmine*
> *Christi docentis praemonet*

adesse iam lucem prope,
ne mens sopori serviat . . . .

> But the voice of Christ our teacher forewarns us from the
> high summit that the light is already near, lest our mind be
> enslaved to slumber.[17]

Here Christ, like the watchman in his *specula*, conveys to mankind
the teachings necessary for our salvation; he gives us knowledge,
which we must translate into action. Just as in the case of the
prophet, what Christ knows and tells us is the word of God, and
the action we are to take on that knowledge is the action of repent-
ing and turning toward the light.[18]

We come now to a series of figures who, while not fully equivalent
to the sort of watchmen we have been speaking of, nevertheless
perform a number of specifically watchman-like duties. We have
spoken before of various medieval castle and cloister allegories, with
their valuable interiors, their inimical surroundings, and the openings in their walls that permit the evil outside to enter in. Many of
these allegories include an allegorical guardian, placed at the door
of the castle or cloister, and given the assignment of warning against
approaching dangers. In the sermon on the Abbey of the Holy
Spirit, which we have quoted from before, Damoiselle Peur is por-
tress, "and shall guard well the cloister of conscience." Her duty
is to make sure that the conscience sees no evil, hears no evil, and,
apparently, eats no evil.[19] In other words, a proper sense of shame
and modesty will keep us from looking at sinful pleasures and being
tempted by them, from listening to flattering words and being
seduced by them, and from being overly attracted by food and eating
too much. What Damoiselle Peur does, that is, is to perceive the outside world, censor out any impure sensations, and transmit only the
safe ones inward to the soul. In her mediating capacity between two
worlds she resembles the prophet-as-*speculator*, although there are
considerable differences between the two metaphors. The prophet-
as-*speculator* transmits the truth of a higher world (God) to a lower
world (sinning mankind) to provoke action (repentance, conversion).
Peur as doorkeeper censors knowledge of a lower world (the fallen

world), and then transmits this purified and partial knowledge to the potential inhabitant (the soul) of a higher world (heaven) in order to maintain the soul's purity and enable it to reach that higher world. Both the prophet-as-*speculator* and Fear-as-doorkeeper, however, share a concern for mankind's spiritual welfare, each approaching the problem in a different way: the prophet seeks to turn man toward the good, while allegorical Fear seeks to shield man from the bad.

A doorkeeper thus has an expanded function as compared with a *speculator*. A *speculator* perceives and transmits knowledge of what he has perceived. A doorkeeper does this too, but he also shields and protects, for when a doorkeeper perceives evil or danger outside he can shut the door.[20] An allegorical doorkeeper can even shut the door to keep harmful *knowledge* out. A *speculator* cannot do this, first of all because his duty is to transmit *all* knowledge, so as to permit those to whom he transmits this knowledge to make a totally rational and informed choice as to the course of action to follow, and second because he is not stationed at a door—an opening between two worlds, which can be either opened or shut—but rather in a tower, a lofty place which overlooks two worlds (his own army and that of the enemy) but which cannot be turned into a physical barrier, such as a shut door, to separate them.[21] A doorkeeper comes closer, in his function, to a *custos*, or actual watchman, than a *speculator* does. The *speculator* is, so to speak, the intellectual half of the watchman; the *custos* not only perceives and transmits knowledge, but also takes up arms against the danger he has perceived. An allegorical doorkeeper such as Damoiselle Peur does not quite come to the point of taking up arms against exterior perils; but she is more than a mere transmitter of knowledge, a mere voice. She also *acts*: she opens the door to safe knowledge and shuts it against unsafe knowledge. The metaphorical action of opening and shutting a door is a way of expressing the fact that this psychological faculty ("peur") consists in an exercise of *judgment*. A *speculator* does not exercise judgment of this sort, and neither does the prophet who is figured as a *speculator*.

The exercise of judgment is the prime function of another

allegorical watchman-like figure we shall now look at. In the fourth
book of the treatise, *De anima*, attributed to Hugh of St. Victor, we
are presented with a castle allegory (actually a house allegory) of
the usual type.[22] The house is conscience, the head of the household
is the soul, his family consists of thoughts, actions, and the senses,
and stored up in the house are the treasures of the virtues. Outside
the house and trying to get in are a number of thieves, the vices, of
whom the foremost is the devil.

> *Contra quem et ejus satellites pater idem . . . domum suam
> forti custodia muniens, prudentiam in primo aditu constituat,
> quae discernat quid sit admittendum, quid vitandum, quid
> excludendum.*

> Against whom and whose henchmen this same father . . .
> fortifying his house with a strong guard, should station
> Prudentia at the main entrance, to distinguish between what
> ought to be let in, what ought to be shunned, and what ought
> to be kept out.[23]

Prudentia, who is appointed doorkeeper, is a personification of, precisely, the faculty of judgment. This faculty perceives, classifies
knowledge, and judges which aspects of experience are acceptable
and which are unacceptable. Prudentia is not alone at the doorway,
however:

> *Secus hanc fortitudo locetur, ut hostes, quos prudentia venire
> nuntiaverit, repellat.*

> Next to her Strength should be placed, to drive off the
> enemies Prudentia has seen approaching.

Prudentia makes a judgment as to whether what she sees outside is
an enemy or not; she then passes the information along to Fortitudo,
who acts on it by taking up arms to drive the enemy away. In a
certain sense, then, Prudentia is like the *speculator*, who passes information along for others to act on, although unlike the *speculator*
she plays an active role as judge. Or, to look at the allegory from
another point of view, Prudentia is only part of the guard placed at the

door. The other part is Fortitudo, who actively opposes the enemy. Prudentia and Fortitudo combined (along with Justitia, who is somewhat
of a supernumerary here) make up the *custodia*, which is the collective noun for 'the watch, the watchmen'. This *custodia* has the full
set of functions we have noted in the various terms for watchman
we have spoken of (*custos, vigil, guaita, wahter*): on the one hand,
perceiving and transmitting knowledge, on the other, actively defending and protecting—in short, both knowledge (the province of
Prudentia) and action (the province of Fortitudo).[24]

The word *prudentia*, it should be added, means something more
than Modern English 'prudence'. 'Prudence' suggests the calculation of advantages and disadvantages, the avoidance of those acts
which are judged to be disadvantageous and the choice of those
acts which are judged to be of calculable benefit. *Prudentia* involves
moral choice, not merely calculation of benefits; it distinguishes
between right and wrong, not merely between the safe and the unsafe. When the watchman of the erotic *alba* advises the knight to
leave because the dawn has come and the *gilos* may return, he is
exhibiting prudence but not *prudentia*. Admittedly, there is a strong
pressure on the Latin word *prudentia* to shed its moral implications
and come to signify mere calculation for benefit. In *Sawles Warde*,
the Middle English version of *De anima*, *prudentia* is translated as
warschipe,[25] a word which has a meaning something like 'wariness',
and in which the suggestion of moral judgment is minimal. And so
far as the allegory of the watchman or doorkeeper goes, it is evident
that literal watchmen and doorkeepers are required to exercise prudence, not to make moral judgments.

But the analogy between the *alba* watchman and allegorized
prudentia is a bit closer than this would indicate, since the knight,
to whom the watchman conveys his knowledge along with much
prudent advice, is then faced, as I shall indicate later, with a choice
closely analogous in its structure to a moral choice, a choice between values. I am not suggesting that the *alba* watchman is an
allegorical representation of Christian *prudentia*, nor that Christian
prudentia plays any part in the *alba*. What I am suggesting is that a
complex of associations similar to that involved in Hugh's

doorkeeper-allegory is involved in the meaning of the *alba* watchman, with the common element from which these associations spring being the notion of a *watchman*. A watchman discerns and distinguishes; and this leads to an association with the act of judging; which in turn leads to an association with moral choice. The logical or narrative relationships among the various associations are not quite the same in the two cases, and of course the moral implications are quite different. But the complex of associations is very much the same, in *De anima* and in the *alba*.

Before leaving these examples of allegorical watchmen, we might briefly note the Gospel text which served as a basis for Hugh's allegory:

> *Hoc autem scitote, quoniam si sciret paterfamilias, qua hora fur veniret, vigilaret utique, et non sineret perfodi domum suam.*

> But of this be assured, that if the householder had known at what hour the thief was coming, he would certainly have watched, and not have let his house be broken into. (Luke xii.39)

This passage is part of a series of admonitions to be prepared for the Second Coming of Christ. What is notable, for our purposes, is the set of ideas and images that are associated here: the notion of being on watch, the notion of having a precise knowledge of the time, and the (by this time quite familiar) image of a threatening external force penetrating into an enclosed house. The idea that a man on watch has, and must have, a precise knowledge of time is an especially important one, as we shall see.

We turn now to watchmen in medieval literature who are presented not as allegorical figures but as literal members of society, performing a social function. The earliest of our examples includes, along with literal watchmen, the metaphor of God as watchman which we noted earlier in Psalms cxx and cxxvi.

> *O tu qui servas armis ista moenia,*
> *nolli dormire, moneo, sed vigila!*
> *dum Hector vigil extitit in Troïa,*

non eam cepit fraudulenta Graecia:
prima quiete dormiente Troïa
laxavit Synon fallax claustra perfida:

per funem lapsa occultata agmina
invadunt urbem et incendunt Pergama.
vigili voce avis anser candida
fugavit Gallos ex arce Romulea,
pro qua virtute facta est argentea
et a Romanis adorata ut dea.

nos adoremus celsa Christi numina;
illi canora demus nostra iubila,
illius magna fisi sub custodia
haec vigilantes iubilemus carmina:
divina, mundi rex Christi, custodia
sub tua serva haec castra vigilia.

tu murus tuis sis inexpugnabilis,
sis inimicis hostis tu terribilis.
te vigilante nulla nocet fortia,
qui cuncta fugas procul arma bellica.
tu cinge nostra haec, Christe, munimina,
defendens ea tua forti lancea.

sancta Maria, mater Christi splendida,
haec cum Iohanne, theotocos, impetra;
quorum hic sancta venerantur pignora
et quibus ista sunt sacrata limina;
quo duce victrix est in bello dextera
et sine ipso nihil valent iacula.

fortis iuventus, virtus audax bellica,
vestra per muros audiantur carmina;
et sit in armis alterna vigilia,
ne fraus hostilis haec invadat moenia:
resultet echo "comes, eia vigila,"
per muros "eia" dicat echo "vigila."

O you who keep these ramparts with arms,
do not sleep, I warn you, but remain on watch!
While Hector stood watch in Troy
deceitful Greece could not capture it;
but when Troy was sleeping in the first slumber of night,
false Sinon unfastened the treacherous bolts [of the
        wooden horse];

the hidden hordes, slipping down a rope,
invade the city and burn Pergamum.
A bird, a white goose, with its watchful voice
puts the Gauls to flight from the citadel of Romulus;
for which valor it was modeled in silver
and worshipped by the Romans as a goddess.

Let us worship the lofty Godhead of Christ.
Let us offer Him our melodious songs of jubilation.
Trusting in His great protection,
let those of us on watch sing these jubilant songs:
Divine protector, Christ, king of the world,
keep this city under Your watchful guard.

Be an impregnable wall to Your people.
Be a terrible enemy to the foe.
With You on guard no force can cause harm,
You Who drive all warlike arms far away.
Christ, gird these fortified walls of ours,
defending them with Your powerful spear.

Holy Mary, glorious mother of Christ,
you who bore God, obtain (with the help of Saint John)
       these things for us [by praying to
       Christ].
Holy relics of both of you are venerated here,
and these thresholds are consecrated to you both.
With Christ as leader the right hand is victorious in war,
and without Him spears are of no value.

Brave youths, bold in warlike strength,
let your songs be heard along the walls;
and let the watch take turns in arms
so that no enemy's deceit may invade the ramparts.
Let the echo resound, "Ho, comrade, be watchful!"
Let the echo speak along the walls, "Ho, be watchful!"[26]

This poem, which comes from Modena and dates from around the end of the ninth century, is evidently related to the defenses of the town necessitated by the depredations of the Magyars in Northern Italy at that period.[27] The key to the structure of the poem lies in the lines of the next-to-last strophe:

quo duce victrix est in bello dextera
et sine ipso nihil valent iacula.

There are two kinds of warriors, the human and the divine. It is necessary that the human warriors be valiant and attentive to duty, but their efforts are in vain unless Christ makes one with them in their battle. Hence the poem is alternately a monition to the soldiers and a prayer to Christ: both are to cooperate in the great cause. (That is why my translation distinguishes between "you" and "You.") Troy was protected, for a time, by a heroic man; Rome was saved by a goose who was subsequently worshipped (although in error) as a god; Modena will be saved by the combined efforts of the true God, Christ, and of the heroic men of the town. The defense of the town, of course, means the defense of the fortified walls ("moenia," "muri," "munimina") that surround the town. The soldiers on watch, the "vigilia," are posted on these walls; their job is to be awake and watchful ("vigilantes") and also to be prepared to fight ("in armis") in case it should be necessary. Christ metaphorically shares all these duties. He is the protector ("custodia") of the town; He, too, stands watch ("te vigilante"); He, too, will fight off the enemy with his weapons ("lancea"). Moreover, Christ is not only figured as the men who guard the walls; He is also figured as the walls themselves, as an impregnable wall ("murus inexpugnabilis") of divine power that is placed round ("cingit") the stone walls.

Christ and the soldiers thus possess or are urged to possess all of the watchman-characteristics we have already noted: wakefulness, watchfulness, readiness to fight to protect the town, and both strength and clear-sightedness to keep the exterior enemy from penetrating inside by force or by stealth. (The necessity for all these qualities, with a special emphasis on clear-sightedness and wakefulness, is brought home with considerable poetic intensity by the urgent reiteration of various forms of the root *vigil*: seven different forms, with one of them, the imperative *vigila*, appearing three times. The command in the final two lines that "vigila" should echo along the walls simply makes explicit, on the realistic level, what has been one of the dominating poetical techniques of the whole poem: "vigila" echoes through it from the very beginning.)

Watchmen appear frequently in fictional narratives in the Middle Ages. In the Middle High German life of Saint Oswald, for example, we find:

> *ûf iegelîcheme turne ein wahtaere . . .*
> *darûfe si tac unde naht lâgen,*
> *der bürge si schône pflâgen.*

> on each tower a watchman . . .
> they lay up there day and night,
> they took good care of the castles.[28]

Of interest here is the specific location of the watchmen in towers, which would have provided them with a view of the surrounding countryside as well as of the town (or castle) itself. The exact duties of the watchmen are not made clear, however. We cannot tell whether their duties relate to what is outside the town, or to what is inside, or to both; and *pflegen* is a verb of only the most general meaning.

Herbort von Fritzlar's version of the story of the Trojan War provides us with a more detailed picture; indeed, it gives us two different passages involving the watchman.

> *Do der wechter entsup*
> *Daz sich der tac uf hup*

Und grawen begunde
Er kunte die stunde
Sin stimme harte lute erschal
Der tac schinet uber al
Wol uf rittere ez ist tac
Daz die burc alle erschrac . . . .

When the watchman became aware
that the day was coming up
and beginning to grow gray,
he announced the time.
His voice rang out very loudly:
"The day is shining everywhere!
Get up, knights, it is day!"—
So that the whole town took alarm . . . .[29]

Here it is the watchman's function to announce the hour, specifically the hour of dawn. In the context, his act is associated not only with the passage of time, but also with warfare, since at his call the Trojan warriors rise and go out to do battle with the Greeks.

The association with war is even stronger in the other passage (an earlier one in Herbort's poem):

Des morgens fil fru
Segelten sie zu troyge zu
Ie baz und baz
Der wechter uf der zinnen saz
Sine tageliet er sanc
Daz im sin stimme erklanc
Vom grozme done
Er sanc ez taget schone
Der tag der schinet in den sal
Wol uf ritter uber al
Wol uf ez ist tag
Do er gesanc sin herze erscrac
Sere und harte
Er gesach uf der warte

Blicken gegen dem mer wert
Halsberg schilt helm swert
Und die baniren manicfare
Er en wiste wannen oder ware
Sie waren oder solden
Oder waz sie tun wolden
Er schrei also sere
Daz alle die wechtere
Die uf den zinnen stunden
Schrigen begunden
Er rief und klagete
Daz die burc alle wangete
Fursten frigen dinstman
Scutten ir wappen an . . . .

Very early in the morning
they sailed to Troy,
closer and closer.
The watchman was sitting on the battlements.
He sang his dawn-song
so that his voice rang out
from his great effort.
He sang, "It is already dawning.
The day is shining in the hall.
Get up, knights, everywhere!
Get up, it is day!"
As he was singing his heart was shocked,
violently and extremely.
From his watch-post he had caught a glimpse
of hauberks, shields, helmets, swords,
and many-colored banners
gleaming from the direction of the sea.
He did not know where they came from
or where they were going to
or what their purpose was.
He cried out so violently

that all the watchmen
who were standing on the battlements
began to cry out.
He called and lamented
so that the whole town staggered.
Princes, free men, serving men,
hurried into their armor . . . .[30]

The watchman exercises two functions here. First, he announces
the dawn and urges the knights to get up. The language describing
this function so closely resembles that of many German *albas* (indeed, the watchman's song is specifically called a "tageliet") that it
is natural to suppose that Herbort was acquainted with the *alba*—or,
alternatively, that writers of the early German *albas* were acquainted
with Herbort's poem![31] The establishment of this sort of genetic
relationship is not our purpose here, of course. What is interesting
is that we have in this passage a watchman singing a "tageliet" to
awaken knights, without any lady, love-affair, or *gilos* being involved.
He is awakening them not from love but from sleep, and calling
them out not in order for them to save themselves from the jealous
husband but in order for them to get ready for battle with the
enemies of their city.

The watchman's second function is closely connected with this.
From his lofty position on the battlements, which of course are on
the walls that surround the town and separate it from the battleground outside, he sees the Greek fleet approaching over the sea,
and he conveys this knowledge of imminent danger to the knights
inside the city, impelling them to take action against the external
threat. His first function—seeing and announcing the dawn—merely
makes men rise to their daily work, which in this case happens to
be fighting. His second function—seeing and announcing an approaching danger—is distinct from the first, although in both cases
those to whom he conveys his knowledge are called upon to go out
and fight. There is no suggestion that the watchman himself does
any fighting. He is more of a *speculator* than a full-fledged *custos*.

The watchman also appears in narratives devoted to subjects

other than war. Here are two typical passages from Heinrich von dem Türlin's vast compilation of medieval narrative clichés, *Diu crône:*

> *Vil kûme ir ieglîcher entslief,*
> *Unz daz der wehter rief*
> *Unde kundete in den tac.*
> *Artûs mit sîn gesellen lac*
> *Unz nâhe zuo der nône,*
> *Dô was ime vil schône*
> *Der imbîz bereit*
> *Nâch des hoves gewonheit.*

> Scarcely had they all gotten to sleep
> when the watchman called
> and announced the day.
> Arthur and his companions lay asleep
> almost until midday.
> Then their meal was very nicely
> prepared for them,
> after the custom of the court.[32]

> *Hie mite er ze hant entslief.*
> *Dar nâch vil snelle rief*
> *Der wehter an der zinne.*
> *Nâch der âventiure gewinne*
> *Verslief er den morgen . . . .*

> Hereupon he immediately fell asleep.
> Very shortly afterwards
> the watchman on the battlements gave his call.
> [But] after the successful adventure
> he [the knight] slept the morning away . . . .[33]

These are watchmen in peaceful romance castles, and their only function (or, at least, the only function we are shown) is to announce the time of sunrise. Even in that function, the watchmen are merely decorative background details from the normal social life of the town and play no role in any significant action. In both passages, we notice, the watchman's call is ignored: the knights do *not* get up. The watchman is nothing more than a sentient clock, and the information he transmits to those inside the town, while useful, does not urgently demand action.*

Medieval literary watchmen, to sum up, have two different kinds of functions. First of all, they are figures in a picture of society at war. They look out for military threats approaching from outside the town, and they give warning to their own people. Their only necessary physical equipment consists of eyes and voice—the ability to acquire knowledge and the means to transmit it. They serve as a point of contact between an inner center of civilization, surrounded by walls, and the external enemies of that civilization. They do not usually take any action themselves to repulse the danger; they are, above all, channels of information, *speculatores*.

But watchmen in medieval literature are also figures in a picture of society at peace. Here, too, their necessary equipment is eyes and voice, and here, too, they serve as mediators between the inner world of the town and an outer world they are assigned to report on. But

* Other examples of watchmen in medieval narrative performing their various duties are given by Bartsch, "Die romanischen und deutschen Tagelieder"; Schultz, *Das höfische Leben*, I, 47–48; and Walter de Gruyter, *Das deutsche Tagelied* (Leipzig, 1887), pp. 148 ff.—but there is a crucial methodological difference between the way they treat such examples and the way I have been treating them. Bartsch's list of examples leads him to the conclusion that the dawn-announcing watchman was a real figure in German town life, such a common figure, indeed, that he could be introduced quite casually into a narrative and be easily recognized by the audience (Bartsch, p. 267); and Schultz takes all these pictures of watchmen as accurate records of social history. My own intention, in these pages, is not to ascertain the watchman's actual role in medieval town life but to analyze the various characteristics and functions attributed to him in literary works other than the *alba*. Whether we may treat these literary works as giving us a true picture of real watchmen does not concern us here. Medieval literature gives us two sorts of pictures of the watchman—the watchman as a social figure, and the watchman as an actor in the *alba* situation—and it is these two *literary* pictures that we are comparing. (We ought to note, however, that the picture of the watchman in his social roles does have a certain verisimilitude; it does not show us something quite improbable in real history, as the picture of the watchman in the *alba* does.)

the outer world is not a world of society (enemy armies); it is the universe of nature, with its heavenly bodies and natural cycles. The watchman relates civilization to time.*

What does all of this tell us about the *alba* watchman? We have already pointed out that the *alba* situation has a striking element of the unreal about it, and much of this air of unreality is due to the watchman and his actions. We do not find the watchman tapping gently at the door of the lady's chamber to whisper his warning to the knight. We find him stationed on the battlements, his voice with its warning ringing out over the whole castle. A great many of the German *albas*, especially, are quite specific about the watchman's location. He is on the *zinne*, the "battlements," just as the watchmen in the passages from Herbort von Fritzlar and Heinrich von dem Türlin were.[34] Often his exact location is not given, but the context and the fact that he is a watchman almost always strongly suggest that he is delivering his message from out on the walls. The absurdity of this, if it is taken as a literal record of reality, is occasionally hinted at in the *albas*, even when the watchman is playing his role most vociferously:

> "*Ich wache umb eines ritters lîp*,"

cries the watchman in an *alba* by the Margrave of Hohenburg,

---

* A ninth-century Arabic poem about lovers parting at dawn (Hatto, *Eos*, p. 232, No. 13) employs a watchman-like figure in the person of the crier calling from the mosque tower to summon the faithful to prayer. The *arabisants*, those who derive all of troubadour poetry from Arabic sources, can point to this *muezzin* as a possible "source" for the *alba* watchman. (For a survey of the Arabizing thesis, see the works listed in Note 9 of my Introduction, above.) The resemblance between the *muezzin*'s function in this poem and the watchman's function in the *alba* is certainly striking, although any actual connection between the two figures cannot be anything but conjectural. In any case, ninth-century Arabic poetry is irrelevant to the present discussion. What I am concerned with here are the meanings and associations the *alba* watchman carried with him; and even if the watchman really was a literary descendant of the *muezzin*, in the Western Christian societies where the *albas* were written and heard the watchman cannot possibly have carried the slightest hint of the meaning: "one who calls the Moslem faithful to prayer at dawn." No Arabic source, therefore, can have played a role in the *meaning* of the watchman figure as he appears in the *alba*—or in the meaning of the *alba* as a whole.

"und umb dîn êre, schoene wîp:
wecke in, frouwe!
got gebe daz es uns wol ergê,
daz er erwache und nieman mê . . . ."

"I am on guard for the sake of a knight's life
and for your honor's sake, beautiful woman.
Wake him, lady!
May God grant that everything go well for us,
that he awake, and not anyone else . . . ."[35]

And another watchman, from a later period, pauses in the middle
of his outcry to observe:

Hört mich der claffer singen,
Ze arg wurd er es pringen . . . .

If the tale-bearer were to hear me singing
he would cause a lot of trouble . . . .[36]

We must recognize, in short, that the watchman's role is not
realistic but symbolic, and that the symbolic meanings the *alba*
watchman carries with him are related to the functions of "realistic"
literary watchmen, those whose job is not to warn lovers but to take
part in the social and military life of a town.[37] The watchman on
the *zinne*, in the narratives we have looked at, functioned to protect
the center of civilization within the walls from the hostile military
forces outside. In the *alba*, the center of civilization and value has
shrunk to the room in which the knight and the lady are making
love, and the hostile forces include all of society, all of nature, and
perhaps even God himself—everything which is *not* the lovers,
everything which lies outside of their enclosed chamber. The walls,
with their battlements on which the watchman stands, are no longer
the real walls surrounding a real town. They are symbolical walls
around the little inner world of the lovers, protecting them from the
outer world foreign to their love. The watchman in the *alba* mediates
not between a town and an outside army but between the inner world
of love and the enemies of love. Just as a realistic watchman stands
on the barrier separating an inner and an outer world, so the fact

that it is a watchman who announces the dawn in the *alba* emphasizes the division of the *alba* universe into two worlds of value. To worry about whether the *alba* watchman can be heard by everyone else in the town, as a number of later treatments of the *alba* do (see below), is to take the whole situation literally, instead of understanding that the watchman and his call and his *zinne* exist and have meaning in a world of symbols. They are physical, narrative symbols of the *ideas* of the *alba*: the union of the two lovers as everything that counts, their centrality, their isolation, the danger they are in, the hostility they are surrounded by.

The watchman's raised position, on the *zinne*, is also significant in terms of the *alba*'s symbolism. The watchman sees into both worlds, as it were: the inner world of love with which he is in sympathy, and the outer world of hostile society and threatening nature. He accepts the high value of the inner world, but he is in a sufficiently elevated position—not enclosed and encircled, as the lovers are—to have knowledge of outer reality as well, and to see that this outer reality has claims which cannot be denied. His dramatic function in the *alba* is to tell the lovers that he sees the dawn; his symbolic function is to perceive the reality of the outer world, to transmit his knowledge of outer reality to those who, enclosed in their inner world, are attempting to ignore any reality but that of their love, and, finally, to rouse the inner world to action: the knight must get up and leave. He is like the *speculatores* we have spoken of, and like the prophet figured as a *speculator*: he transmits knowledge of one world to the inhabitants of another world, requiring them to take action lest they fall victim to physical and spiritual disaster. The knight must turn from one world of value to a quite different world, just as the sinners warned by Ezekiel must turn to the true path of righteousness.

In the *alba*, of course, the conversion is not from wickedness to virtue but from pleasure to safety, and the two worlds, although in conflict, are not mutually exclusive, as the paths of virtue and sin are. Indeed, the significance of the watchman's position on the battlements is that from there he can see and accept both worlds at once. In short, he is in the position of the audience of the *alba*, who accept the supreme value of love but at the same time remain aware of the ineluctable reality of society, nature, and time. The watchman's knowledge and sympathies are those of the audience; and in a certain sense—perceived and exploited by some of the later *alba* poets—the watchman's vision of the good and the real constitutes the whole meaning of the *alba*, and, indeed, the poem itself.

In analyzing the appearances of watchmen in narratives we distinguished between two sorts of functions: those related to warfare, and those related to the announcing of the time of day, mainly the hour of sunrise. In representations of the watchman as an actual social figure these two sorts of functions are clearly distinguished, even when, as in the second passage from Herbort von Fritzlar, one sort succeeds immediately upon the other. In the *alba* the two functions are fused. The watchman announces the imminence of dawn, and so puts the lovers into contact with the great natural processes that mark off the intervals of human time. But this dawn carries with it great danger for the lovers. The sighting of dawn is equivalent, in the dramatic situation of the *alba*, to the sighting by Herbort's watchman of the Greek fleet gleaming in the waters off the Troad.

Nevertheless, the watchman's peacetime function as an announcer of the time contributes a certain distinct layer of symbolic meaning to his presence in the *alba*. Time, as it is announced by watchmen, is a principle of social order. It is a way of dividing the life of the community and the life of the individual members of the community into fixed compartments, fixed categories of activities, each of which is assigned its proper time. The night is assigned to sleeping, the dawn to rising and working (whether in arms or in peaceful industry). The time-ordering of social life is similar to the class-ordering of society: just as each time of day has its proper activity, so each social class has its proper place and function. For society to function in general, each class must know and play its proper part; for a town to enjoy an orderly daily life, each category of activity must come at its proper time.

The *alba* watchman's second symbolic function, then, is in his role as an upholder of the social order, of the orderly processes of civilization. He is an emblem of rule and order, and, especially, of limitation—because the orderly time divisions of the day and night put limits on the propriety of any particular kind of activity. The lovers are opposed to these ordering and compartmentalizing concepts, symbolized in the watchman's time-announcing function. There is no opposition to the class order of society. That is accepted as a necessary precondition for love of the sort the courtly *alba* portrays: the lover and the lady must be members of the only social class to which literature of this period accords the capability of real love. But there is intense opposition, on the part of the lovers, to the limitations time imposes on them. Their love is as radically against limitations as it is radically antisocial; it is against all orders and rules except its own. Consequently the watchman, who as part of his meaning symbolizes this social orderliness, must bear the brunt of the lovers' protests and curses.

That the lovers are also opposed to time as a metaphysical principle, and that the watchman's awareness of time is also a metaphysical awareness, we will see in Chapter Four.

The symbolic watchman is a crucial element in the meaning of the courtly *alba*. He is not a real social figure; he is a pair of eyes and a voice. Once he begins to be treated as a man, and the *alba* situation begins to be looked at critically from the point of view of its verisimilitude, the watchman's symbolic meaning becomes much attenuated, and the *alba* turns into a rather different sort of poem. The Margrave of Hohenburg, as we have seen, is aware of the difficulties inherent in having the watchman cry out the lovers' secrets from the battlements, but that does not prevent him from maintaining the fiction, with all of its symbolical import. Some later authors exhibit interests of a different kind. The Swiss poet Steinmar, for example, poses a painful question: how can the lover trust the watchman, since in betraying his own lord (the lady's husband) the watchman has shown himself so deeply untrustworthy?[38] An acute sense of real human psychology is at work here. The poet treats the *alba* situation as though it were a part of the real world, and the watchman as though he were possessed of full psychological existence and a full set of motives. The psychological reality attributed to the watchman thus lays him open to the sort of shrewd psychological observation and practical moral judgment Steinmar treats him with.

Steinmar does not carry this fine psychology through to the corollary observation that a woman who betrays her husband is *also* not very worthy of trust. But what he does do is quite sufficient to undermine much of the symbolic meaning of the *alba*, along with the symbolism of the watchman and of his role. It is true enough that the watchman, considered as a real social being, has a problem of divided loyalties—on the one hand to his lord and on the other hand to the lovers—and that in choosing to be loyal to the lovers he is forced to be disloyal to his lord. It seems quite evident, however, that the writers of courtly *albas* (such as Wolfram, Hohenburg, and Cadenet, to mention only those poets we have looked at specifically) did not intend the watchman's choice to be interpreted as a reflection on his untrustworthy character. The fact that a loyal servant will break his bond of loyalty to his lord—in medieval ethics an immensely strong bond—in order to further the intimacy of a pair of lovers is really significant not for a picture of the watchman's character but for an illustration of the values that obtain in the *alba* world. The watchman's disloyalty to his lord reinforces the notion of the values of erotic love as having a greater claim than any social values can have: honor, loyalty, duty, or the like. The watchman is a representative of the social order, who, in his changed loyalty, affirms that the love relationship is superior to the whole social order. His decision to aid the lovers rather than to be dutiful to his lord shows the dissolution of social bonds effected by the very existence of an exclusive, passionate, erotic love; it shows the profound opposition, not of one pair of lovers to one cuckolded husband, but of erotic love to society as a whole. Erotic love, indeed, sets up its own society, with its own loyalties, and in choosing that society above the other, the watchman is not exhibiting his treachery but rather proving himself a wise judge of what constitutes real value. Hence, by focusing on the watchman's character rather than on the ethical significance of the watchman's choice, Steinmar greatly weakens the basic idea of the *alba*, namely, that there are two worlds of value in unalterable opposition, and that the world of erotic love is morally superior to the other world.

Just as Alwin Schultz, in a later age, took the *alba* watchman to be a real person and judged his behavior as realistic, so Steinmar took the *alba* watchman to be real and judged his behavior as realistic and *bad*. Other poets of the thirteenth century judged his behavior as *unrealistic*, and corrected it. One way to eliminate the watchman's lack of verisimilitude was to eliminate the watchman altogether and replace him by someone more believable. This is what Ulrich von Lichtenstein, for example, does in his *Frauendienst*: for reasons of verisimilitude, he gives the role of the watchman to a female dependent of the lady's.[39] This makes the situation more realistic. No highborn lady, as Ulrich observes, would confide her illicit love to a watchman, who would necessarily be of a lower class; a "maget," on the other hand, a female retainer of the lady's own class, could quite believably be let in on the secret. And of course (Ulrich does not say this, but his *alba* demonstrates it) the "maget" would not be professionally required to be out on the *zinne* as she announced the daybreak, which would eliminate that glaringly unbelievable element. These changes do indeed result in a decided gain in social verisimilitude, but also in a decided loss of suggestiveness. The elevated position from which one can see into two worlds of value, the vital protective function, the association with the orderly temporal arrangement of civilized life—all are gone. The story becomes a purely personal romance—which is what it is, fundamentally—but loses the symbolic force of its parallelism to the epic conflict between society and its external enemies.[40]

A third kind of variation in the person and role of the watchman can be seen in those *albas* where the lovers are awakened by the song of birds. Unlike the previous two examples, this is not a matter of intentional alteration by later poets of a previously established convention. On the contrary, the *albas* in which the lovers are awakened by birds seem to constitute a separate tradition going back at least as far as the tradition of *albas* with watchmen.[41] Typical of this tradition (which, it should be mentioned, is much less extensive than that with the watchman) is the Old French "Entre moi et mon

amin."[42] The scene here is out of doors, in a wood adjacent to
Béthune. Dawn is announced to the lovers by the song of the lark,
whose warning the man attempts to reject:

> "*Il n'est mie jours,*
> *Saverouze au cors gent;*
> *Si m'aït amors,*
> *L'alowette nos mant.*"

> "It is not day at all,
> sweet lady of noble body.
> So help me Love,
> the lark is lying to us."[43]

This is a poem of great freshness and charm, similar in some of
its effects to Walther von der Vogelweide's song of outdoor love-
making, "Under der linden."[44] But it is very different from the other
albas we have been speaking of. The sense of two opposed worlds of
value, reinforced in those other *albas* by the inside-outside topographical structure, is hardly to be found here. The lovers themselves are outside in the midst of nature, not enclosed within walls
that protect them from the natural world. The watchman, with his
function of mediating between the two worlds and his implied role
as a protector of civilization from external enemies, plays no part.
Instead of a human watchman to voice in words the dangers of a
hostile society and of a great natural—almost supernatural—force,
the sun, we have only the lark, itself a part of nature, and moreover
a small and graceful part of nature that cannot serve to symbolize a
terrible, overwhelming threat. Along with the walls, the castle, and
the watchman, society as a force in the poem has virtually dis-
appeared. The only sort of dualistic opposition that remains is that
between the attitude of the lovers toward the dawn and the attitude
of the lower creatures, as in Wolfram's lines, quoted earlier:

> "*owê tac,*
> *wilde und zam daz fröit sich dîn*
> *und siht dich gerne wan ich eine.*"

"Alas, day,
wild and tame creatures rejoice in you
and are glad to see you, except for me alone."[45]

But even that opposition is muted, in that the lark merely responds to the daylight, with only the faintest suggestion that its response is an expression of joy.

There are a number of intermediate forms between the watchman-*alba* and the bird-*alba*, each with its own kind of meaning. In the Provençal "En un vergier sotz fuella d'albespi,"[46] for example, the love-making takes place outside, and birds are present; but there is also a watchman, and the *gilos* is mentioned (as he was not in "Entre moi et mon amin"—there is no suggestion in the French poem that the lady is even married). It is of course not possible here to analyze all the permutations and combinations of these various elements in all of the extant *albas*. We may say, however, that the two extremes of meaning are represented by the *alba* in a castle with a watchman, and the *alba* in a wood with birds, and that the meanings of the other combinations lie somewhere in between.

The treatments of the watchman as a real social figure, to be criticized on grounds of his unethical or unrealistic behavior, go along with a treatment of the whole *alba* as a fiction, an artifact, a thing poets make. Ulrich von Lichtenstein treats the *alba* in precisely this way, telling us how earlier poets wrote one kind of *alba*, and how he will write a different kind, and why. A later poet indicates the artificial, literary quality of the *alba* form in a more subtle —or perhaps a more naive—way. The poet begins in his own voice:

> *Frölich so wil ich singen*
> *Mit lust ein tageweyss,*
> *Ich hoff, mir sol gelingen . . . .*
>
> Happily I want to sing
> an *alba*, with joy;
> I hope I do a good job . . . .[47]

He then recedes into the role of omniscient narrator, and we have twenty-five lengthy strophes of perfectly objective narrative, recounting the usual *alba* plot. Strophe 25 brings the lover (he is only a "knabe" in this late, bourgeois version of the *alba*) out of the castle and sets him on the road of escape.

26

Do sprang der selbig knabe
Gleich als ein hirsch so stoltz
Durch manchen tieffen graben,
Er sang wol inn das holtz.
Do kam ich dar geritten
Gar heymlich und gar leyss,
Er saget diss geschichte;
Do hub ich an zu dichte
Hie dise tageweyss.

Then that self-same young man
like a stag so proud
sprang through many deep moats.
He sang out into the woods.
Then I came riding that way,
all secretly and softly.
He told this story.
Then I began to write down as a poem
this *alba* you have here.

After having hidden himself for twenty-five strophes behind the curtain of objective narration, the poet, whom by this time we have completely forgotten, suddenly reappears. The *alba* story the audience has been involved in as an immediate experience is suddenly twitched away; it becomes a narration, a story, a "geschichte" told by one of the participants in it; and then it becomes even less real, even more of a literary artifact: a "tageweyss," a conventional literary form set into poetic language by the poet—just what he had told us it would be from the very first strophe. The effect, whether intended or not (this poet does not inspire a great deal of faith), is quite striking, with its contrast between the illusion of reality created by the narrative, and the poet's voice, at the beginning and end, telling us it is all a fiction.

Even more striking is the effect produced, in other *albas* (and not all of them late), by the notion that the entire *alba* is a song sung by the watchman, who is at the same time a character in the song he sings. We noted this idea earlier in Wolfram's "Der helden minne ir klage." It appears in a particularly interesting way in what is usually referred to as the "Kerenstein Ballad."[48] The story recounted in this poem is a narrative episode expanded from the basic *alba* plot. The hero is a knight in love with the daughter of the Lord of Kerenstein (note the lack of the adulterous element, so important to the courtly *alba*). He sends a messenger to her, then meets her himself that night, under a linden tree outside the castle gate. The dawn comes; the girl expresses her anguish that the knight will desert her; but—as never happens in the courtly *alba*—instead of leaving her, he puts her on a horse and rides off with her.

> *Da hueb sich in der purge   wol wundergrosser schall,*
> *der wachter an der zinen   der sang: "die burg ist auffgeton!*
> *hat ymant hie verloren,   der sol sein nemen war."*
> *da sprach der edel von kerenstain: "ich hab meine*
>   *schöne dochter verloren."*

> *"Nuen wais es Crist uon himel wol,   das ich vnschuldig pin.*
> *vnd ist mein schone junckfraw   mit ainem anderen dohin,*
> *das wass ir bayder wille,   sy waren einander lieb."*
> *der wachter an der zinnen   der sang so wol ein tagelied.*

Then a marvelously great noise arose in the castle.
The watchman on the battlements sang, "The castle is
                    opened wide!
If anyone has lost something here, he ought to become
                    aware of it."
Then spoke the Lord of Kerenstein, "I have lost my
                    beautiful daughter."

"Now, Christ in Heaven knows well that I am guiltless;
and if my young mistress has gone away with another,

that was what they both wanted; they loved each other."
The watchman on the battlements was singing—so very
well—an *alba*.

The watchman's declaration that he is guiltless of his mistress's
flight cannot constitute the "tagelied" the last line has him singing.
A *Tagelied* is a fixed poetical genre, telling the story of illicit lovers,
their night together, and the coming of the dawn. The only *Tagelied*
the watchman can be singing—provided it is not one completely
extraneous to the rest of the poem—is the whole poem itself. (The
manuscript in which the poem appears specifically calls it "ein tag
weyss."[49]) The whole narration, if my analysis is correct, is discovered to be a song of the watchman, who takes the role not only
of a figure in a fictional drama, but also of a *jongleur* singing a poem
of well-known, fixed content. From an analogue of a prophet,
transmitting the painful truth, the watchman has turned into an
analogue of an entertainer, transmitting a pleasant fiction.

The symbolism of the watchman in the courtly *alba*, as we spoke
of it earlier, constitutes only part of the meaning this figure conveys.
There is also considerable significance for the meaning and structure
of the poem in the watchman's dramatic relationship to the other
main active character, the lady.

THE LADY

The lady's character and function in the *alba* are even more
invariable than those of the watchman; through the whole history
of the genre she remains very much the same. She is much more
passionate than the knight, and much more eloquent in her expression of feeling. Her joy in the pleasures of love is usually more intense, as is her grief at the separation. Her antagonism to the day is
more violent. She lives only for love: she is the chief upholder of the
erotic values of the inner world, having no real existence anywhere
else. The knight at least has a social function in the outer world,
although not much is said about it. When he goes out into the world

of everyday life he does not cease to exist, for there is something for him to do there. The lady does not leave the chamber of love, so far as we can tell from the poems themselves. She remains in the inner world, which is her only world, and since that inner world has meaning only when it is the scene of love-making, the lady must go into a kind of inanimate suspension during the daylight, when her lover is away.

Along with the lady's exclusive preoccupation with love goes her other chief characteristic, her opposition to whatever interferes with that love. Both the lovers, of course, are opposed to the day, to society, to the whole outside world, as we have shown. But the lady's opposition is more uncompromising, more unreasonable than that of the man. Both oppose the dawn, both try to deny that it really is dawn, but while the knight is usually the first to give in and accept reality the lady usually accepts it only grudgingly, if at all, and only when the man is already taking his leave. In a few *albas* the lady is much concerned with the knight's safety, and seconds the watchman's urgings that he leave. But this is so unusual a state of affairs that we are probably justified in considering it a conscious reversal (on the part of the poet) of the norm. Normally the lady fights as hard as she can against the daylight and the separation it causes; she tries to quiet the watchman with threats or bribes; she tries to persuade the knight to remain, in spite of the danger. Her passion is so strong, so much the very essence of her being, that from her point of view the realities of day and danger cease to have any reality at all. Her concern is not with what is but with what she would like things to be.

Consequently, one of the most characteristic rhetorical devices of the *alba* can be seen as a perfect expression of the lady's character. This is the use of the vernacular equivalents of the optative subjunctive—the wish that something were so that in fact is not so, the wish that the future course of events will bend to one's will:

> *Plagues a Dieu ja la nueitz non falhis*
> *Ni·l mieus amicx lonc de mi no·s partis*
> *Ni la gayta jorn ni alba no vis!*

Might it please God that the night never end,
nor that my best friend ever go far away from me,
nor that the watchman ever see day or dawn![50]

Ach das ich nit gewünschen mag,
Das es werd nymmer liechter tag,
So läg ich noch in heldes arm verpunden.

Alas, that I may not have my wish
that the bright day never come.
Then would I still be lying embraced in the hero's arms.[51]

Het ich den tag in meinem schrein,
so muost er mein gefangner sein!

If I had the day in my closet,
then he would have to be my prisoner![52]

Although the passages above are spoken by the lady, these optative subjunctives (as we may call them, although they are not all
precisely that) are by no means confined to her alone. Both the
lovers make use of them, with the lady perhaps doing so more
often.[53] Nevertheless, the optative subjunctive, with what it signifies,
belongs more to her than to the knight, because her wishes are
stronger than his and her opposition to reality is more radical. The
knight's wishes-contrary-to-fact are only part of his attitude toward
the separation; the lady's desire to make reality subject to her will
constitutes *all* of her attitude. It is the only possible attitude of a
person devoted entirely to love, in a world containing so many
powerful forces opposed to love.

In her passion, her exclusive concern with love, her upholding of
erotic values above all others, and her violent opposition to reality,
the lady of the *alba* merely shares the qualities attributed to women
by almost all of the literary traditions known to the Middle Ages.
The anti-feminist tradition of the theologians and their followers
consistently upbraids women with having no interest but in wantonness, and with being deficient in reason, that is, in the faculty that

distinguishes between the wish and the fact.[54] Classical literature, too, portrayed most women as passionate and unreasonable. Ovid's *Heroides* present us with a *catalogue raisonné* of this type of woman: Phyllis, Briseis, Phaedra, Oenone, Hypsipyle, Dido, Ariadne, Medea. Medieval romances, while they present a number of different kinds of pictures of women, give ample space to the fairy mistresses and their human derivatives, seducing men by their sexual charms to a life of dalliance in a world perpetually sheltered from day, death, and necessity. The *Frauenstrophen*, those monologues expressing the passion and grief of ladies during the various ups and downs of love affairs, are dominated by the representation of the female character as obsessively erotic and passionate. (Indeed, it is the character of these *Frauenstrophen* ladies that has given rise to the theory, discussed earlier, that the *alba* is an outgrowth of the *Frauenstrophen*; the female character in the two genres is identical.) If these *Frauenstrophen* are of folk origin, as has been suggested,[55] then the folk must have had the same notion of what women were really like as did Euripides, Ovid, and Saint Jerome. Even the Arabs conceived of women in this same way.

The watchman, on the other hand, has a quite different approach to reality. This is something apart from his symbolical function, his association with prophets and protectors of cities. He has a characteristic attitude toward what is real and what is good that distinguishes him radically from the lady. The lady rejects the outer reality of the world; the knight rejects it, and than accepts it; the watchman accepts it from the very beginning. We noted earlier that one of the functions of the full-fledged watchman, the *custos*, was to take arms against the enemies attacking his town: not only to see, but also to fight. The *alba* watchman does not have this function. What he sees is the rising of the sun, something it is impossible to fight against. With the sunrise is associated the *gilos*, representing all of conventional society; and the watchman has no thought of taking up arms against society either. He may help to outwit the *gilos*, but he does not attempt any active resistance against him. He accepts the realities of nature and society, as indeed he must.

This is not a moral decision on the watchman's part, but merely one of practical prudence. So far as his idea of the good goes, he favors the ethical system of the inner world, the world of the lovers, over the ethical system of the outer world, the world of the husband. His actions in the poem make this quite evident. But, unlike the lady, the watchman distinguishes between his notion of what is good and his notion of what is real. He may feel that the love of the knight and the lady is morally superior to the social bonds between husband and wife and between master and servant; he may even feel that this love is morally superior to Christian law. But he does not decieve himself into thinking that such a love can make the sun stand still. The lady, all passionate and unreasonable, tries to bend reality to her will; the watchman, with his practicality and prudence, gives voice to unavoidable outer reality, which will not submit to being bent.

This attitude is closely connected with the watchman's social class. In the aristocratic literature of the High Middle Ages only aristocrats can experience real love, and only they can give themselves fully to love's values. The lower classes are automatically cut off from this full understanding of the meaning of love. The watchman is not of the proper social class to be able to uphold the erotic values as single-mindedly as the wellborn lady does. The poets who treat the watchman as a real social figure inevitably emphasize this class-difference. Ulrich von Lichtenstein, as we mentioned before, called the watchman a peasant, and said that such a person was much too low in the social scale to be allowed to take part, even from the side-lines, in the love affair of an aristocratic lady. The watchman in the *alba* by Heinrich von Frauenberg demands money from the lady before he will consent to aid her, showing that he has no instinctive nobility of heart to appreciate the high moral value of the love affair, and that his values are those of a less exalted, more materialistic class.[56] In the courtly *alba*, the watchman is generally given a kind of intermediate set of values, with the implication of an intermediate social class. His attitudes are not those of a fully low-class character, who, according to courtly ideas, would be guided entirely by practical realism, appetites, and greed. He has been affected by courtly erotic values and sympathizes with them. He has chosen to aid the knight and the lady not for personal gain but because he appreciates the value of their love. Nevertheless, something of his lowborn status remains with him in his down-to-earth insistence on the practical realities of the situation. The aristocratic lovers, especially the lady, are concerned with love. The watchman, of lower class, is also concerned with such practical things as the time of day, the keys to the castle gate, and the knight's physical safety. Brangaene, in Gottfried's *Tristan*, plays a very similar role and has similar limitations, although she herself is highborn. Her concern throughout is with practical arrangements and safety, while the lovers themselves, in their mystical devotion to each other and to the love goddess, "die gottinne Minne," can hardly be concerned with such trivia. She sympathizes with the lovers, yet is incapable of understanding the nature of their love. Highborn or not, she is of inferior status, just as the *alba* watchman is.*

THE PROBLEM OF CHOICE

These two points of view, these two attitudes toward reality, correspond to two fundamental and universal psychological principles. On the one hand, we have desire, attempting to create the world in its own image, unwilling to accept any limitations imposed on it from without. On the other, we have the sense of an external reality which dominates and limits all human actions and which cannot be controlled by desire. Freud called these two principles the pleasure principle and the reality principle.[57] The *alba* can be construed as a debate or battle between the two.

In the *alba*, both points of view appear dramatically, each voiced by a different character. The watchman's speeches are mainly an

* That is why she is excluded from the *Minnegrotte*, in the same way that the watchman always remains *outside* the chamber of love. See William T. H. Jackson, "The role of Brangaene in Gottfried's *Tristan*," *Germanic Review*, XXVIII (1953), 290–96: Brangaene cannot be admitted to the *Minnegrotte* with Tristan and Isolde because she "would be unable to grasp the ideals which they are seeking" (p. 293). Both Brangaene and the watchman belong to the long tradition of sympathetic, helpful, and spiritually inferior servants, with their earthiness, practicality, and lack of comprehension of the ideal. Juliet's nurse and Sancho Panza have similar functions, on a more complex level.

expression of the reality principle; the speeches of the lovers—and most often of the lady—are expressions of the pleasure principle, which tries to deny and reject reality. The polarity between the points of view actually expressed in the *alba* is not so absolute that the characters can be taken as allegorical figurations of the two psychological principles. The watchman, although he urges the cause of reality, sympathizes with the desires of the lovers; the lady, although she wishes to ignore reality, is ultimately forced to give way to it. But the main thrust of the watchman's words is clearly the furthering of the claims of reality, while the lovers' attitude is dominantly that of the pleasure principle, only slightly tempered by the final acceptance of necessity. The psychological and ideological drama of the *alba* is based on the dialectic between these two points of view, each point of view made concrete by embodying it in the actions and words of one of the fictional characters. The dramatic conflict really takes place in the hearts of the lovers: the pleasure they do not wish to give up, versus the knowledge that they do live in a real world which cannot be controlled by their desires. Even more so, the conflict takes place in the hearts of the poem's audience; it is the living-through of this conflict that constitutes our experience of the *alba*, as we shall see later on.

This kind of conflict between two attitudes appears with exceptional simplicity and clarity in the *alba* of Giraut de Bornelh. Six strophes are devoted to the speech of the watchman-like friend, detailing the real conditions and real perils of the situation. The seventh strophe contains the answer of the lover, asserting the higher reality of the world of desire and refusing to bow to external reality. The fact that the role played in most *albas* by a watchman is here taken by a friend of the lover contributes to the simplicity of the way the conflict of attitudes is presented. Giraut is not interested, even marginally, in showing us a contrast of class viewpoints: the low-class prudence of a watchman versus the high-class passion of the lovers. He wants to emphasize the contrast of the two attitudes without reference to any social determinants of such attitudes. The *albas* in which the claims of the reality principle are expressed by an actual watchman have more of a connection with the notion of social reality we find in most medieval (and modern) narratives: the notion that class and attitude go more or less automatically together. Giraut's dramatization of the conflict of viewpoints is more abstract and idealized. The emphasis is not on painting a scene or portraying novelistic characters, but on exposing and contrasting, in as clear-cut a way as possible, the two psychological principles we have been speaking of.

(We may note here, in passing, the difference between what Giraut was doing and what Cadenet did in his *alba*. In Cadenet's poem there is none of the abstract opposition of two attitudes toward reality which makes up the drama of Giraut's *alba*. In Cadenet, indeed, there is no conflict at all, and consequently no drama. The situation itself is full of conflict, as any *alba* situation must be; but none of this conflict appears actively within the poem, because the lady and the watchman are not expressing opposed attitudes toward reality and are not arguing with each other. So far as the actual poem goes, the pleasure principle is supreme and unopposed.)

Giraut's *alba* is unusual in many respects: the simplicity of the contrast of the two attitudes; the lack of resolution between them at the end; the fact that the reality principle is embodied in a friend, rather than in a watchman; and, especially, the fact that the expression of the pleasure principle is assigned to the knight rather than to the lady. We have seen how strongly the Middle Ages identified passion, erotic love, opposition to reality—in short, all the concomitants of the pleasure principle—with women. Men, with their greater reasoning powers, while they are subject to being tempted by sensual desires, are nevertheless not usually regarded as being totally devoted to them. It is more in keeping with the general medieval attitude toward woman to make her the proponent of the pleasure principle, and such in fact is what we find in the great majority of *albas*. In these *albas* the lady is the advocate of the pleasure principle, the watchman is the advocate of the reality principle, and the knight is a more passive figure in between them, not so much advocating a position of his own as forced to choose between the two opposing principles being advocated. *Albas* of this type have a structure of ideas more complex than that found in Giraut's *alba*. In them, the two attitudes toward reality are not simply juxtaposed and contrasted, as in Giraut; instead, they become dynamic principles of an unfolding drama, each offering a proposed course of action for a third figure, the knight, to follow.

This is not, of course, the only kind of structure that can result from the opposition, in the *alba*, of the two attitudes. Giraut de Bornelh's structure is one example among many of other forms that the conflict can take. The two attitudes are almost always there, and almost always in conflict; Cadenet's *alba* is one of the few exceptions. But the actual dramatic conflict that expresses this conflict of fundamental psychological principles can vary considerably. The knight versus the watchman; the lady versus the watchman; the lady and the knight together, versus the watchman; the lady and the knight versus each other—all of these divergent structures can be found. Each of these structures could be shown to be analogous, in different ways, to certain forms of medieval thought. For the purposes of this study, however, I should like to confine myself to pointing out some analogies to the most common structure we find in the *alba*: the lady versus the watchman, with the knight, expressly or by implication, choosing between them.

Let us look, first of all, at a more or less typical example of this sort of *alba*: the *alba* by the Margrave of Hohenburg, which we have already referred to.

> "*Ich wache umb eines ritters lîp*
> *und umb dîn êre, schoene wîp:*
> *wecke in, frouwe !*
> *got gebe daz ez uns wol ergê,*
> *daz er erwache und nieman mê:*
> *wecke in, frouwe !*
> *est an der zît,   niht langer bît.*
> *ich bite ouch niht wan dur den willen sîn.*
> *wiltun bewarn,   sô heiz in varn:*
> *verslâfet er, sost gar diu schulde dîn.*
> *wecke in, frouwe !*"

" Dîn lîp der müeze unsaelic sîn,
wahtaere, und al daz singen dîn!
slâf, geselle !
dîn wachen daz waer allez guot:
dîn wecken mir unsanfte tuot.
slâf, geselle !
wahtaere, in hân   dir niht getân
wan allez guot, daz mir wirt selten schîn.
du gers des tages   dur daz du jages
vil sender fröiden von dem herzen mîn.
slâf, geselle !"

" Dîn zorn sî dir vil gar vertragen:
der ritter sol niht hie betagen,
wecke in, frouwe !
er gap sich ûf die triuwe mîn:
do enpfalch ich in den gnâden dîn.
wecke in, frouwe !
vil saelic wîp,   sol er den lîp
verliesen, sô sîn wir mit im verlorn.
ich singe, ich sage,   est an dem tage,
nu wecke in, wande in wecket doch mîn horn.
wecke in, frouwe !"

"I am on guard for the sake of a knight's life
and for your honor's sake, beautiful woman.
Wake him, lady!
May God grant that everything go well for us,
that he awake, and not anyone else.
Wake him, lady!
The moment is at hand. Delay no longer.
I do not ask it but for his sake.
If you want to protect him, tell him to go.
If he oversleeps it will be all your fault.
Wake him, lady!"

"May you be accursed,
watchman, and all your singing too!

Sleep, beloved!
Your standing on watch would be all to the good;
your calling to awaken pains me.
Sleep, beloved!
Watchman, I have done nothing to you
but good things, yet I scarcely see any sign of it.
You are longing for the day, and by so doing you chase
many poignant joys out of my heart.
Sleep, beloved!"

"Your rage can be fully forgiven;
but the knight must not remain here after dawn.
Wake him, lady!
He put himself in my hands, relying on my loyalty,
and I then commended him to your gracious kindness.
Wake him, lady!
Most blessed woman, if he should lose his life
we are lost with him.
I sing, I cry, 'The day is at hand.'
Now wake him, for my horn will wake him anyway.
Wake him, lady!"[58]

The proponents of the two attitudes toward reality are engaged here in active controversy about the course of action the third character, the knight, is to take. The watchman is concerned with the demands of outward reality, with physical danger, with the status of individuals in society ("êre"). The lady refuses to accept any of these realities; her only concern is with maintaining and prolonging the erotic joys she and the knight have been sharing. The knight himself does not speak. He is, in a certain sense, absent from the dispute, because he is asleep while it is going on. But the dispute is about him and his future actions, and the arguments are directed ultimately at him. The watchman's refrain, "wecke in, frouwe," presents one possible course of action for the knight: waking to outward reality, accepting the day and the light with all their symbolic meaning, taking practical steps to deal with the dangers of the situation. The lady's refrain, "slâf, geselle," expresses the opposite course of action: remaining passively in the world of sleep, the unreal world in which all desires are satisfied by means of fantasy, the world of darkness, night, and sensual pleasure. The lady is trying to keep the knight asleep in spite of everything. The watchman, while he appeals to the lady to help him wake the knight, intends to wake him himself no matter what the lady may do.

The knight, being asleep, is not actually faced—on the dramatic, narrative level—with a choice between these two types of reaction to the external situation. When he wakes, however, he will be faced with such a choice, as is the case in numerous other *albas*; and these two voices, arguing over what he should do, represent symbolically the two attitudes he must choose between. He must either let himself be guided by the lady and act according to a total indulgence in the pleasure principle, or let himself be guided by the watchman and act according to the demands of the reality principle. He must choose one course or the other, and it is the choice he makes that will determine the outcome of the plot. Thus, while the lady and the watchman speak all the actual words of the poem, it is really the knight who is its central character.

The debate between two points of view or two ways of life is a common form in the literature and thought of the Middle Ages.[59] There are numerous poems in which such opponents as the rose and the lily, or youth and age, or water and wine, dispute with each other, each vaunting its own qualities and depreciating those of its opponent. These poems are mainly rhetorical exercises on frivolous subjects, and their purpose is mainly to display the eloquence and wit of the poet in the arguments he invents for the fictional debaters. Much the same purpose and technique inform those formal oratorical exercises familiar to schools from the Renaissance onwards.[60] The formal philosophical dispute, a particularly characteristic literary form in the Middle Ages, closely resembles these debates in form, although its intentions were serious rather than merely rhetorical.

The literary debate sometimes consisted of a simple presentation of the two opposed points of view. Frequently, however, the cases, once presented, were turned over to an umpire for judgment, so that the debate could also resemble a judicial process.[61] This is the case, for example, in the Carolingian "Conflictus veris et hiemis,"[62] where the debate between spring and winter is turned over to the shepherds Palaemon and Dafnis for judgment; the Latin debate between Phyllis and Flora over the merits of soldier and cleric as lovers,[63] turned over to Cupid himself; the Middle English *The Owl and the Nightingale*,[64] where the relative merits of the two birds are to be judged by a certain Nicholas of Guildford; and the Middle English *Wynnere and Wastoure*,[65] in which the two approaches to life, money, and property, named in the title, are judged by the king. Characteristic of the judge in these debates is his disinterestedness. He is someone of greater wisdom and authority than the disputants: the shepherd who is really a philosopher, the clever Nicholas, the King of England, the god of love. Except perhaps in *Wynnere and Wastoure*, which is somewhat unclear in this regard, the judge is not himself affected by the debate; he is above it, rather than involved with it.

We find something quite different in the tradition of debates between the body and the soul. In the Middle English representative of this genre, for example,[66] the narrator has a dream-vision of a debate between the body and soul of a knight who has just died. This is not a witty debate on a frivolous subject, as most of the above are. It is a deeply earnest quarrel between the two ways of life open to man; and the consequences of the choice made between these two ways of life extend beyond the grave to all eternity. The soul is the spiritual part of the knight, which made him capable of knowing the true good, God, and of attaining salvation and heaven. The body represents his sensual appetites, his lust for the false goods of the flesh. Their debate is long and bitter, but so far as the knight is concerned it is not a debate which can result in a choice between the two principles involved. The knight made his choice long ago: he chose the life of sensual indulgence, which, as the soul tells the body, has doomed him—body and soul together—to hell. There is a choice still to be made, however, although not by the knight. It is the narrator—and the audience—who must choose between the two ways of life represented in the debate. This debate between body and soul, in other words, is a moral exemplum. It presents the two ways of life, shows or suggests their consequences, and then leaves the choice between the two up to the audience. The narrator, who represents the audience of individual Christians confronted with this great moral choice, is consequently the chief character of the poem, although he speaks in his own voice only at the very beginning and the very end.

This notion of the Christian having to decide between two courses of life—the sinful and sensual on the one hand, or the virtuous and spiritual on the other—is of course fundamental to Christian thought. It is the dominant idea of the New Testament; we encountered it earlier, in the form of metaphor, in our study of the Pauline symbolism of night and day. It reappears constantly throughout the Middle Ages, in the visual arts, in literary works, in homilies, in theological texts. We can see it in its simplest, clearest, and most striking form in the morality plays, where it provides the basic structure of the drama.[67] In *The Castle of Perseverance*, for example, a play that dramatizes so many medieval thought patterns, we are shown Humanum Genus between Bonus Angelus and Malus Angelus, listening to each one state his case, and finally making his choice between them. The good angel counsels mankind to turn to Christ; to which the bad angel replies:

> "*Pes, aungel! Thi wordis are not wyse!*
> *thou counselyst hym not a-ryth.*
> *he schal hym drawyn to the wer[l]dis seruyse . . . ."*[68]

After much disputing between the angels, Humanum Genus chooses the wicked angel to be his guide, and goes off with him.

> Bonus Angelus:
> "*I weyle, and wrynge, and makë mone!*
> *this man with woo schal be pylt.*
> *I syë sore, and grysly grone,*
> *for hys folye schal make hym spylt . . . ."*[69]

It is just the sort of structure we see in Hohenburg's *alba*. Indeed, the last quoted speech could easily have been spoken by an *alba* watchman; and suppose the speech of Malus Angelus had begun,

"Pes, *watchman*! Thy wordis are not wyse!" The choice the *alba* knight must make is certainly of a different nature from that confronting Humanum Genus in this play, and the lady and watchman are clearly not to be identified with bad and good angels. It is simply that the same kind of dramatic structure, with the same kinds of interrelationships among the characters, naturally tends to call forth similar kinds of dramatic utterances.

The use of this structure in drama is not confined to the Middle Ages. Marlowe's *Doctor Faustus*, so closely related to the morality plays, stages the same Christian icon at several crucial points: Faustus between a good angel and a bad angel, listening to their advice, and choosing. Shakespeare parodies the icon in *The Merchant of Venice*, a play much concerned otherwise with the problem of choice:

Launcelot Gobbo: . . . The fiend is at mine elbow, and tempts me, saying to me, "Gobbo, Launcelot Gobbo, good Launcelot," or "good Gobbo," or "good Launcelot Gobbo, use your legs, take the start, run away." My conscience says, "No; take heed, honest Launcelot; take heed, honest Gobbo; do not run; scorn running with thy heels." Well, the most courageous fiend bids me pack: "Via!" says the fiend; "away!" says the fiend . . . . Well, my conscience, hanging about the neck of my heart, says very wisely to me, ". . . Launcelot, budge not." "Budge," says the fiend. "Budge not," says my conscience. . . .[70]

(Launcelot, like Humanum Genus and Faustus, eventually chooses to obey the fiend.)

The same medieval Christian structure appears, this time in a serious way, in Shakespeare's Sonnet cxliv:

> *Two loves I have of comfort and despair,*
> *Which like two spirits do suggest me still:*
> *The better angel is a man right fair,*
> *The worser spirit a woman colour'd ill.*
> *To win me soon to hell, my female evil*
> *Tempteth my better angel from my side,*
> *And would corrupt my saint to be a devil,*
> *Wooing his purity with her foul pride. . . .*

Here the sexes of the two counselors are specified, and, in accordance with classical, medieval, and Renaissance tradition, it is of course the woman who represents temptation, corruption, and vice. The added notion of the good angel's being himself tempted to vice by the wicked female spirit does not correspond with the Christian icon we have seen in *The Castle of Perseverance*, for there a good angel cannot be tempted. But the *alba*, which in its general outlines so closely resembles that Christian icon, on occasion also offers a parallel to this variation in the basic structure. In the *alba* of King Wenceslas II of Bohemia, for example, the lady, proponent of the pleasure principle, successfully bribes the watchman, proponent of the reality principle, to cease his overprudent warnings.

> *Er sprach "ich bin gemietet:*
> *gêt wider unde nietet*
> *iuch fröiden . . . ."*

> He said, "I am paid off.
> Go back and enjoy
> your pleasures . . . ."[71]

The male counselor has been corrupted by the female (although not perhaps in the way Shakespeare's better angel was corrupted), and, as in Shakespeare, it is the central figure between the two counselors who will have to suffer the consequences: in the sonnet the speaker runs the risk of hell, and in the *alba* the knight runs the risk of being killed by the *gilos*.

The allegorical representation of the soul between a good angel and a bad angel, taken literally (as it no doubt often was) shows us a rather naive superstitious concept of the process of moral choice. On the allegorical level, however, the good and bad angels are not real spirits but psychological urges. The soul between the two counseling voices is thus a representation of the divided will that is characteristic of mankind since Adam's Fall. The most eloquent medieval description of the divided will and the painful psychological conflict it causes is to be found in Saint Augustine's *Confessions*. We should note, in the following passage, not only the same kind of structure we find in the *alba*—the two psychological principles contending over the fate of the central figure—but also a number of close parallels in the imagery used to express the conflict:

> . . . *Velle meum tenebat inimicus et inde mihi catenam fecerat et constrinxerat me. Quippe ex voluntate perversa facta est libido, et dum servitur libidini, facta est consuetudo, et dum consuetudini non resistitur, facta est necessitas. . . . Voluntas autem nova, quae mihi esse coeperat, ut te gratis colerem fruique te vellem, deus, sola certa iucunditas, nondum erat idonea ad superandam priorem vetustate roboratam. Ita duae voluntates meae, una vetus, alia nova, illa carnalis, illa spiritalis, confligebant inter se atque discordando dissipabant animam meam. . . . Ita sarcina saeculi, velut somno assolet, dulciter premebar, et cogitationes, quibus meditabar in te, similes erant conatibus expergisci volentium, qui tamen superati soporis altitudine remerguntur. Et sicut nemo est, qui dormire semper velit, omniumque sano iudicio vigilare praestat, differt tamen plerumque homo somnum excutere, cum gravis torpor in membris est, eumque iam displicentem carpit libentius, quamvis surgendi tempus advenerit: ita certum habebam esse melius tuae caritati me dedere quam meae cupiditati cedere; sed illud placebat et vincebat, hoc libebat et vinciebat. Non enim erat quod tibi responderem dicenti mihi:* surge qui dormis et exsurge a mortuis, et inluminabit te Christus, *et undique ostendenti vera te dicere, non erat omnino, quid responderem veritate convictus, nisi tantum verba lenta et somnolenta: "Modo," "ecce modo," "sine paululum." Sed "modo et modo" non habebat modum et "sine paululum" in longum ibat. Frustra condelectabar legi tuae secundum interiorem hominem, cum alia lex in membris meis repugnaret legi mentis meae et captivum me duceret in lege peccati, quae in membris meis erat. . . .*

. . . The enemy had control of my will, and out of it he fashioned a chain and fettered me with it. For in truth lust is made out of a perverse will, and when lust is served, it becomes habit, and when habit is not resisted, it becomes necessity. . . . A new will, which had begun within me, to wish freely to worship you and find joy in you, O God, the sole sure delight, was not yet able to overcome that prior will, grown strong with age. Thus did my two wills, the one old, the other new, the first carnal, and the second spiritual, contend with one another, and by their conflict they laid waste my soul. . . . Thus by the burdens of this world I was sweetly weighed down, just as a man often is in sleep. Thoughts wherein I meditated upon you were like the efforts of those who want to arouse themselves but, still overcome by deep drowsiness, sink back again. Just as no man would want to sleep forever, and it is the sane judgment of all men that it is better to be awake, yet a man often defers to shake off sleep when a heavy languor pervades all his members, and although the time to get up has come, he yields to it with pleasure even although it now irks him. In like manner, I was sure that it was better for me to give myself up to your love than to give in to my own desires. However, although the one way appealed to me and was gaining mastery, the other still afforded me pleasure and kept me victim. I had no answer to give to you when you said to me, "Rise, you who sleep, and arise from the dead, and Christ will enlighten you." When on all sides you showed me that your words were true, and I was overcome by your truth, I had no answer whatsoever to make, but only those slow and drowsy words, "Right away. Yes, right away." "Let me be for a little while." But "Right away—right away" was never right now, and "Let me be for a little while" stretched out for a long time. In vain was I delighted with your law according to the inward man, when another law in my members fought against the law of my mind, and led me captive in the law of sin which was in my members. . . .[72]

The inner conflict in Augustine's soul is between his will toward the pleasures of the flesh, the *cupiditas* which has dominated his old life, and his will toward the way of God, the *caritas* which will dominate his new life once he has conquered his weakness and has converted. This inner conflict is an epitome of the bipartite structure of his life as he presents it in the *Confessions*: his carnal life before conversion, his spiritual life after conversion. It is also a reflection, in the individual soul, of the perpetual conflict between God and Satan ("inimicus"). But primarily it is a psychological conflict between two principles both naturally contained in the single soul, each principle urging the soul in a different direction, toward a different course of action and a different way of life. The conflict must go on until the soul itself makes its decision, until it chooses one principle and rejects the other. In a brilliantly effective simile, based ultimately on Biblical metaphors of the sort we have spoken of before, Augustine compares this soul in conflict to a man between sleep and waking, trying to awaken fully but unable to do so. Sleep, of course, symbolizes sin, spiritual sluggishness, and carnal pleasures, just as it does in Prudentius's "Ales diei nuntius." Awakening is a common Christian metaphor for conversion, closely related to the symbolism of day and night we discussed earlier. The sleep of sin and spiritual death takes place in darkness and night; understanding of the divine truth and turning toward God is symbolized by light and illumination.[73] Fallen man, while knowing intellectually that the counsels of his spiritual will are the right ones and that to awaken into God's day is the right act, is unable to choose what he knows is right.[74] He wants to postpone acceptance of the necessary truth, and prolong his life of sensual satisfactions even in the face of his knowledge that he must not do so. He wants to postpone the coming of the light and remain in the pleasurable darkness.

This passage from Augustine has so many points of contact with the *alba* that the temptation to see a real connection between them is very strong. In spite of our fallen state, we should do our best to resist this temptation. The *alba* is not an allegory of Augustine's inner conflict before his conversion, or of any conflict between the way of sin and the way of salvation. At least, there is nothing in the erotic *albas* themselves to tell us that they are allegorical, and therefore we have no right to treat them as if they were. The passage in the *Confessions* and the *alba* resemble each other because they share conventional medieval symbolism and conventional medieval forms of thought. It may be that the Pauline and Augustinian notion of the divided will is the source—or, at any rate, the main source— of the kind of psychological structure we see symbolized in the *alba*. But that would simply be because Augustine is the chief psychologist of the Middle Ages, the chief creator of iconic structures to be used in describing the operations of the mind. And if the *alba* lady, proponent of the pleasure principle, tries to keep the knight from waking up in just the way that Augustine's carnal will tried to keep him from waking up, this need only mean that "carnal will" and "pleasure principle" are different names for the same kind of psychological force, which behaves in the same way whether the reality it is trying to resist is that of God or that of an angry cuckolded husband. Furthermore, while the watchman in the *alba* corresponds to Augustine's spiritual will (the will that draws the soul toward the source of all true value, God), the source of all true value in the *alba* is the lady, who corresponds to Augustine's carnal will, the instrument of sin. And, finally, while the choice Augustine had to make was between the values of the city of man and the values of the city of God, the *alba* knight's choice is between two different sets of values both of which are very much of this world: erotic love on the one hand, and physical safety and social honor on the other; or, to use a different terminology, indulgence in the pleasure principle on the one hand and acceptance of the reality principle on the other.[75]

The kind of *alba* we have been speaking of here has a number of meanings that are expressed by—and are distinctive to—the particular kind of dramatic structure we have pointed out. The dramatic conflict of the two chief active characters, the lady and the watchman, carries with it an important idea about the antithetical attitudes toward desire and reality inherent in any human experience. The fact that the central character, the knight, must choose between these two attitudes and take action on his choice carries with it equally important ideas about human freedom and the psychological processes of making decisions—ideas closely related to those found in Augustine. This kind of *alba* is about conflict, choice, decision, and action, in the difficult problem of reconciling passionate erotic love with the demands of external nature and society. It differs in many fundamental ways from poems which, although they present most of the *alba* motifs, relate them to each other in a different sort of structure.

Ovid, for example, has a poem similar in theme to the medieval *albas* we have been discussing, but because of its difference in structure it is a different kind of poem altogether.[76] Ovid's poem (*Amores* I.xiii)[77] is a monolog addressed to the dawn goddess, Aurora. The speaker, in bed with a girl, reproaches the dawn for coming so swiftly and interrupting his pleasures. He goes on, with the usual Ovidian prodigality, to enumerate all those types of men (in addition to lovers) who have cause to dislike the dawn: the seaman, who no longer has the stars to guide by; the peasant, who must go out into the fields and work; the schoolboy, who must go to school; and so forth, for some fourteen lines. He then makes a number of adverse comments on Aurora's own love-life, and concludes the monolog with a delightful display of self-directed irony and playful wit:

> *Iurgia finieram. scires audisse: rubebat—*
> *nec tamen adsueto tardius orta dies!*

> I had ended my reproaches. You could tell she had heard:
> she was blushing.
> Nevertheless, the day did not arise any later than usual!
> (Lines 47–48)

This poem by no means lacks the contrast between the pleasure principle and the reality principle which we pointed out in the medieval *alba*. The pleasure principle is expressed by the speaker's desire to prolong his erotic pleasures; his opposition to the dawn; his attempts to persuade Aurora to slow her pace; and, especially, his use of the optative subjunctive, with its compact grammatical contrast between the desired and the real:

> *optavi quotiens, ne nox tibi cedere vellet,*
> *ne fugerent vultus sidera mota tuos!*

optavi quotiens, aut ventus frangeret axem,
  aut caderet spissa nube retentus equus!

How many times I have wished that night would refuse to
                give way to you,
    that the stars would not be moved to flee at the sight of
                you!
How many times I have wished that the wind would break
                your chariot's axle,
    or that the horse would fall, held back by thick clouds!

                                            (Lines 27–30)

The reality principle finds its expression in the irony of the poem's
final line:

nec tamen adsueto tardius orta dies!

The poet accepts the fact that the processes of nature are not to be
delayed or circumvented by the strength of his desire. Desire is a
mightly force, but reality will always win out. Even the witty remark
about the dawn's blushing expresses what is ultimately a quite
serious thought. Men deceive themselves into thinking that the
phenomena of external nature are responses to the expression of
human feelings and desires: prayers, reproaches, conjurations. But
in fact, nature goes her own way, completely untouched by human
needs, and what men believe to be the result of their own words is
actually a completely independent natural process over which men
do not have the slightest control. The fact that this self-mocking
irony appears only in the final distich is itself an incisive means of
contrasting the pleasure principle (along with the pretensions of
universal power it gives rise to) with the reality principle. The expression of the real in the last two lines effectively punctures all the
eloquent tirade of wishing that forms the poem up to that point.[78]

The pleasure principle and the reality principle are indeed present
in Ovid's poem. But they are present as parts of one mind, as contrary impulses both finding expression in one lyric oration. They are
not given dramatic voices of their own, and the ironic situation of the
speaker, caught between his desires and knowledge of the real, is not

turned into a dramatic situation, with arguing opponents, a decision made between them, and resultant action. The medieval *alba* embodies the psychological conflict in an objective, external drama; Ovid's *alba*—if we can call it that—presents the conflict lyrically, subjectively, internally.

Consequently, the psychological situation in Ovid's poem, totally internalized in the mind of the single speaker and with no suggestion of personification or dramatization,* is much more static than that in the medieval *alba* or in Saint Augustine's portrayal of his divided will. The two attitudes toward reality—the two principles, the two wills—are not in active conflict in the mind of Ovid's speaker. They exist side by side, contrasted, but in perpetual ironic balance. There is no battle between them; no decision is expected; no turning from one to the other is possible. In Augustine, the two wills are in a dynamic relationship with each other and with the soul that contains them; they fight for dominance; and the soul finally chooses, sloughs off the old man, turns toward the right path, converts. In the medieval *alba*, too, where the psychological conflict has been objectified and dramatized, all the relations between the characters are dynamic. The lady and the watchman, championing the causes of the pleasure and reality principles, oppose each other vehemently, arguing over the course of action the knight is to take. The knight himself must eventually make a decision, renounce (if only temporarily) the pleasures of the inner world, turn toward the realities of the outer world, and leave. This is, structurally, a dramatic equivalent to spiritual conversion: both structures necessitate choice, both result in action. In Ovid, the different kind of structure represents a different concept of man and of man's potentialities. Man's ironic predicament, between desire and reality, is permanently fixed. Man's desires are bound to be frustrated by the inevitable movement of natural forces. Much as one would like to, one cannot stay in the chamber of love. But, on the other hand, one does not have to make an *active decision* to renounce pleasure and accept reality: the acceptance of reality is not a matter of will, of inner

---

* External reality—the dawn itself—is, of course, personified, but that is not the point here. There is no personification of *psychological* entities.

choice, but a necessity totally imposed from without. Creatures of nature do not exercise their wills and make a free choice when they submit to nature; they simply submit, because that is the way of creatures of nature. And man is one of them.

Thus, for Ovid, the outcome of the *alba* situation—this situation in which the pleasure and reality principles oppose each other—cannot be an action, a voluntary turning to one principle or the other. The only response a man can possibly make to the conflict of the two principles is to *know* them: to be conscious of their existence and coexistence, their inevitability and irreconcilability. This kind of knowledge is the essence of irony, and the structure Ovid uses to express it—forty-six lines of pleasure principle, punctured by two final lines of reality principle—is virtually an archetype of ironic structure.

If we compare this poem of Ovid's, Augustine's portrayal of his divided will, and the medieval *alba*—all with respect to their structures and meanings—we will note certain suggestive resemblances and differences. For Ovid, reality and value are strictly confined to the natural world. Erotic love is a part of nature, the sunrise is a part of nature, the conflict between the two is a part of nature, and man's psychological predicament is a part of nature. Man himself, with all of his impulses and actions, is nothing more than a part of nature. Augustine's concepts of reality and value are of course radically different. There are two worlds of value and two kinds of reality: a world of the flesh, of inferior reality and value, and a world of the spirit, of superior reality and value. Man partakes of both of these worlds: he is both spirit and flesh, and he is drawn both upwards toward God and downwards toward the earth. He is not merely a creature of nature, as in Ovid; he is two different kinds of creature at once. The conflicting wills which contend within his soul are not merely natural psychological forces, both belonging to the world of nature; each of these two wills comes from a different world—one from the fallen world of the flesh, and the other from the world of God—and the battle of the two wills within the individual soul is at the same time a battle between the two worlds of reality and value over the destiny of mankind.

The medieval *alba* shares with Ovid the sense of an exclusively natural reality. The erotic love between the knight and the lady is part of the natural world; and the opponents of this love—society and the movement of the sun—are also parts of nature. There may be a hint of the supernatural in the sun symbolism, as we pointed out in an earlier chapter, but we cannot be sure of that; and in any case the supernatural plays no vital role in the drama. The situation, the characters, the psychological forces—all are totally secular and natural. But the *structure* of the medieval *alba* has very little in common with Ovid's *Amores* I.xiii, and very much in common with the passage quoted earlier from Augustine's *Confessions*. The conflict of two worlds, the problem of choice, the necessity for action— these ideas are basic to the structure of the medieval *alba* and to that of Augustine's passage on the divided will, while they and the structure they give rise to are absent from Ovid's poem. The naturalism and secularism we see in the *alba* of the High Middle Ages differ from the similar attitudes of much ancient poetry in that the naturalism and secularism of the *alba* are expressed in the thought forms of Christianity.[79] It is not Christian doctrine that we see in the *alba*, not the actual content of Christian thought, but the *forms* of Christian thought, the ways of looking at and structuring reality. Although neither the *alba* lady nor the *alba* watchman, in their argument over the knight's course of action, shows the slightest concern for Christianity, the very structure of that argument tells us that this is a poem of the Christian Middle Ages.

FOUR

TIME

Pou ai geü
En la chambre de joie.

I have lain but a short time
In the chamber of joy.

—"Gaite de la tor"

WE HAVE SAID that the world of the medieval *alba* is a world of nature. An inevitable concomitant to the world of nature is the domination of everything by time. Time is change in nature, and everything natural is subject to change. Change can be of two kinds, as seen from the moralizing point of view of human desires. It can be change for the better: movement toward a higher state, rediscovery of what has been lost, the righting of wrongs, the reuniting of the separated. This is the way time functions in comedy and in those sections of a man's life that are structured in the manner of comedy. But there is another kind of change: change for the worse. States of happiness cannot last; change results in falling away, loss, separation. This is the way time functions in tragedy, and it is also the way it functions in the *alba*.

The plot of the *alba* is, simply, the separation of lovers at dawn. This separation takes place in time, and is due to time. The sun, rising, *is* time; and because of it the lovers must part. If the lovers had their way, if the pleasure principle ruled the universe, nothing would ever change, no one would ever grow old, the love affair— and, indeed, this single night of the love affair—would go on forever. The lovers want to reject time, to blot it out. But the movement of time appears at the very foundation of the dramatic events in the *alba*: the change from night to day, the dawn itself. The lovers hate the dawn, because it symbolizes the hard fact that in reality all things do change, and that ultimately they all change for the worse. The night of union changes to the day of separation; there is no stasis in human life; the joy of love cannot last; and, finally, life itself must give way—in the process of time—to death. The lovers do not want to accept time; but the watchman, proponent of the reality principle, keeps reminding them of the existence of time, keeps telling them that in the world of nature time cannot be avoided.

Thus, one of the main points of conflict between the watchman and the lovers is the difference in their respective attitudes toward time. It might even be said that this difference contains within it all the other differences that separate the two opposed concepts of reality. Time, in the *alba*, is not merely one element among many. It is the basic force behind the events of the story, and the basic medium in which they take place. The different ways that the characters understand and react to time, therefore, in a certain sense sum up their attitudes toward the entire *alba* situation and everything it symbolizes. Furthermore, the way time is treated in each individual *alba* can be seen as a key to the over-all meaning of the poem, its concept of man and of the universe he lives in. In this chapter we will present certain metaphysical, theological, and psychological concepts of time, and then apply these concepts to the analysis of some of the representative *albas* we have been examining.

The chief medieval philosopher of time is of course Saint Augustine.[1] Time, according to Augustine, begins with the Creation, as is shown in Genesis i.1–5. These verses in Genesis describe God's activities on the first day, and the fact that this was the *first* day proves that there can have been no time before it. Moreover, what God does on this first day is to create the day and the night, whose alternation is not only the symbol but also the very substance of time. On the fourth day of Creation (verses 14–19) God reinforces the existence of time by creating the heavenly bodies. Their periodic motion serves to divide time into intervals; and, in addition, the sun and the moon are given the function of ruling over the two main periodic divisions of time, the day and the night.

The sort of time Augustine is speaking of here does not correspond to either of the two sorts of change in nature we indicated above. It is not change for the better or change for the worse. It has no moral meaning whatever. It is change seen without reference to human desires: it neither fulfills them nor frustrates them. This is time as a purely abstract metaphysical principle, and Augustine's concept of it derives from his literal interpretation of the Biblical text, not from any human experience. Time as it is experienced in actual life always has moral consequences. On a small scale it may lead to an increase of happiness. On a large scale it always leads to decay, old age, and death. But the alternation of day and night described in the first chapter of Genesis has neither of these consequences.

For Augustine, time becomes a moral force only with the Fall of Man. Before the Fall, Adam and Eve were not subject to the decaying effects of time:

> *Quae . . . senio non veterascerent, ut necessitate perducerentur ad mortem . . . .*

> . . . they decayed not with years, nor drew nearer to death . . . .[2]

> *Ideo corpus eius . . . ligno vitae a mortis necessitate prohibebatur, atque in juventutis flore tenebatur . . . .*

> And therefore his [Adam's] body . . . by means of the tree of life warded off the necessity of dying, and was thus maintained in the flower of youth . . . .[3]

But Adam's sin and his expulsion from Eden made him and all his descendants subject to time as a destructive force:

> ... *traditus esset tempori vetustatique finiendus, in ea duntaxat vita, quam ... posset in paradiso, nisi peccasset, habere perpetuam.*

> ... he was delivered over to the wasting of time, at least in respect of that life which, had he not sinned, he might have retained perpetually in Paradise . . . .[4]

This is the destructive, tragic time that operates in the *alba*. The *alba* situation would thus not be possible except for the fallen state of mankind. We might digress at this point to note that the *alba* situation, aside from its being a result of the Fall of Man, has numerous analogies of structure and content to the story recounted in Genesis iii. Both situations begin with a man and a woman in an enclosed space of perfect joy (we have previously noted the analogies between the *alba* chamber and the Garden of Eden). In both stories a warning of some sort is given by someone who can see both into the inner world and into the outer world around it: God in Genesis, the watchman in the *alba*. In both there is another voice that expresses opposition to the moral or prudential warning from above. In the *alba*, the lady opposes the watchman's urgings of caution and safety; in the Eden story, the serpent, soon seconded by Eve, opposes God's injunction not to eat from the tree of the knowledge of good and evil. In both stories a central male character —the knight or Adam—is forced to choose between the actions advocated by the opposed voices.[5] In both stories the interior world is (or is felt to be) free of time and of the fear and grief that time, as a destructive force, gives rise to. In both, a great force or being enters into the inner paradise to put an end to the joyful life there: God, in Genesis iii.8, and the sun in the *alba*. In both stories the outcome is exile from the inner paradise, separation from its joys: Adam and Eve are exiled from Eden, and the knight is exiled from the lady's chamber. (The lady herself cannot be exiled, because she is herself the source of the joy in that inner world; in a way she *is* the inner

world, the paradise, that the knight is forced to leave.)[6] In both stories
the exile is accompanied with much grief and fear, and is associated
with time as a tragic moral principle. Both stories are, indeed, potential tragedies; but in both, the tragic consequences are tempered by
future events. The knight's separation from the lady is only temporary: they expect to be reunited in the near future. Similarly, the exile
from Eden lasts only a measured length of time, until Adam's sin
is redeemed by Christ's sacrifice, and the possibility of man's entering
into paradise is restored.

These similarities in structure (there are, of course, many differences as well) connect the *alba* with the story of the Fall of Man
as it appears in the Bible. There is also an important similarity of
content that connects the *alba* with the Christian—specifically the
Augustinian—interpretation of the Biblical story. The sins of Adam
and Eve in the Bible are disobedience and ambition. But the first
result of their eating of the fruit has to do with sexuality: they
realize that they are naked, and cover themselves. The avid interest
in sexuality (although in a negative way, let it be said) of the early
Fathers of the Church led them to make much of this hint; and
Augustine especially, with his particular personal history, always
tended to give strong emphasis to the sin of sexual lust. A significant
proportion of his commentaries on the Fall of Man, therefore, is devoted to the sexual aspects of the story. Having experienced sexual
lust while at the same time trying to escape it, Augustine was aware
that lustful feelings can be independent of the will, that they constitute in themselves a kind of bodily will which a man may feel to
be opposed to his own will and not subject to his control. The
psychological model, in this notion, is of course quite similar to
that of the divided will, which we discussed earlier. Since the
prelapsarian Garden of Eden was a place of perfect harmony, a
disharmony in the human will would not have been possible there.
It follows, according to Augustine, that in Eden before the Fall the
sexual organs were under the complete control of the will—that is,
they had no will of their own. Lust did not move them. Their purpose,
as sexual organs, was solely for reproduction. Had they been used
sexually there (they were not so used until after the Fall), the act

would have been a clear act of the will, deriving from a conscious intention to produce children; no lust would have initiated the act, and no sexual pleasure would have been felt during it. (To understand just how deeply opposed this Augustinian ideal is to actual human experience, we should describe it even more specifically: in Eden, according to Augustine, man would never have had a sexual erection without a conscious act of the will; and this act of the will would never have had anything to do with the desire for pleasure.)[7]

With the Fall, however, this state of things was changed. The genitals acquired a will of their own. They ceased to obey man's will, and instead obeyed only their own lust. Sexual contact became an object of desire in itself. Sexual intercourse produced pleasure. And along with sexual lust and sexual pleasure, man acquired sexual shame. He covered his genitals because he was ashamed of the fact that they were no longer under the control of his will. But why, we might ask, was sex involved at all in the punishment of Adam and Eve for their transgression, and why should the punishment have consisted in making the genital organs independent of the control of the will? Augustine's answer seems to attribute to God a kind of ironic wit: the shameful way the genitals *disobey* the will is a just retribution for the first couple's *disobedience* of God's command.[8]

This association of the Eden story with sexuality adds to the numerous similarities that story shows to the *alba* situation. We cannot really speak of a structural similarity here, but only of a similarity of motif and association. The notion of sexuality in the *alba* is not parallel to Augustine's notion but antithetical to it. Augustine's ideal—which he sees as having been real in Eden—is for the will to have complete control over sex, and for there to be no sexual passion whatever. The ideal of the *alba* lovers, in *their* paradise, is to will what their bodies will, to experience passion, and to satisfy desire. The exile from Eden, according to Augustine, first brought passion and lust into being. The exile from the chamber of love in the *alba* frustrates passion and denies satisfaction. Thus—and this brings us back to the main subject of this chapter—Augustine associates freedom from the destructive power of time with freedom from sexual desire and sexual pleasure: destructive time and sexual concupiscence are both characteristics of the fallen world. The *alba*, on the contrary, associates freedom from time (or a willful ignoring of it) with sexual *satisfaction*, and the destructive power of time with the *ending* of a sexual union.

Just as Augustine's ideal of the way the genital organs ought to behave is an intentional reversal of actual human experience, so too his association of time with sex (in the fallen world) and timelessness with nonsexuality (in Eden) reverses the associations brought about by nature. One of the most characteristic phenomenological aspects of sex is the loss of awareness of the passage of time during sexual activity.[9] The sense of timelessness is at its height during actual orgasm. After withdrawal and separation, however, perceptions of the outer world and of time reassert themselves. The structure of the *alba* parallels this sequence in the subjective experience of sex. A period of erotic union (not necessarily devoted entirely to sex) is accompanied with an ignoring of time; the watchman's reminding the lovers of the time goes along with the ending of their erotic union and with their subsequent separation. This structural analogy between the *alba* and the events of actual sexual intercourse, along with the fact that the *alba* is itself a poem about sexual love, may be said to reinforce an audience's emotional experience of the poem. To be more precise: the structure of the usual *alba* is analogous—with more or less completeness, depending on the particular poem—to the structure of the psychosexual experience of interrupted orgasm, and the reaction provoked by the poetic experience is to a certain extent analogous to that produced by the sexual experience.[10] The topographical similarity between the two structures—both involve a separation, in which the male must withdraw from and leave an enclosed inner place of erotic pleasure —strengthens the analogy.

Let me say at once that I am not claiming that the *alba* is a symbolical representation of an interrupted orgasm, a kind of dream-elaboration of an unpleasant sexual fantasy or experience. The *alba* is not reducible to a particular kind of sexual experience any more than it is reducible to an allegory of psychological faculties.

But its structural similarities to the sexual experience play a part—exactly how great a part it is impossible to say—in its meaning and effect. Just as two waves of the same wave length will reinforce each other, even though each may come from a different source, so the poetic structure is reinforced by the similar structure of the sexual experience, without our needing to assume that the sexual experience is the "source" of the poetic structure. The analogy is one of large structure, not of precise content. There is no medieval *alba* in which the watchman's announcement actually comes in the middle of a moment of sexual intercourse. The watchman's reminder of the time interrupts a night of erotic joy which may contain sexual intercourse but which evidently contains much else. It is not a moment of intercourse that is interrupted, but the whole being-together of the lovers. The separation that results is analogous to post-coital separation but is itself something much less specifically sexual. It is a separation not of sexual organs but of bodies and souls and hearts. Only in Wagner's version of the *alba*, in the second act of *Tristan und Isolde*, does the analogy with an interruption of sexual intercourse seem to become an analogy of content as well as an analogy of structure. The words of the lovers about their rapture are accompanied by an enormous climax in the orchestra, with wave after wave of sound piling up in greater and greater excitement, until, exactly at the moment when a harmonic and melodic resolution to this great build-up would be expected, Brangäne screams, and the orchestra stops short with a horrible discord: Isolde's husband, King Marke, has returned. This is not merely a structural analogy with an interrupted orgasm; it is the symbolic, musical representation of an interrupted orgasm. The medieval *alba* does not go so far. But the analogy is there, and it plays its part.

I now want to present, in brief outline, a psychoanalytical theory of time and time-perception based on the—admittedly hypothetical —experiences of infants with respect to time. The imaginative life of infants is scarcely subject to scientific verification, and a theory of this sort must be seen as a hypothetical construct to be judged not on the basis of its objective validity but rather on the basis of its utility in explaining and ordering other products of the imagination.

My intention, in sketching this theory, is mainly to provide a convenient classificatory scheme for some of the attitudes toward time we find in literature (particularly, of course, the *alba*), and in philosophy and theology (particularly the concepts of time we see in Augustine).

As a first stage we may posit a sense of total timelessness experienced by the infant in the womb. There are no periodic changes to mark off intervals of time: no changes from dark to light or from light to dark, and not even a periodic recurrence of hunger. Feeding is relatively continuous and uninterrupted, as are darkness, insideness, and, to a great degree, freedom from discomfort and unpleasantness of all kinds.

A second stage would begin with birth and continue for some time thereafter. Time now must have a certain real existence for the infant. Intervals of light and dark and of hunger and satisfaction introduce a periodicity into his existence. To what extent the infant's separation from the womb is felt by him as a sorrowful event is of course impossible to say. This event—the beginning of time, so far as the infant is concerned—is analogous to Creation in the Augustinian scheme. Before it, there was no time. For a certain period after it, time has an existence, but an existence which is perhaps not felt by the infant to have any moral meaning—that is, it may be felt as mere periodicity, without any sense of its leading to good things or bad things. On the other hand, the beginning of time for the infant—the separation from the womb—may be felt as the first experience of time in its tragic, separating capacity; and the periodic recurrence of painful hunger and pleasurable satisfaction of that hunger may give time a tinge of moral meaning. But, provided that the hunger is always satisfied, there can be no sense of time as leading preponderantly in one direction or the other, that is, as consisting mainly of change for the better or change for the worse. Time, in this stage, would remain to a great extent morally neutral—as in the period between the Creation and the Fall of Man, according to Augustine.

During this second hypothetical period, the infant does not make a clear distinction between himself and the world around him. He is not aware of an inside (himself) and an outside (not himself), but only of a unity in which inside and outside are not distinguished. He is in particularly close association with his mother, whose love and presence encompass him, who is associated with pleasure, and who is felt to be part of himself. At some time, however, he is forced to become aware of an outside reality which is not subject to his will and cannot be manipulated by his desires. He becomes aware of an inside and an outside; of an external periodicity he cannot—or cannot totally—control (day and night, his mother's sleeping and waking); and of the fact that his mother is distinct from himself. All of this constitutes a kind of separation: a separation from the sense of all things being one, a separation from external reality, and at least a partial separation from the mother.[11]

This sense of separation would be reinforced at the time of weaning, when the child is even more decisively separated from his mother, the source of pleasure, love, and nourishment. Time now assumes a more fully external quality; it becomes associated with fixed hours of eating and going to sleep, time-intervals over which the child himself has little control. Time also begins to assume its quality as a moral force, and particularly as a tragic force associated with separation from the mother. It is time that causes the separation, and separation is loss of love, loss of identity, even—symbolically—loss of life. "Partir, c'est mourir un peu" accurately represents the psychological experience of the child separated from the source of his joy—except that we might eliminate the "un peu."[12] For Augustine, the Fall of Man is a spiritual death, an exile from paradise. For the infant, the moment of tragedy is his exile from the encompassing paradise of his mother's total presence, and it, too, is felt as a spiritual death. In the *alba*, the moment of grief and tears comes when the lover must leave the joyful interior dominated by the love of the lady and go out into a harsh external world. In all of these parallel structures there is a contrast between absolute or relative timelessness in the inner world, and subjection to time as a tragic force in the outer world. The moment of separation is the transition from a relatively timeless world to a world dominated by time.

To this series of hypothetical stages in the infantile development of time-consciousness we might add a final stage—a stage which lasts for many years, often for decades. It is during this period that the growing person gradually comes to realize fully the dominance of time over all human activity and achievement. He becomes aware that time is operative in everything, that it always has a moral effect, that its over-all movement is downwards, that no joy can last forever, that men really do grow old, and that the end is death. These realizations are the result of increasing experience of the world of nature, and they are reflected (if only lightly) in the *alba*. This stage in the development of time-consciousness is greatly modified by Christian theology, as we shall see in a moment.

It may be that men maintain a racial memory of the timelessness of Eden, which they seek in various ways to return to; or it may be that each individual subconsciously recalls the various stages of relative timelessness in his infancy and longs to recover that lost freedom. Or perhaps it is mere logic at work, or a category of the autonomous imagination, completely independent of any psychological or religious "origin." Whatever the cause, man's history exhibits constant attempts, in all the media of human thought, to portray the world in a way that would deprive time of its sway over the events of nature and of human life. Of particular interest for our purposes is the Western philosophical-theological tradition in this universal campaign against time. Ancient Greek philosophy sought to discover an impersonal permanence underlying the flux of phenomena: Parmenides's One, Plato's Ideas, Aristotle's Order of Nature. Plato and his Christian followers added to the philosophical notion of an impersonal permanence the related notion, already established in the mystery religions, of a personal permanence, an indestructible soul in each individual, which enjoys a timeless, eternal existence after having passed through the time-bound changes of earthly life. Let us look at this Platonic-Christian concept of eternity more closely, focusing on the analysis of it given by Augustine.

Augustine begins, as is usual with him, with a description of psychological experience. Time is a destructive force, continually separating us from joy:

. . . tempora surripiunt quod amamus . . . .

. . . time seizes and carries away the things we love . . . .[13]

This time is a constant flux, never ceasing during the course of human life. We experience it as something always moving, incapable of being held on to. The present tense—a stability of being, without change—is impossible in earthly life; earthly life is all future and past tense. Man desires to find a present tense, but cannot do it on earth. The future, which is unreal because it has not yet come, dominates his desires. The present immediately becomes past. The past is unreal because it no longer exists. Only God can truly be spoken of in the present tense, for He is eternal, immutable, timeless:

> *Nam in omnibus actionibus et motibus nostris, et in omni prorsus agitatione creaturae duo tempora invenio, praeteritum et futurum. Praesens quaero, nihil stat: quod dixi, jam non est; quod dicturus sum, nondum est: quod feci, jam non est; quod facturus sum, nondum est: quod vixi, jam non est; quod victurus sum, nondum est. Praeteritum et futurum invenio in omni motu rerum: in veritate quae manet, praeteritum et futurum non invenio, sed solum praesens, et hoc incorruptibiliter, quod in creatura non est. Discute rerum mutationes, invenies Fuit et Erit: cogita Deum, invenies Est, ubi Fuit et Erit esse non possit.*

> For in all our actions and movements—indeed, in every motion of a created thing—I find two tenses: the past and the future. I look for the present tense, but there is none. What I have said, no longer exists; what I am going to say, does not exist yet. What I have done, no longer exists; what I am going to do, does not exist yet. What I have experienced, no longer exists; what I am going to experience, does not exist yet. I find a past and a future in every natural event. But in the unchanging Truth I find no past and no future, but only the incorruptible present, which does not exist in any created thing. Analyze the events of the natural world and you will find "Was" and "Will be." Consider God and you

will find "Is," where there can be no "Was" and no "Will be."[14]

It is only in eternity that a man can truly possess joy. A joy which is subject to time, which cannot last but must pass away, is an incomplete joy. Only a joy which lasts forever is a complete joy, and it is this kind of joy that men long for:

> *Cum ergo beati esse omnes homines velint, si vere volunt, profecto et esse immortales volunt: aliter enim beati esse non possent.*

> Therefore, since men desire to be happy, if they desire rightly they must also desire to be immortal. For in no other way could they be happy.[15]

True blessedness can only be conceived of as blessedness outside of time. In God's eternity, which all men long for, there is stability rather than change, the present tense rather than the continually moving past and future, and full and eternal enjoyment rather than partial and momentary enjoyment.

The nature of eternity, and the relation of eternity to time, are almost beyond the grasp of the human intellect:

> ... *conantur aeterna sapere, sed adhuc in praeteritis et futuris rerum motibus cor eorum volitat et adhuc vanum est. Quis tenebit illud et figet illud, ut paululum stet et paululum rapiat splendorem semper stantis aeternitatis et conparet cum temporibus numquam stantibus et videat esse inconparabilem et videat longum tempus nisi ex multis praetereuntibus motibus, qui simul extendi non possunt, longum non fieri; non autem praeterire quicquam in aeterno, sed totum esse praesens; nullum vero tempus totum esse praesens: et videat omne praeteritum propelli ex futuro et omne futurum ex praeterito consequi et omne praeteritum ac futurum ab eo, quod semper est praesens, creari et excurrere? Quis tenebit cor hominis, ut stet et videat, quomodo stans dictet futura et praeterita tempora nec futura nec praeterita aeternitas? ...*

They attempt to grasp eternal things, but their heart flutters among the changing things of past and future, and it is still vain. Who will catch hold of it, and make it fast, so that it stands firm for a little while, and for a little while seize the splendor of that ever stable eternity, and compare it with times that never stand fast, and see that it is incomparable to them, and see that a long time cannot become long except out of many passing movements, which cannot be extended together, that in the eternal nothing can pass away but the whole is present, that no time is wholly present? Who will see that all past time is driven back by the future, that all the future is consequent on the past, and all past and future are created and take their course from that which is ever present? Who will hold the heart of man, so that it may stand still and see how steadfast eternity, neither future nor past, decrees times future and those past?[16]

But this metaphysical timelessness, described by Augustine as virtually ineffable, acquires a wonderful concreteness in medieval portrayals of paradise. Here, for example, is Jean de Meun's timeless (and typically prolix) paradise, where there is no rising or setting of the sun—that primal indicator of the passage of time—and where the past and future tenses give way to the eternal present, just as in the passages from Augustine quoted above:

> *Qu'onques n'i virent naistre nuit;*
> *Si n'ont il qu'un jour seulement,*
> *Mais il n'a point d'avesprement,*
> *Ne matins n'i peut comencier,*
> *Tant se sache l'aube avancier;*
> *Car li seirs au matin s'assemble*
> *E li matins le seir resemble.*
> *Autel vous di de chascune eure:*
> *Toujourz en un moment demeure*
> *Cil jourz, qui ne peut anuitier,*
> *Tant sache a lui la nuit luitier;*

N'il n'a pas temporel mesure,
Cil jourz tant beaus, qui toujourz dure,
E de clarté presente rit;
Il n'a futur ne preterit,
Car, se bien la verité sent,
Tuit li trei tens i sont present,
Li queus presenz le jour compasse;
Mais ce n'est pas presenz qui passe
En partie pour defenir,
Ne don seit partie a venir;
Qu'onc preteriz presenz n'i fu.
E si vous redi que li fu-
Turs n'i ravra jamais presence,
Tant est d'estable parmanance . . . .

For never have they seen night come on there,
and they have only a single day,
but it has no twilight.
Nor can the morning ever have a beginning there,
however much the dawn may assert itself,
for the evening is one with the morning,
and the morning is like the evening.
I can say the same about every hour.
That day, which can never become night
however much the night may battle with it,
always stays at a single moment.
Nor does it have any intervals of time,
that lovely, everlasting day,
and it laughs in the brightness of the present.
It has neither future tense nor past tense,
for (if I understand it correctly)
all three tenses are the present tense there,
and this present tense rules the day.
But it is not a present of which a part passes by
and comes to an end,
or of which a part is still to come;

for the past was never present there,
and I tell you once again that the future will never be present there,
so stable and permanent is [the time] . . . .[17]

This paradise is not an abstract construct but a real, concrete place, where an eternity of blessedness can be enjoyed by every virtuous Christian. For the contrast of time and timelessness in Christianity is not only a matter of metaphysics; is also involves the life of every individual and his destiny after death. History, as we have already indicated, is cradled in timelessness. Before history began at all, that is, before the world was created, there was no time. At the very beginning of history, between the Creation and the Fall, time existed, but without a moral meaning—which is really to say that time, as we know it, did not yet exist. At the end of history lies the Day of Judgment, and beyond that—timelessness once again. But while timelessness lies before and after history, it also lies above it. Since Christ's atonement, it is possible for men to enjoy that eternity from the moment of their death, to ascend from the world of destructive and tragic time, with all its necessary separations, to the world of timelessness, with its perpetual union.

The time scheme in the Christian concept of human life is thus antithetical to the time scheme forced upon us by natural experience, and hence to the time scheme we find in the erotic *alba*. The *alba*'s time scheme is naturalistic in several ways. It follows the natural movement of daily time from night to dawn to day. It also parallels the stages in the natural growth of the human consciousness of time. It begins with a time-denial analogous to that of the infant, a total devotion to the pleasure principle, such as we have supposed it to exist in the early stages of infancy; it moves along, like the child, to the experience of time as an ineluctable external force; it ends in separation from the beloved lady and an acceptance of time as the governing principle of the real world—stages, both of these, in the natural process of human growth and aging. In the *alba*, the analogies with the time scheme of human life (childhood, weaning, adulthood) are thus in harmony with the diurnal time scheme of the natural world (night, dawn, day). The two are parallel time movements, reinforcing each other, giving us a sense of the ineluctable movement of all nature—man and the stars—in time, along with a great sense of regret that time moves that way, that time leads to separation and loss and eventually to death.

The Christian time scheme moves in the opposite way, from a state analogous to adulthood—namely, the world of separation in time—to a state analogous to infancy—namely, a world of union in timelessness. The idea of death as a second birth, so common in Christian thought, reinforces this analogy we are pointing out between the infant's experience of timelessness and the Christian concept of God's timeless paradise. The joys looked forward to by the Christian are in certain ways similar to the joys of one's infancy, except that they are seen not in the past but in the future. The Christian metaphor reverses the time scheme of nature and brings us back to being born.

This reversal of the natural time scheme makes for an entirely different sort of dramatic movement in literary works based on the Christian world view as compared with works based on an acceptance of natural processes and of nothing beyond them. The time scheme of the *alba* is that of naturalistic tragedy: acceptance, under duress, of the movement of time that leads to separation (although the *alba* falls short of the full movement of tragedy). The time scheme of the Christian picture of reality is that of divine comedy: a negation of the destructive processes of natural time, and an assertion of a supernatural, reverse time, which leads to unification and eternal blessedness. As Christ reversed Adam's Fall, that Fall which initiated the destructive temporal movement of history and of individual lives, so Dante's *Purgatorio* shows us a reversal of the individual's history of sinning. The various sins, acquired in the course of natural time on earth, are purged away, one by one, restoring the soul to its unfallen state. (The soul's new innocence is analogous to the innocence of the infant, or of Adam before the Fall, but we must note that it is by no means identical with that earlier innocence. The experience of sin and purgation enriches the soul: that is why the children in the divine amphitheater of *Paradiso* xxxii are ranked lower than the adults. The Christian reversal of time in Dante is thus not a simple matter of backtracking. Included within the over-all reversal are the beneficial effects of life in time, so that the soul's eventual state in the timelessness of paradise is a result of both kinds of movement: tragic, downward-moving time on earth, and reverse, upward-moving time in purgatory.)

We have been speaking of the Christian alternative to the notion of destructive natural time. There is another sort of attitude toward the destructive power of time which has found frequent literary expression. This is an attitude which completely embraces the reality principle, accepts time as it is, imagines no escape from its tragic movement, and simply tries to make the best of things. It is the philosophy of *carpe diem*, a phrase which makes the characteristic point that no interval of time longer than a day ought to concern us. The Augustinian idea that no joy is a true joy unless it is an eternal joy may correspond to an innate yearning of the human heart; but if the poets of *carpe diem* experienced this yearning they did not attempt to erect a philosophical system that would satisfy it. They accepted the fact that such a yearning must always be frustrated in this world, and they did not posit the existence of another world in which time would play no part and joy would be eternal. Time presses irreversibly forward, and leads to decay and death:

> *Eheu fugaces, Postume, Postume,*
> *labuntur anni, nec pietas moram*
> *rugis et instanti senectae*
> *adferet indomitaeque morti . . . .*

> Alas, Postumus, Postumus,
> the years slip fleetingly by, nor will piety
> cause any delay to wrinkles, and imminent old age,
> and unconquered death . . . .[18]

> *Like as the waves make towards the pebbled shore,*
> *So do our minutes hasten to their end;*
> *Each changing place with that which goes before,*
> *In sequent toil all forwards do contend.*

Nativity, once in the main of light,
Crawls to maturity, wherewith being crown'd,
Crooked eclipses 'gainst his glory fight,
And Time that gave doth now his gift confound. . . .[19]

Le tems s'en va, le tems s'en va, ma Dame,
Las! le tems non, mais nous nous en allons,
Et tost serons estendus sous la lame . . . .

Time is passing, time is passing, my lady—
alas! not time, but it is we who are passing,
and soon we will be laid out under a stone . . . .[20]

Even cities, and the great civilizations represented by them, are
decayed and destroyed by time:

Et querimur, cito si nostrae data tempora vitae
*   diffugiunt? urbes mors violenta rapit. . . .*
Et te (quis putet hoc?), altrix mea, durus arator
*   vertet et:—Urbs—dicet—haec quoque clara fuit.—*
Fata trahunt homines. Fatis urgentibus, urbes
*   et quodcumque vides auferet ipsa dies.*

And do we complain if the time given to our life
    flees swiftly? Violent death ravages [even] cities. . . .
Even you (who would think it?), my foster-mother, the
                    pitiless plowman
    will turn up, saying, "This city too was famous."
The fates carry men away. Pressed on by the fates, the day
                    alone
    will carry off cities and everything you see.[21]

Giace l'alta Cartago; a pena i segni
De l'alte sue rüine il lido serba.
Muoiono le città, muoiono i regni;
Copre i fasti e le pompe arena ed erba . . . .

High Carthage lies waste; the shore shows only
the merest traces of its lofty ruins.

Cities die; kingdoms die;
sand and grass cover the splendor and pomp . . . .[22]

In the face of this destructive power of time, the only rational thing
to do is to try to experience the passing moments as intensely as
possible, to enjoy the pleasures of union with the object of desire
before tragic time brings on the inevitable separation:

Donc, si vous me croyez, mignonne,
Tandis que vostre âge fleuronne
En sa plus verte nouveauté,
Cueillez, cueillez vostre jeunesse:
Comme à ceste fleur la vieillesse
Fera ternir vostre beauté.

Therefore—if you believe me, my sweet—,
while your years are blooming
in their greenest freshness,
pluck, pluck your youth.
As it has done to this flower, old age
will make your beauty fade.[23]

Quant'è bella giovinezza,
  che si fugge tuttavia!
Chi vuol esser lieto, sia:
  di doman non c'è certezza.

How lovely youth is!—
  youth, which is always fleeing.
Let him who wishes to be gay be so!
  There is no certainty in tomorrow.[24]

Sapias, vina liques, et spatio brevi
spem longam reseces. Dum loquimur, fugerit invida
aetas: carpe diem, quam minimum credula postero.

Be wise, attend to straining your wine, and cut back
              long-ranged hopes
to a brief period. While we are speaking, envious time

is already gone. Pluck the day; put as little trust as possible
in the future.[25]

An apparent exception to the impossibility of permanence in this
world is the special sort of immortality reserved for the great poets
—their work will live on after them:

> *Exegi monumentum aere perennius . . . .*
> *Non omnis moriar multaque pars mei*
> *vitabit Libitinam . . . .*

> I have completed a monument more lasting than bronze . . . .
> Not all of me shall die; a large part of me
> shall escape death . . . .[26]

> *Not marble, nor the gilded monuments*
> *Of princes, shall outlive this powerful rime . . . .*[27]

But even this sort of immortality is illusory:

> *Nous devons à la Mort et nous et nos ouvrages;*
> *Nous mourons les premiers, le long reply des âges*
> *En roulant engloustist nos oeuvres à la fin:*
> *Ainsi le veut Nature et le puissant Destin.*

> We owe to Death both ourselves and our works.
> We shall die first; the long cycle of the ages,
> rolling along, swallows up our works in the end.
> That is the way Nature and the force of Destiny
> command it.[28]

The greatest of men—poets, soldiers, or statesmen—will one day be
forgotten. And even if this were not so, what real pleasure can a
man receive from posthumous fame?—:

> *Quant à moy, j'aime mieux trente ans de renommee,*
> *Jouyssant du Soleil, que mille ans de renom*
> *Lors que la fosse creuse enfouyra mon nom . . . .*

As for me, I prefer thirty years of renown
while I am enjoying the sun, to a thousand years of fame
when the hollow tomb has buried my name . . . .[29]

The mutability of everything earthly, being a self-evident truth of nature, is a commonplace of poetic treatments of time in all ages. It is quite as frequent in the Middle Ages as in the Renaissance or in classical antiquity. But the conclusion drawn from this fact is not always the same. For the Middle Ages, the world of time was not the only world; for many important poets and thinkers of antiquity and the Renaissance, it was. For the Middle Ages, the alternative to time was a real timelessness with God; but from the other point of view, there could be no real alternative to time. The medieval Christian sought to achieve eternity. The Epicurean had to be content with plucking the day.

Let us now turn to the *alba*, and see where it stands in relation to these two very different attitudes toward time. We will remember that Augustine's theory of time worked from phenomenology (the subjective experience of time) to metaphysics (the nature of time and of God's timelessness). The *alba* presents us only with experience; it does not draw any specific metaphysical conclusions. In order to elicit the time metaphysics tacitly underlying the actions and speeches of the *alba*, we will have to analyze the poems in close verbal and grammatical detail.

We begin with the *alba* of Giraut de Bornelh. Here is the full text:[30]

I

Reis glorios, verais lums e clartatz,
Deus poderos, Senher, si a vos platz,
Al meu companh siatz fizels aiuda;   3
Qu'eu no lo vi, pos la nochs fo venguda,
     Et ades sera l'alba.

II

Bel companho, si dormetz o velhatz,   6
No dormatz plus, suau vos ressidatz;
Qu'en orien vei l'estela creguda

C'amena·l jorn, qu'eu l'ai be conoguda,   9
    Et ades sera l'alba.

III

Bel companho, en chantan vos apel;
No dormatz plus, qu'eu auch chantar l'auzel   12
Que vai queren lo jorn per lo boschatge
Et ai paor que·l gilos vos assatge
    Et ades sera l'alba.   15

IV

Bel companho, issetz al fenestrel
E regardatz las estelas del cel.
Conoisseretz si·us sui fizels messatge;   18
Si non o faitz, vostres n'er lo damnatge
    Et ades sera l'alba.

V

Bel companho, pos me parti de vos,   21
Eu no·m dormi ni·m moc de genolhos,
Ans preiei Deu, lo filh Santa Maria,
Que·us me rendes per leial companhia,   24
    Et ades sera l'alba.

VI

Bel companho, la foras als peiros
Me preiavatz qu'eu no fos dormilhos,   27
Enans velhes tota noch tro al dia.
Era no·us platz mos chans ni ma paria
    Et ades sera l'alba.   30

VII

Bel dous companh, tan sui en ric sojorn
Qu'eu no volgra mais fos alba ni jorn,
Car la gensor que anc nasques de maire   33
Tenc et abras, per qu'eu non prezi gaire
    Lo fol gilos ni l'alba.

I

Glorious king, true light and brightness,
Powerful God, Lord, if it please you,

be a faithful help to my comrade,   3
for I have not seen him since night came,
      and in a moment it will be dawn.

II

Handsome comrade, whether you are sleeping or awake,   6
do not sleep longer, wake yourself gently,
for in the east I see the star rising
that brings the day, for I have certainly recognized it,   9
      and in a moment it will be dawn.

III

Handsome comrade, I call you by my singing,
do not sleep longer, for I hear the bird singing   12
that goes seeking the day in the foliage,
and I am afraid that the jealous one may attack you,
      and in a moment it will be dawn.   15

IV

Handsome comrade, come out to the window,
and look at the stars of the sky;
you will learn whether I am a faithful messenger to
                        you;   18
if you do not do this, yours will be the harm,
      and in a moment it will be dawn.

V

Handsome comrade, since I left you,   21
I have not slept nor risen from my knees;
on the contrary, I have prayed God, the son of Saint Mary,
that He might give you back to me for loyal companion-
                        ship,   24
      and in a moment it will be dawn.

VI

Handsome comrade, out there at the entrance-steps
you begged me that I not sleep,   27
that, on the contrary, I stay awake the whole night until the
                        day;

now neither my song nor my friendship pleases you,
and in a moment it will be dawn. 30

VII

Handsome sweet comrade, I am in such a precious resting-
place
that I would not want there ever to be dawn nor day,
for the most noble lady that ever was born of mother 33
I hold and embrace; for which reason I do not care at all
about the foolish jealous one or the dawn.[31]

The poem, as it is presented here, can be divided into two parts.
Strophes I–VI are spoken by the friend, while VII constitutes the
reply of the lover. I–VI are spoken in the outside world and voice
the claims of reality. VII is spoken in the inner world and voices
the claims of the pleasure principle (here upheld by the knight,
rather than—as is usual in the *alba*—by the lady). The two speakers,
in their opposing worlds of value, have very different attitudes toward time, as we may see in the verb forms each one uses.

The friend—or perhaps we may speak of him as a watchman,
since that is his function—has a clear consciousness of the movement of time. Lines 4–5 present the entire time-range of the action,
from the previous evening ("la nochs fo venguda") to the imminent
dawn ("ades sera l'alba"). The past and future tenses, along with
forms that imply the future, dominate the watchman's part of the
poem. The watchman remembers (lines 21–23) the past—his parting
with the knight the previous evening, his praying during the night
(note the preterits: "parti," "dormi," "moc," "preiei"). He antici-
pates the future ("vostres n'*er* lo damnatge," "ades *sera* l'alba");
indeed, the refrain, six times repeated, is an urgent reminder that
the future is continually pressing into the present, destroying present
joy and bringing grief and danger in. In addition, the watchman employs imperatives: "no dormatz plus," "ressidatz," "issetz," "regardatz"—forms which, although they are not in the future tense,
point toward the future, toward action which has not yet been
undertaken.

In each strophe the order in which the verb forms appear follows the natural movement of time: first the past (in some of the strophes); then the present and imperative; finally the future, which is always there in the refrain, and which is sometimes reinforced by another verb with future meaning. In III, for example, the watchman begins with a mixture of presents and imperatives ("apel," "dormatz," "auch," "vai," "ai"). The last of these, the present "ai," leads to the subjunctive "assatge," which of course points toward the future: he fears (in the present) that the *gilos* may attack the knight (in the imminent future). The strophe closes with the future tense of the refrain.

Strophe VI gives an even more complete picture of natural time in its inexorable movement. It begins with a past ("preiavatz"), it continues in the present ("era no·us platz," "*now* it does not please you"); and the refrain takes it into the future. This is time in nature: the *Fuit* that is only remembered, the *Est* that is not a real *Est* because it is continually turning into a *Fuit*, the *Erit* which is pressing upon us to become an *Est*, yet which, when it comes, rushes through *Est* in no time and turns into a *Fuit*.*

The lover previously shared with the watchman this sense of real time, which is a necessary part of an adherence to the reality principle. Last night he asked his friend not to sleep but to stay on watch all night long. The rule for sequence of tenses has turned this event into a past tense ("preiavatz") followed by imperfect sub-

---

* The *alba* of Heinrich von Morungen (*MF*, pp. 189–90) presents a love union which has receded entirely into the past tense and thus has ceased to exist except in the memory. (Time, as Augustine observes in *Confessions* XI.xiv.17, can be characterized by the fact that it always tends toward nonbeing.) The two lovers, separated from each other, and each one speaking only to himself, *remember* their night of love and their separation at dawn. What, in the usual *alba*, is present experience—the fight against the moment of separation which is pressing ever nearer from the future—has here become a fixed, unchangeable event of the past. We do not see the lovers being separated; we see them as already separated, each of them alone with his memories. Time has done its destructive work; the love union that was once real, in the present tense, has changed to the nonbeing of the past tense, where the state of being separated is the only reality. See Kurt Ruh, "Das Tagelied Heinrichs von Morungen," *Trivium*, II (1944), 173–77. I reproduce the text of this beautiful and poignant poem in Appendix C.

junctives ("fos," "velhes"); but when the request was spoken it must have consisted of a present, plus present subjunctives pointing toward the future, or of an imperative, commanding future action.

Now, in the inner world of love (Strophe VII), the knight has given himself up to the pleasure principle and has lost or discarded his sense of natural time. (We might note that according to Freud the *id*, the repository of desires that are unlimited by a sense of reality, is free of any notion of time or sequence.[32]) In this Eden of erotic joy there is no past or future, no change, no loss, no separation. It is like the universe we have supposed the infant to be conscious of, an eternal present of love and comfort; it is like the *Est* that Augustine told us could only be found in God, "ubi Fuit et Erit esse non possit"; it is like the paradise described by Jean de Meun and numerous other medieval writers (except that here, in accordance with the erotic reversal of Christian night-day symbolism, we have not a perpetual day but a perpetual night). What counts is what is happening *now*, the present tense: "sui," "tenc," "abras." The future is not to be thought of; from the point of view of the pleasure principle, indeed, the future does not exist. The urgent, perilous, imminent future, repeated again and again in the refrain of I–VI, is eliminated in VII. The dawn is no longer seen as an active force, rushing toward the present from the future. Only the upholder of the reality principle sees the dawn that way. For the upholder of the pleasure principle, only his own will counts, and his will denies anything but the present. Hence "l'alba," which in I–VI was the subject of the future verb "sera," in VII becomes (along with the *gilos*, that other representative of reality) the object of the present verb "prezi." The lover himself is the subject of this verb. He (whose own emotional life constitutes all the reality he will accept) does not (in the present tense, the only tense the pleasure principle knows) care about the husband or the dawn (who are thus not only the passive objects of the verb; they are, in addition, *negated* by it). The change in the refrain is one of the most striking signs of the change in the attitude toward time, as we pass from the first six strophes to the last.

The optative subjunctive, with its opposition to reality, also appears in the last strophe (line 32). The negation of time, found according to the Christian world view only in God, is here to be effected by erotic love. The lover, like Augustine, knows that a joy which is subject to time, which cannot last, is not a full joy. But the pleasure principle demands the utmost perfection and fullness of joy: hence there can be no time here. The eternal joy Augustine spoke of and sought was the beatitude of the saved in heaven; the eternal joy the lover in Giraut's *alba* seeks—and, in a certain sense, all lovers seek—is the continuation, forever, of union with a beloved human being.[33] It is the emotional equivalent, in terms of a total love relationship, to the physical experience of an orgasm that never ends—that not only is not interrupted by some clock-like watchman, announcing the time, but that never even comes to its own natural completion and subsidence; it goes on, at the height of ecstatic pleasure, forever.

The two attitudes toward time and reality appear in Giraut's poem side by side, paratactically, without any real communication between them, and without any resolution to their conflict. The friend describes reality, with its full set of tenses; the lover simply denies that reality, and insists on the *Est*—really the "sui"—that has no end. Yet he does not deny reality entirely. The optative subjunctive is already an admission that there is a conflict between desire and reality, and that the undesired reality exists. The lover says he does not care about the *gilos* and the dawn, but he does not deny that they exist. He wishes there were no dawn or day, but the verbs—"volgra," "fos"—tell us that dawn and day are real, and that the wish is contrary to fact. The lover is devoted to the pleasure principle: he wants things his own way. But he is not an allegorical representation of the *id*, and he is not a madman. He knows there is an outer reality; yet his desire to remain with the lady is so strong that he refuses to bow to that reality.

The audience of the poem is in much the same state. They know that what the watchman-friend says is true. Nights do not last forever; the dawn always comes; and cuckolded husbands are dangerous. But how pleasurable it is to deny all this—vicariously, in the person of the knight—or at least to refuse to bow to it. We bow to such truths every day; here, however, is a chance to indulge our pleasure principle. On the other hand, reality is not excluded from Giraut's *alba*, as it would be from a pure wish-fulfillment fantasy of the sort we find in pornography, for example. Pornography totally eliminates the reality principle; in pornography an orgasm really can last forever. Giraut's *alba* is more sophisticated than this, and its psychological effect is more complex. It satisfies our desire to deny time, to escape from time; and yet reality is also there, with its *Fuit* and *Erit*, its danger, its call to action. The two principles— pleasure and reality—remain in unresolved tension. The poem does not tell us what happened afterwards; the story ends with the friend still anxiously waiting outside, and the knight still making love inside. In Giraut's *alba*, the conflict between the two attitudes toward reality can never come to an end.

In a way, this kind of poetic structure gives an accurate picture of human reality. The reality principle and the pleasure principle remain in unresolved tension during the whole life of the human psyche—at least in this world. There is always an inside of desiring and an outside of unmanipulable otherness. There is always a longing for stasis, and yet everything is always in flux. Giraut's *alba*, with its very simple dualistic structure, mirrors this conflict. The friend speaks for reality, the lover speaks for desire—and how could the two ever be reconciled? How could the plot ever be brought to a harmonious end?

When the *alba* has three characters, however, rather than two, something more is possible. The two attitudes—spoken for, usually, by the lady and the watchman—may remain unreconciled. But there is a third character who participates in both attitudes, and whose freedom of action can carry the plot to some kind of conclusion. This is the case in Wolfram's "Sîne klâwen," whose treatment of time we will consider next. (The reader is asked to refer to the text, reproduced at the beginning of this book.)

The five strophes of this poem give us a sense of a complete dramatic action. Strophes I and III are spoken by the watchman, upholding the reality principle; Strophes II and IV are spoken by the lady, upholding the pleasure principle; and after their cases have been stated and the polar opposition of the two principles has been established, a strophe of objective narrative (V) resolves in dramatic terms what cannot be resolved in argument.[34]

The watchman has the characteristic qualities and attitudes we have spoken of. He is conscious of the realities of nature (the powerful natural force of the dawn) and of society (the knight's honor—line 20). He realizes that the dawn brings with it great danger: the knight's very life is threatened (line 20). He has a clear awareness of time ("ez ist nu tac: naht was ez do"—line 23): what could be done at night cannot be done in the morning; times moves on; pleasure must give way to reality. He sees into both worlds and is attached to both. He is attached by "triuwe" ("loyalty") to the lady and her desires and pleasures (line 14); but he is also attached by "triuwe" to the knight's safety, and consequently he must give voice to those realities of the outer world that will compel the knight to leave the chamber of love (lines 21–22).

The lady, upholder of the pleasure principle, is concerned not with safety but with "fröide" ("joy, pleasure"—line 9). She objects to the claims of reality as interfering with her intimate joys. She does not want to hear about reality; she simply wants to ignore it; and she is angry about having it forced on her ("diu solt du mir verswîgen gar"—line 13). Like the knight in Giraut's *alba*, however, she is aware of external reality even though she opposes it. She knows that frequently in the past the watchman has taken her lover from her arms. She knows that, no matter how passionately she may want the love-union of this night to endure forever, the knight is going to have to leave.

Yet, if the actual night of love cannot be eternal, the love itself can be—so she believes. Lines 31–32 express this idea in a compact figure of speech:

> *du hâst in dicke mir benomen*
> *von blanken armen, und ûz herzen nieht.*
>
> You have often taken him
> from my white arms, but not out of my heart.

This is a form of the figure *zeugma*. In its use here, it yokes together, as complements of the same verb ("hâst benomen"), two expressions, one of which ("von blanken armen") goes with the verb literally, while the other (" ûz herzen nieht") goes with it figuratively. There is a world of nature and outer reality in which watchmen do take lovers from the white arms of their ladies. But there is also a world of interior feeling, a world of the heart, from which the lover cannot be taken away. The world of nature is subject to time, but the world of feeling is not. Although their physical union cannot last, their feelings for each other are eternal.

This *zeugma* thus yokes together the two worlds of reality and value. The outer world of time and separation, that is, the world as seen by the reality principle, and the inner world of eternal union, where the wish is truth, are linked with each other in the rhetorical figure just as they are linked with each other in the events of the final strophe of the poem.

Strophe V begins with a summing-up of the pressures of the outer world: the dawn, symbol of time, breaking through into the inner world; and the voice of the watchman, spokesman for time, giving his warning. The lady finally begins to accept the fact that the situation is full of danger; she becomes alarmed for the knight's safety. To this extent she has been won over by the reality principle. In this moment of awareness of reality, the lovers make love once again, before parting. The knight—the third character, who is not a proponent of either of the two psychological principles, but who is called upon to take action by choosing between them—does indeed take action. Which of the two does he choose? In a way, he chooses both. He accepts the fact that a leave-taking is inevitable. The "urloup," already decided upon as a course of action, hurries closer and closer from the future. Yet, along with this acceptance of the destructive power of time, he also satisfies his erotic desire. Desire and reality are asserted simultaneously, as it were.

Giraut's *alba*, too, showed us the reality principle and the pleasure principle simultaneously, in pure, unresolvable opposition. But Wolfram connects them by more than mere simultaneity. The last two lines of the poem offer grammatical difficulties, but it is evident that the proper translation would lie somewhere between the following possibilities:

Their parting, coming near and yet nearer,
with kissing, and other things, gave them the reward of love.

With their parting coming near and yet nearer,
Love, with kisses and other things, gave them their reward.[35]

In either case, it is the approaching separation that is responsible for the joys of love-making. The love-making is inspired by the separation, by the consciousness of swiftly passing time. It is the very fact of being imbedded in reality, time, and danger that makes the pleasure so poignant and so intense. Part of the love ideal in this poem may be the longing for a secular, erotic equivalent of God's timeless paradise. But the part that prevails in the end has much in common with the naturalistic philosophy of carpe diem, although idealized, and invested not with the Horatian or Renaissance melancholy—"Seizing the moment is the best we can do"—but with a peculiar optimism of its own, as if to say, "Being forced to seize the moment makes the moment that much the more wonderful."

Love, in "Sîne klâwen," is seen as a psychological force which tries to oppose itself to time and reality, tries to create a higher, timeless reality (that is what the lady, like the knight in Giraut's alba, wants), but in fact is part of temporal reality and achieves its own full reality and meaning in time and because of time. Love is real only under the shadow of the changes in nature symbolized by the dawn and the parting. The joys of satisfied desire and the griefs of frustrated desire are inseparable in this world. (In its simplest form, this is a commonplace of Minnesang. "Liep âne leit mac niht gesîn" ["Love without suffering cannot exist"], says Dietmar von Aist in his alba,[36] and the Burggrave von Lüenz, adding the notion of destructive, downward-moving time, says, "Nâch liebe kumt et dicke leit" ["After love there often comes suffering"].[37] Gottfried von Strassburg, in his Tristan, pushes this notion even further, and tells us that the suffering inextricably bound up with love is not to be shunned; it is rather to be embraced, because it is only in suffering that love achieves its highest intensity and reality. And Wolfram, in a more down-to-earth way, tells us something very similar: that *liep* is sweetest because of *leit*, that desire lives in the shadow of reality and shines more brightly because of that shadow.)

The resolution of the dramatic situation, which we see in Strophe V, suggests that the psychological or philosophical conflict has been resolved too. The watchman's point of view and the lady's point of view have been superseded by the knight's actions, just as the parochial first-person speeches of the two opposing voices have been superseded by the all-embracing third-person narrative of the last strophe. The pleasure principle and the reality principle have been combined in the love-making that is inspired by the separation. But there really is no resolution of the two principles, only a demonstration (scarcely found in Giraut's *alba*) of their indissoluble connections. In Wolfram's poem there is a submission to the reality principle: the lovers accept the fact that they must part. But even in the moment of submission there is an assertion of the unquenchable will to pleasure. The two principles are both asserted in all their force—the great force of the sun, which separates, and the great force of love, which unites—but they remain in conflict. In the nature of things, they cannot be resolved in this life.

They can only be resolved in death. Love-tragedies, such as *Tristan* or *Antony and Cleopatra*, achieve a sense of peaceful, harmonious resolution that the *alba* cannot attain to. The *alba* does not press the separation of the lovers to the permanent separation, which is death. Far from making the separation lead to death, the *alba* does not even make the separation permanent in this life, which would be a forceful symbol of death. The separation is thought of as only temporary; the knight will return, and they will take up where the watchman's cry made them leave off. The time scheme of an *alba* like Wolfram's "Sîne klâwen" is thus very much of this world. It does not lead into an eternity of union after death, the sort of union Tristan and Isolde long for. The *alba* lovers, too, are very much of this world. They do not long for death; they do not speak of union after death; they are interested only in union in this world, and they look forward to their next night together. And just as the *alba* separation is only a minor, temporary tragedy, so the love in the *alba*, in its opposition to the outer world and the forces of separation and destruction, never takes on the power of a great universal principle that can triumph over everything, even over death. The love is never called upon to meet a total, tragic separation; hence it can never exhibit the grandeur of tragic love. And for the same reason, the lovers can never achieve the stature of the heroes and heroines of tragedy: they suffer from—and respond to— a temporary sentimental setback, not a permanent tragic loss. Tristan and Isolde are seen almost as saints; Antony and Cleopatra virtually become gods; the lovers in the *alba* remain on the purely human, purely earthly level of their audiences.

Wolfram's *alba* shows us a world of nature, dominated by time. There is no suggestion in it that another world exists, outside of time and beyond death, where the imperfections of this world will be made perfect. The notion of the special sweetness of the moment in the inevitable, destructive flux of time would be simply irrelevant in an Augustinian picture of the universe. From the Augustinian point of view, the *alba* could be said to contain a very different sort of notion, namely, the didactic moral that all earthly joy based on *cupiditas* is necessarily impermanent. To love an earthly creature in the way the *alba* lovers love each other is to deliver oneself over to the destructive force of time.[38] The night of love must come to an end, and the lovers must be separated. The drama of the *alba* shows us—implicitly in Giraut, explicitly in Wolfram—that the attempt to turn the chamber of love into a secular equivalent of God's eternal paradise must always fail. The Augustinian conclusion would be: since all things earthly are subject to time and must come to an end, turn to God, Who alone is changeless and timeless.

In Wolfram's poem, the hope that the night may last forever is decisively abandoned. Yet the suggestion remains that the love itself, the feeling of the lovers for each other, is eternal. The notion that feelings of love are eternal, a perfectly common one in courtly love poetry, is of course a retreat from the demand that the single night of erotic union go on forever. It is a retreat from full devotion to the pleasure principle toward an acceptance of the fact that outer reality, at least, is subject to time. The idea of eternity is preserved only for the feelings: the love that will last forever. But from an

Augustinian point of view, this too is *cupiditas* and illusion. We will not find in Wolfram's *alba*—or in any serious erotic *alba* of the courtly period—the slightest intimation that love itself, this interior world of feelings, might be subject to time.

That further retreat toward an acceptance of reality is to be found in Chaucer's *Troilus*, where an elaborate *alba* at the very center of the poem (iii.1394–1533) epitomizes the basic structure of the plot: the union and separation of lovers. As Troilus and Criseyde are separating, they vow eternal love and faithfulness, in the manner common to the lovers in the courtly *alba*.[39] Criseyde vows:

> *That first shal Phebus fallen fro his spere,*
> *And everich egle ben the dowves feere,*
> *And everi roche out of his place sterte,*
> *Er Troilus out of Criseydes herte. . . .*
> *But herte myn, withouten more speche,*
> *Beth to me trewe, or ellis were it routhe;*
> *For I am thyn, by God and by my trouthe!*

Yet, as the story goes on, not only are the outer conditions of life shown to be subject to tragic, destructive time, but Criseyde's inner "trouthe" is found to be unstable and mutable as well. Chaucer's *Troilus* demonstrates, as none of the earlier *albas* does, that every earthly phenomenon, from a night of passion to the feelings of a lovely lady, inevitably turns into a *Fuit*. The sentiment of erotic love is as impermanent as everything else on earth. *Est* is to be sought in only one place—God's eternity:

> *And of youre herte up casteth the visage*
> *To thilke God that after his ymage*
> *Yow made, and thynketh al nys but a faire*
> *This world, that passeth soone as floures faire.*[40]

It is a moral which could be drawn from any erotic *alba*, seen from a Christian point of view. But before Chaucer, no author of an *alba*

---

* *Troilus* iii.1495–98 and 1510–12. The entire text of the *alba* scene in *Troilus*, in many ways the culminating point in the medieval development of the genre, is reproduced in Appendix A, below.

does look at the *alba* situation from such a point of view. There are, indeed, Christian versions of the *alba*, as we have noted. But these do not draw a Christian moral from the grief of the *alba* lovers at their separation; they eliminate the lovers entirely, along with the whole *alba* plot. All that is left is the call to sinners to awake, so strongly reminiscent of the dawn-hymns of Ambrose and Prudentius. Chaucer was the first to use the erotic *alba*, with its plot and characters intact, as a Christian exemplum. The attitude toward time and reality and value that we find in "Sîne klâwen," and in most of the courtly *albas* of the twelfth and thirteenth centuries, is not a Christian attitude.

FIVE

THE *ALBA* AND THE *CHANSON*

WE COME, FINALLY, to an explicit comparison of the *alba* with the dominant form of medieval lyric, the *chanson*. It should be said, first of all, that the poems comprised under this category are far from uniform. I earlier described the *chanson* as the poem of hopeless, endless, frustrated love by a humble and faithful lover for an exalted and inaccessible lady. Although the great majority of *chansons* are based on a more or less fixed set of motifs revolving around this theme, individual representatives of the genre combine and exploit the motifs in different ways, much as the individual *albas* do. There are *chansons* in which the lover rejoices at signs of favor (sometimes even the greatest intimacies) that the lady has granted him. There are others in which she has once loved him but has now ceased to do so. Sometimes the lover represents himself as more than worthy of the lady's grace and expresses indignation at her for being so parsimonious with it; occasionally, indeed, his indignation is so great that he resolves to repay her for her indifference by abandoning her entirely. To speak of "the" *chanson*, then, is to speak of an abstraction, an average, an amalgam, rather than of an actual poem.

In speaking of "the" *alba*, of course, I have been doing much the same thing. But the generalizations that are, in a sense, the aim of a study such as this one—a study of a literary type or genre—have been qualified and nuanced throughout by the attention we have been able to give to individual poems, individual variants from the "norm." In dealing with the *chanson*, we will have to be more summary: a typology of the various distinctions of structure and meaning within this immense genre would require another book— one far longer than this one. "The" *chanson* I will be speaking of admittedly does no justice to the variety of real medieval *chansons*. But if it is merely an abstraction, it is an abstraction whose details will be perfectly familiar to all readers of medieval and renaissance love lyrics as well as of their literary offspring in narrative and drama. Therefore, a comparison between the *alba* and this composite or "average" *chanson*, while it cannot be totally valid for every actual *chanson* (or every actual *alba*), will nevertheless have at least some validity for virtually every member of the two genres. Between any *alba* and any *chanson* there are significant similarities and differences, and it is the general nature of such similarities and differences that I want to point out. This comparison, on the basis of the categories I have used in investigating the *alba* alone, should also indicate a useful approach to individual *chansons*, even though I do not analyze any individual *chansons* in detail. In addition, the comparison will enable us to consider with greater profit certain aspects of the *alba* which we have touched on only briefly, if at all, in the earlier chapters.

The relationship between the man and the woman in the *alba* is one of equality. They are evidently on the same social level, and they are in love with each other. This relationship is quite different from that found in the *chanson*. There, the lady is portrayed as greatly superior to the man, both in social status and in human worth. He is passionately in love with her, while she is cold, distant, indifferent, disdainful, and sometimes positively hostile. The relation is not one of equality and mutuality, but rather one of superiority and inferiority. It is a vertical relationship rather than a horizontal one:

> *Totz tems volrai sa onor e sos bes*
> *e·lh serai om et amics e servire . . . .*

I shall always seek to maintain her honor and her well-
being,
and I shall be vassal to her, and lover, and servant . . . .[1]

> *qu'eu l'am d'amor coral,*
> *ela·m ditz "no m'en chal";*
> *enans ditz que per al*
> *no m'a ira mortal.*

Because I love her with heart-felt love,
she says to me, "I don't care";
on the contrary, she says that, for no other reason than
that,
she has a deadly anger against me.[2]

> *Tan m'a salvatge cor e dur*
> *Cela que·m bat de sos verjans,*
> *Qu'on plus li sui humilians,*
> *Adoncs me dona plus d'esglai.*

She has a heart so cruel and hard towards me,
She who beats me with her switches,
That the more submissive I am to her
The more pain she causes me.[3]

We have noted that the knight in the *alba*, being somewhat more open to the demands of the reality principle than the lady is, sometimes seems to play a less passionate role in the love relationship. This would indicate a certain degree of reversal of the relationship that obtains in the *chanson*, where the man is passionate and the lady is cold. But the man's lack of passion in the *alba* ought not to be exaggerated. The lady's role in the drama is to advocate the pleasure principle with all the persuasiveness and vehemence she is capable of. The knight's role is merely to make a choice between the two courses of action proposed to him. It is natural that his feelings should seem more subdued than hers, since her role is, specifically, to express her feelings, while his role is of a different sort. But there is never any clear indication in *albas* of the courtly period that the knight is less in love with the lady than she is with him. His passion may be tempered by reason, as hers is not, but it is not necessarily diminished thereby. If, indeed, the relationship is slightly more heavily weighted on one side, there is nevertheless no question of its being completely (or even predominantly) one-sided and "vertical," the way the *chanson* relationship is.

The kind of horizontal, mutual love relationship we see in the *alba* is scarcely unique in medieval literature. It is found with great frequency in the romances. All of the romances of Chrétien de Troyes, for example, with the exception of the *Lancelot*, include (and sometimes center upon) relationships of this sort. The equality of the lovers and the equality of their passion may be said to constitute one of the fundamental ideas of Gottfried's *Tristan*, where the continual rhetorical pairing of the lovers serves to emphasize this relationship:

> *ein man ein wip, ein wip ein man,*
> *Tristan Isolt, Isolt Tristan.*

> a man, a woman; a woman, a man;
> Tristan, Isolde; Isolde, Tristan.[4]

(Indeed, the whole plot of *Tristan* is based on the fact that *both* the lovers have drunk the magic love potion.) The horizontal, mutual relationship is, in fact, the norm in medieval romance.

The same relationship is found in a number of the lyrics of Walther von der Vogelweide, where it is put in intentional opposition to the sort of vertical relationship found in the *chanson*—particularly in the love songs of Walther's rival, Reinmar von Hagenau.

This sort of love, called by Walther "ebene minne," pairs the man with a girl of equal or even inferior rank who truly and frankly reciprocates his love; the notion of adoring a cold and lofty lady from below is scornfully rejected.[5]

Another traditional genre of the twelfth and thirteenth centuries, the crusade song, depends for much of its emotional effect on the mutuality of the lovers' feelings. The basic situation is that the knight and the lady must part because he is required to go to the Holy Land on a crusade. They love each other equally, and are equally grieved at the parting. (We might note that the knight's decision to leave frequently comes after a painful struggle between his love for the lady and his sense of religious duty—a psychological and dramatic structure familiar to us from the *alba*. There are other similarities of motif between the two genres.[6])

The mutual, *ebene minne* relationship is also to be found in some of the *Frauenstrophen*. Like the crusade songs, these love laments of women have much in common with the *alba*; the similarities include the passionate character of the lady (which we spoke of earlier), the less outspoken feelings of the man, the mutuality of love (except where it is the lady who loves, and the man who is standoffish), and the motif of separation.[7] We indicated earlier that a large number of scholars consider these poems to be of folk origin.[8] An interesting reason for this supposition, given frequently by nineteenth-century medievalists, is the notion that the relationship of mutuality and equality found in the *Frauenstrophen* (and also in Walther, Gottfried, the romances, the crusade songs, and of course the *alba*) is a "natural" relationship, whereas the relationship shown in the *chanson* is "artificial." Romantic veneration of the *Volk* as the source of all that is authentic and sincere led these scholars to suppose that the "natural" relationship must indicate a folksong origin.[9] The *chanson*, on the other hand, with its "artificial" relationship, was evidently a product of aristocratic and courtly—and hence unrealistic—ideals and manners.

Neither of these suppositions, however, is based on anything more than Romantic fantasy. There is not the slightest reason for thinking that a mutual love relationship is more in conformity with nature than is the adoration and idealization of a lady by a man she does not love. Mutual love is certainly more pleasant than the other kind, but it is no more "natural." It is perfectly common for a man to fall in love with a woman who does not return his feelings. It may be unnatural, or at any rate unhealthy, for him to persist in such a hopeless love for a great length of time, but this has been known to happen; and the *chanson*, after all, pictures this condition at its height of intensity, when it is natural enough for a man to feel that he will love the lady hopelessly forever, will never be able to leave her, will never be able to love another, and so on. The fact that he believes, at this moment, that his emotions will never change does not mean that that is the way things are going to be in reality. The *chanson* communicates a state of feeling; it does not narrate the story of a life.

In any case, whether natural or unnatural, there is no legitimate reason for attributing *chanson* love to the court and *ebene minne* to the peasantry. Surely highborn persons in the Middle Ages could have enjoyed satisfactory love affairs—that is, those in which the love was reciprocal—without having to imitate the passions and ideals of the lower classes; and if a poet had to look for such an affair to model his *albas* or *Frauenstrophen* on, he could have found it easily enough without leaving the court. In fact, the *alba*, with its mutual love relationship, is just as courtly as the *chanson*: the manners it shows are as refined, the feelings as idealized, the atmosphere as aristocratic, as any we may find in the *chanson*. It is only a preconceived and erroneous idea about the values of the various social classes that insists on seeing it as a derivative of folk-songs.[10]

The love relationship in the *alba* and that in the *chanson* cannot be differentiated on the basis of naturalness or of social class. They are structurally different, but they also have much in common. They might be said to be two possible states of the same aristocratic love affair. The structure of the relationship is simply the result of the lady's attitude. If she does not return the man's love, that automatically lifts her above him and creates the vertical relationship of the *chanson*. If she does return his love, that puts her on his level, and we have the horizontal relationship of the *alba* and the other genres we spoke of above. The exalted position of the *chanson* lady is not absolute; it depends on her refusing her love, or on her granting it only sparingly. If she were to conceive a passion of her own for her adorer, she would swing right down from her exalted height to a position of equality. The Renaissance loves to play with this kind of transformation from vertical to horizontal, from *chanson* love to *ebene minne*. Angelica in Ariosto (*Orlando Furioso* XIX.xviii ff.), Armida in Tasso (*Gerusalemme liberata* XIV.lxv ff.), Olivia in Shakespeare's *Twelfth Night* (III.i)—all undergo this descent.* Medieval lyrics do not show the transformation taking place, but that is no reason for supposing that the *alba* lady and the *chanson* lady live in two totally different worlds. If we think of them as the same lady, at one time in love and at the other time not, would we be attributing an impossible change of character to either of them?

As to the man's love, that needs no transformation. It is very much the same in the *alba* and the *chanson*. The love relationship in the *chanson* bears a striking similarity to the Christian idea of the relationship between man and God.[11] A man's love for God is *eros*, a desire, based on the value of the love object, to possess that object, along with a sense of incompleteness until the object is possessed. God's love for man is *agape*. This kind of love is independent of the value of the love object: God loves man not on account of man's worth but in spite of man's worthlessness. *Agape* does not seek to possess, but is given gratuitously. It is not caused by need and incompleteness, but by an overflowing abundance of love. The relationship of God and man is of course a vertical relationship: man's desiring *eros* strives upward from below, God's gratuitous *agape* flows downward from above.[12] Similarly, in the *chanson*, the man desires to possess the lady, who is thought of as of infinite value and indeed as the source of all value. The love he hopes or imagines she

* In *Twelfth Night* and in the later stages of the love affair in Tasso's epic, there is really something of a total reversal of the relationship: the vertical relationship is turned upside-down, when Rinaldo and "Cesario" refuse to return their ladies' love. The same pattern may be observed in Pushkin's *Eugenii Onegin*, where, however, it is the *man* who is transformed from rejecter to rejected.

will give him, however, is freely given, desiring nothing, and not dependent on his worthiness. He continually emphasizes his lack of worthiness, and how the lady's love would be that much the more noble in that he is much too low to deserve it. His love is *eros*, proceeding from incompleteness, need, and longing; hers—if she were to give any—would be *agape*, proceeding from superabundant goodness and unconstrained condescension.

In the *alba* there is nothing resembling *agape*, since the lady is herself in love with the man and the relationship is horizontal. But the man's love is the same *eros* he feels in the *chanson*. He desires to possess the lady; he is drawn to her by her excellent qualities; he needs her; and he feels incomplete without her (that, after all, is why he is sorry to leave her). And the lady's love for him is of the identical sort. *Alba* love is mutual *eros*. It does not show a totally different kind of love from that found in the *chanson*. *Eros* appears in both genres, although in the *alba* it constitutes all the love, while in the *chanson* it constitutes only part.

At this point we should speak of just what it is that is desired, in both the *alba* and the *chanson*. What is the object of this *eros*?[13] As for the *chanson*, it seems perfectly clear that the desire, in many *chansons* at least, is for a union of minds and hearts, accompanied with some kind of union of bodies.[14] It is not merely a spiritual desire; it is a sexual desire as well:

> *Ara cuit qu'e·n morrai*
> *del dezirer que·m ve*
> *si·lh bela lai on jai*
> *no m'aizis pres de se,*
> *qu'eu la manei e bai*
> *et estrenha vas me*
> *so cors blanc, gras e le.*

> Now I think that I shall die
> of the desire that comes to me,
> if the beautiful one, there where she lies,
> does not make me welcome next to her,
> so that I may caress and kiss her

and clasp against me
her white body, plump and smooth.[15]

The exact kind of sexual union that is desired, however, is not clear, in spite of what the above quotation might make us think. Andreas Capellanus, in his influential (perhaps overly influential) treatise on love, distinguishes between pure love ("amor purus")— which involves all sorts of spiritual and physical satisfactions, up to and including the lovers' embracing each other while both are totally unclothed—and another type of love, going somewhat beyond this, which he calls "mixed" love ("amor mixtus"). *Amor purus* excludes actual sexual intercourse and consummation; if these occur, we are dealing with *amor mixtus*. This most peculiar distinction, due entirely to Andreas, has created considerable controversy in the assessment of the object of *eros* in the *chanson*. When we read that Jaufré Rudel would like to have his beloved lady to himself "dinz vergier o sotz cortina" ("in an orchard or under a curtain"),[16] we are likely to suppose that he is talking of country matters. But if we have read Andreas Capellanus, we are thrown into confusion. Does Jaufré want to embrace the lady naked and go no farther? Or does he want more than that? For that matter, what is there in this line to prove that he wants anything more than to look at her and speak with her? Being together with a lady in an orchard or beneath curtains (that is, in bed) does not absolutely necessitate making love to her. And even Bernart de Ventadorn, who certainly indicates some physical action, does not mention anything beyond caressing, kissing, and clasping.

If we are in doubt about the sort of desire the *chanson* is based on, this doubt is not essentially due to the poems themselves. Sometimes they talk only about love; sometimes, as in Jaufré's line, they imply some sort of sexual relationship, but without making anything specific; sometimes, as in the lines of Bernart, they are definitely "suggestive," but still leave something to be imagined. These reticences, if they can be called that, are hardly evidence for the existence of so odd a phenomenon as *amor purus*. From the point of view of normal modern notions of love, a man's love for a woman is accompanied by sexual desire, and the ultimate aim of that desire is genital intercourse. It is not necessary for a love poem to be specific about the kind of physical intercourse desired, or even to mention physical things at all. Physical desire, and the object of that desire, would seem to be implicit in any romantic attachment of this sort. It is only because we have read Andreas Capellanus and heard strange theories about Catharist heresies and the like that we feel unsure of what the singer of the *chanson* wants. Leo Spitzer has gone so far as to suppose that the lack of consummation of the *eros* in the *chanson* is not a misfortune but rather an ideal, something in itself desirable, the aim of some quasi-Augustinian asceticism.[17] This seems to me a great distortion of these poems. The object of the *eros* in the *chanson* is kind words and loving looks from the lady, conversation with her, going to bed with her, and all the further perquisites of *amor mixtus*. The *chanson* does indeed show this *eros* frustrated of its object—not, however, because of some ascetic renunciation of sex on the part of the man, but simply because the lady is not willing.

Emil Nickel—to give another example of what I consider a misinterpretation of *chanson* love—makes the following contrast between the love of Tristan and Isolde and the love portrayed in the *chanson*: courtly love is idealized and spiritualized, while the love of Tristan and Isolde is earthy, bodily, sensual, and real in its foundations.[18] I cannot accept this distinction. The love felt by Tristan and the love felt by the man in the *chanson* is the same love. It is a love which is earthy, bodily, sensual, real in its foundations, idealized, and spiritualized, all at once. It is precisely this mixture of sensual desire and spiritual passion that characterizes *chanson* love and distinguishes it from Ovid on the one hand and Dante on the other. The difference between *Tristan* and the *chanson* is not in the kind of love felt by the man, or in its object. It is a difference of situation: in Tristan the love relationship is horizontal, because Isolde has drunk the potion too, while in the *chanson* the relationship is vertical, because the lady is not experiencing any *eros* of her own.

The sexual nature of the love in the *alba* is much less subject to dispute. The *chanson* shows us a love whose character, since circumstances prevent the love from being consummated, we are forced to infer from the expressions of the lover's hopes and longings. In the *alba*, the love has already been consummated, and we are often given a graphic description of it:

> *ir liehten vel diu slehten*
> *kômen nâher. . . .*
> *sus kunden si dô vlehten*
> *ir munde, ir brüste, ir arme, ir blankiu bein.*

> Their white skins, the smooth [skins],
> came nearer [each other]. . . .
> Thus could they then intertwine
> their mouths, their breasts, their arms, their gleaming
> thighs.[19]

> *si heten beide sich bewegen,*
> *ezn wart sô nâhe nie gelegen,*
> *des noch diu minne hat den prîs:*
> *obe der sunnen drî mit blicke waeren,*
> *sin möhten zwischen si geliuhten.*

> They both took up such a position
> that never had any [two persons] lain so close [before].
> Love is still renowned for this.
> If there had been three suns peering in,
> they could not have shined between them [the lovers].[20]

It is no doubt possible that this proximity does not result in anything beyond the bounds of *amor purus*, but the tone of Wolfram's lines seems to suggest otherwise. In any case, it is important to realize that although the sexuality is much more explicit here than it is in most *chansons*, the love depicted in the *alba* is not mere gross sexuality (as it is, for example, in the *pastourelle*—the contemporary lyric genre in which a knight seduces a country wench), but the same kind of mixture of the physical and the spiritual we spoke of in connection with the *eros* of the *chanson*. What we see in the *alba* is the consummation the lover in the *chanson* so longs for: mutual love expressed in words, looks, and sexual acts.

The prominence of sexual description in the *alba*, however, made the genre painfully ripe for parody, once the audience for medieval lyrics began to change. From the thirteenth century onwards, there is an anti-idealizing tendency in certain literary works which rejects the combination of tenderness, exaltation, and sexual passion characteristic of the earlier love lyrics. The methods of these parodies are of three kinds, closely interconnected. The aristocratic characters are replaced by peasants; the physical aspects of the erotic union are emphasized at the expense of the spiritual and emotional aspects; and the setting and action are associated with brute animals. These methods are really only one method, because of the general association in much medieval literature of the peasantry, gross sexuality, and lower animals.

Although many of these parodies are quite funny, a discussion of their various devices would have to carry us far beyond the courtly *alba* into a study of the devices of medieval satire in general. But the following quotation from a parody of the *alba* is pertinent because, in its indelicate focusing on the sexuality of the love affair, it brings home, by contrast, the greater scope and value of the love in the courtly *alba*. Aleyn, the young cleric in Chaucer's *Reeve's Tale*, has spent much of the night in the bed of the miller's daughter, Malyne. (Note the lowering of the social class from the aristocratic level of troubadour poetry.) The dawn arrives, and we are shown one of the regretful partings we are by now so familiar with. But the reference to what the "lovers" have actually been doing during their night of union is a great deal more specific than Giraut's romantic "tenc e abras" ("I hold and embrace") and Wolfram's sly but decorous "mit kusse und anders" ("with kissing, and other things"):

> *Aleyn wax wery in the dawenynge,*
> *For he had swonken al the longe nyght,*
> *And seyde, "Fare weel, Malyne, sweete wight!*
> *The day is come, I may no lenger byde ...."* [21]

The idea—quite realistic, of course—that the lover may be exhausted from his sexual labors and may almost welcome the dawn as a chance to put an end to them decisively punctures the idealizations of the courtly *alba*.

The courtly *alba* shows us two noble human beings united in the bliss of a full love relationship. Chaucer's parody shows us two lower-class persons enjoying animal pleasures with each other. The slight veneer of imitation courtliness that overlies this animality serves to emphasize its coarseness. Chaucer's parody also throws a mocking light on the desire of the lovers in the courtly *alba* that the night may last forever. If Aleyn waxes weary after only part of a night of normal length, what would happen to the *alba* knight's "ellen" ("battle-zeal") if the night never came to an end at all? But in the love lyrics of the courtly period this is not the sort of question that is asked.

The courtly *chanson* and *alba* are not radically different in their concept of love. They are both idealizing, and they both give sexuality its due. They differ in the situation of the lovers with respect to each other, and this difference depends on the different attitude of the lady in the two genres. When she feels the same *eros* as the knight, we have a horizontal relationship and *ebene minne*. When she does not return his love, we have a vertical relationship analogous to the relationship of man to God, or of vassal to lord. This difference in the structure of the relationship makes for a great difference in the structure of the physical and moral universe portrayed in each of the genres. In the *alba*, the large dramatic conflict is between the lovers—together—and the whole universe. On the one side, we have the idealized values of human love, personal and intimate; on the other side, the impersonal forces of nature, society, and time, great and powerful realities which dwarf the lovers physically if not morally. The man and the lady share the same desires and the same ideals; they are together in their joy, in their grief, and in their opposition to the values of the outside world. In the *chanson*, the drama is of a different sort entirely. The conflict is between the man and the lady, his desire opposed by her refusal. It is mainly a personal drama, with the chief forces of the conflict being these two opposed wills. Society, represented by the spies and slanderers who try to damage the relationship of the two main characters, plays only a subsidiary part; it is the lady herself who is the chief enemy. Cosmic forces play no part at all; nature appears only as a decorative background to harmonize or contrast with the lover's feelings. Nor is there any sharing of experiences and emotions, as there is in the *alba*—no sense of two persons united against their opponents. The lover is alone with his hopes and suffering. Only the lady can end his isolation, but she refuses to do so.

This difference in the kind of conflict is reflected in the differing treatment of space in the two genres. In the *alba* the lovers are together in an interior; a vast, hostile exterior encircles them. The interior and the exterior are separated by walls, the walls of the chamber or the castle; but the outside forces (the sunlight, the watchman's voice) penetrate within through openings (chinks, windows) in the walls. In the *chanson*, the lover is alone, and the lady is at a great distance from him. Sometimes this distance is physical, geographical —as in Jaufré Rudel:

> *Luenh es lo castelhs e la tors*
> *On elha jay e sos maritz . . . .*
>
> Far is the castle and the tower
> where she and her husband lie . . . .[22]

It is also social, the great vertical distance between the lady's exalted social status and the lower social position of the man. (The man's lower social position is a traditional element of the *chanson* fiction; it appears even when the author of the poem is actually a member of the higher nobility.) This vertical distance has a moral meaning, too: the distance between the lady's metaphorical loftiness as the source of all value, and the man's abject unworthiness (as he describes himself). And all of these distances—geographical, social, moral—symbolize the emotional and spiritual distance caused by the lady's refusal to love.[23]

The universe of the *alba* consists of an interior world of great value, where both the lovers are, surrounded by an exterior world of great, active force, and of inferior value. The universe of the *chanson* consists of a place of great value, where the lady is; a place of inferior value, yet of great emotional reality, where the man is; and, in between the two, an enormous void of meaningless, alien, spiritually empty space. The lover is in an emotional interior (and sometimes a physical interior as well) of his own, isolated in himself and his desires. The lady is outside of his interior world of feeling, untouched by it, refusing to be part of it. She is outside of it and at a great distance from it. Or—to look at the situation from the point of view of the lover, and of the usual medieval valuation of insides and outsides—the lady herself is an inside, a center, and the man revolves around her at a great distance, feeling starved and excluded and outside, grateful for the faint light that occasionally reaches him from his distant sun.

The imagery of inside and outside varies in the *chanson*, like those optical illusions that seem now a stairway, now a cornice, or like the interplay of the Ptolemaic and Neoplatonic schemes in Dante's *Paradiso*. The sense of spatial distance, however, is constant. Furthermore, the spatial relationships—the two human worlds, divided by a great dead distance—are fixed and static. In the *alba*, the outer world penetrates into the inner world, and the knight leaves the inner world and goes out into the outer world. The *alba* shows us movement in space, the dynamic effect of one world on the other. In the *chanson*, the nature of the relationship between the man and the lady precludes any movement, any interaction of the worlds. The lady's lack of love and the man's feeling of worthlessness make him keep his distance, literally or symbolically. He is not permitted to enter the world of her affection. That is why there is no action in the *chanson*; nothing ever happens. The *chanson* portrays the state of emotional suspension and frustration of a man in love with a lady who will not love him in return, while he himself is unable to stop loving her. The spatial relationship that symbolizes this emotional situation is a permanent, immutable state of separation. The *alba* moves, dynamically, from union to separation. The *chanson* shows us a separation which is already there and which cannot change or end.

The static quality of the spatial relationships in the *chanson* is also characteristic of its narrative technique.

In general, the Provençal love-song has not, in the Aristotelian sense of the term, an end nor, strictly speaking, a beginning. This is not terminology appropriate to its structure any more than it would be suitable to the analysis of a stained-glass window. The song has a point of inception, and necessarily a termination, but not necessarily a conclusion. The strophes are conceived of as autonomous and collateral units; they do not develop syllogistically.[24]

The *chanson* does not get anywhere; it says the same thing over and over, in different forms, and, were it not for certain formal traditions about the number of strophes, the poem seemingly could go on forever. There is a sense of "piétinement sur place" (Spitzer). But this is only natural, since the *chanson* portrays a psychological state of suspension and frustration. "C'est comme si la 'situation sans issue' se reflétait dans une forme à jamais stagnante."[25] The love affair is not moving toward a consummation; the distance between the lover and the lady remains fixed; he goes on loving her in the same way, and goes on receiving the same cool indifference. The strophes of his self-revelation are merely juxtaposed paratactically, without any sense of development, because there is no change or development in his feelings and no change or development in the situation that causes those feelings. He is always the lover, and always the lover scorned.

The *chanson* is psychological and paratactic. The *alba*, in contrast, is dramatic, and it proceeds not by parataxis but by cause and effect. The *alba* is not the subjective expression of unchanging feelings but the objective narration of changing events. These events are connected causally: in "Sîne klâwen," for example, the sunrise causes the watchman to give his warning; the watchman's warning evokes a response from the lady; the watchman replies; the lady replies; the sunlight penetrates into the room, causing the lovers to be afraid; their awareness of time and danger leads to their making love one final time; and the whole dramatic series of events results in the knight's departure. Certainly, not all the strophes of every *alba* follow a sequence dictated absolutely by causality. Especially in the longer *albas*, there is often considerable repetitiveness and elaboration in the speeches of the lady and the watchman, and in these speeches the arrangement of elements may be more or less paratactic. But the poem as a whole follows a story from beginning to end, whereas the *chanson* presents us not with a story but with a "situation sans issue." The *chanson* is interested in the psychology of a man hopelessly in love; the *alba* is interested in the dramatic events of a specific night of love interrupted by the dawn.

There is thus a close connection between the narrative technique in the *alba* and the concept of time we have found there. The notion of cause producing effect, of a sequence of events, of the possibility of there being such a thing as a story, is dependent on an acceptance of the reality of time. The events of the *alba* take place in time; indeed, as we have shown, the whole poem is to some degree *about* time: time which is real, time which causes separation, time which must be accepted. Consequently, the verb forms in the *alba*—those, that is, in the speeches of the watchman and in the sections of objective narrative—indicate the movement of time, from future to present to past. In the *chanson* there is a sense of temporal stasis, just as there is a sense of spatial stasis:

> Lo tems vai e ven e vire
> per jorns, per mes e per ans,
> et eu, las! no·n sai que dire,
> c'ades es us mos talans.
> Ades es us e no·s muda,
> c'una·n volh e·n ai volguda,
> don anc non aic jauzimen.

> Time goes and comes and turns
> through days, through months and through years,
> and I, alas, do not know what to say,
> for my desire is always the same.
> It is always the same and does not change,
> for I want and have wanted one woman,
> from whom I have never had joy.[26]

The predominant tense in the *chanson* is consequently the present— not the present of endless bliss, asserted by the lovers in the *alba* as a denial of the movement of time, but the present of endless grief, endless separation, unchanging frustrated love. Where the past tense appears—and it does not appear often—it frequently refers not to a real event in the past, but to the present state of the lover or the beloved. This is evidently so in the passage from Bernart de Ventadorn just quoted. To give some examples from another poet— in Jaufré Rudel's "Quan lo rius de la fontana,"[27] all of the verbs are in the present tense, with only one exception:

> . . . *anc genser crestiana*
> *Non fo . . . .*

> . . . never was there a more noble Christian lady . . . .
> (Lines 17–18)

The past tense here does not indicate a past event, but rather emphasizes the lady's timeless superiority. In Jaufré's "Lanquan li jorn son lonc en may,"[28] the past tense appears twice:

> *Dieus que . . .*
> *. . . format sest' amor de lonh . . . .*

> God Who . . .
> . . . formed this distant love . . . . (Lines 36–37)

> . . . *lo pairis*
> *Qe·m fadet q'ieu non fos amatz!*

> . . . the god-father
> who enchanted me so that I should not be loved!
> (Lines 51–52)

Neither of these passages is really referring to events in the past. The past tense is used mainly to indicate a sense of fatality in the present: the divine fascination of the lady, which can only be attributed to God, and the lover's inability to make her love him, which he sees as part of the destiny fixed at his birth. How different these uses of the past tense are from

Bel companho, la foras als peiros
Me preiavatz qu'eu no fos dormilhos . . .

Handsome comrade, out there at the entrance-steps
you begged me that I not sleep . . . ,

or from

naht was ez dô
mit drucke an brust dîn kus mirn an gewan. . . .

it was night then,
when, as you pressed him to your breast, your kiss won him
from me. . . ,

both of which refer to actual events that took place at a more or
less precise moment in the past.

A verb form which does appear with some frequency in the
chanson is, as one would expect, the optative subjunctive. The love
and unlovedness go on in an endless present, but the lover still
hopes for a resolution. He hopes that the lady will one day grant
him her love; in other words, he hopes that what is now a subjective
psychological state will turn into an objective event, a story. This
hope is sometimes expressed in conditional sentences, sometimes in
the future, but usually in the subjunctive:

Amors, enquera·us preyara
qu·em fossetz plus amoroza . . . .

Love, once again I would pray you
that you be more loving to me . . . .[29]

Ai! car me fos lai pelegris,
Si que mos fustz e mos tapis
Fos pels sieus belhs huelhs remiratz!

Ah, if only I were there as a pilgrim,
so that my staff and my mantle
could be looked upon by her beautiful eyes![30]

The optative subjunctive contrasts the present state of separation
with an erotic union hoped for in the future. This erotic union would
negate the spatial distance and the barriers that keep the lover and
the lady separated:

> *Ai Deus! car no sui ironda,*
> *que voles per l'aire*
> *e vengues de noih prionda*
> *lai dins so repaire?*

> Ah, God! why am I not a swallow
> who might fly through the air
> and come in the depth of night
> into her chamber?[31]

The lover wishes to fly across the distance that separates him from
the center of all value, the lady's chamber; he wishes to penetrate
from the outside, where he is alone, into the inner world of love,
where he will be with the lady.

Such a movement from one world to another cannot actually take
place in the static, timeless universe of the *chanson*. It can only be
wished for—or dreamed of. The dream is a frequent device in the
chanson for indicating the intensity of the lover's desire, and the
unreality of its fulfillment. The dream is a product of the pleasure
principle, and it is contrasted with the acceptance of reality that
must come when the dreamer awakes:

> *Minne, diu der werlde ir fröide mêret,*
> *sêt, diu brâhte in troumes wîs die frouwen mîn*
> *dâ mîn lîp an slâfen was gekêret*
> *und ersach sich an der besten wünne sîn.*
> *dô sach ich ir werden tugende, ir liehten schîn,*
> *schône und für alle wîp gehêret . . . .*
> *ôwê leider, jô wând ichs ein ende hân,*
> *ir vil wünneclîchen werden minne:*
> *nu bin ich vil kûme an dem beginne.*
> *des ist hin mîn wünne und ouch mîn gerender wân.*

Behold: love, who increases the joys of the world,
brought my lady in the manner of a dream
where I was lying asleep,
and I looked upon my greatest joy.
Then I saw her noble virtues, her shining brightness,
beautiful, and exalted above all women . . . .
Alas the misfortune! I thought I had reached a consummation
in her noble, joy-bringing love.
Now I am scarcely at the beginning.
Because of this I have lost my joy, and also the delusion
born of my desire.[32]

Thus, although the *alba* and the *chanson* differ in their treatment of
time, they nevertheless share the contrast of desire and reality. In
both genres, moreover, the supreme time of the pleasure principle is
the night, and in both genres it is usually the dawn that forces the
reality principle to function once again:

> *Anc tan suau no m'adurmi*
> *Mos esperitz tost no fos la . . .*
> *E quan mi resveill al mati*
> *Totz mos bos sabers mi desva, a a.*

I never fall asleep so sweetly
but that my spirit is immediately there [with the lady] . . .
and when I awaken in the morning
all my knowledge of this goodness vanishes, ah, ah.[33]

> *Mich dûhte daz mir nie*
> *lieber wurde, danne mir ze muote was.*
> *Die bluomen vielen ie*
> *von dem boume bî uns nider an daz gras.*
> *Seht, sô muoste ich von fröiden lachen.*
> *dô ich sô wunneclîche*
> *was in troume rîche,*
> *dô taget ez und muos ich wachen.*

236 THE ALBA AND THE CHANSON

It seemed to me that I had never
been happier than I felt [then].
The flowers kept on falling
from the tree near us down onto the grass.
Behold, I had to laugh from joy.
When, in my dream,
I was so marvelously rich,
the dawn came, and I had to awaken.[34]

The contrast of the joyful dreams of night with the cold reality of dawn is of course a commonplace of poetry long after the Middle Ages:

Methought I saw my late espoused Saint
Brought to me like Alcestis from the grave . . . .
But O, as to embrace me she inclin'd,
I wak'd, she fled, and day brought back my night.[35]

It is a contrast especially beloved of the Romantics. Hölderlin's Hyperion, passionately in love with Diotima, gives way during the night to joyous fantasies of their union:

Die sternenhelle Nacht war nun mein Element geworden. . . .
Wie aber am Strahle des Morgenlichts das Leben der Erde
sich wieder entzündete, sah ich empor und suchte die Träume
der Nacht. Sie waren, wie die schönen Sterne, verschwunden. . . .

The star-bright night had now become my element. . . . But as, in the rays of the dawn-light, the life of the earth was once again kindled, I looked upwards and sought the dreams of night. They had, like the beautiful stars, vanished. . . .[36]

Both the *alba* and the *chanson* show the pleasure principle and the reality principle in conflict. In both, the pleasure desired is that of erotic union, and in both, the reality that is to be escaped from is the reality of separation. But the issue (if we may call it that) over which the conflict takes place is not the same in the two genres. We can see this simply by contrasting the way the optative subjunctive is used in each. In the *alba*, the lovers wish to be outside of time; they wish time to cease its movement, so that the present moment may go on forever. In the *chanson*, the lover wishes that the present, with its endless, motionless state of frustration, its "piétinement sur place," may give way to the motion of time; that there may be change that will bring him to his beloved. The lovers in the *alba* and the lover in the *chanson* are at different stages of a love relationship, and they therefore conceive of time in antithetical ways. The *chanson* lover, who has never yet had his lady in his arms, and whose present reality is one of solitude and unhappiness, looks toward the future with desire and hope; he thinks of time in its role of fulfiller and uniter, the role it plays in comedy. The lovers in the *alba*, whose present is one of utmost fulfillment and joy, look toward the future with anguish; they see time in its tragic role of separator and destroyer.

Regarded in this way, separately, the *alba* and the *chanson* seem quite different in their attitudes toward time. But if we look at them from a broader point of view, as stages in the same love affair, we will see that in a deep sense they are very closely connected. A man loves a lady who refuses to love him in return. He is in a timeless present of unhappiness, and at a great distance from her. But let us suppose that, as he wishes, comic time begins to operate. The lady changes her mind and accepts him. The distance is annihilated, not in wish or dream this time, but in real life. He enters into her inner world, and spends a night of bliss with her. His desire has finally become reality. But time, once started, is not to be stopped. The time that brought the lovers together now tears them apart. The sun rises, the watchman makes his announcement, the lover must leave the inner world and go out into the outer world again. Now the lovers want time to stop, to leave them on their pinnacle. They want an eternal present of joy. Ignoring their desires, however, time—now transformed into tragic time, the separator—goes on with its work. The knight leaves—although with a promise to return. Time can still function in the comic way and bring the lovers together again. Yet when they come together they will have to part once more. So, alternating its comic and tragic roles, time will play with the lovers' desires, now satisfying them, now frustrating them. But in the long run time's movement must be downwards, and the separation one day will turn out to be permanent. Beyond the grave there is an end to time, and there is a timeless place of bliss in heaven, close to the center of all true value, God. But it is not that sort of bliss that these lovers desire, in the *chanson* or in the *alba*, although their idea of bliss may sometimes be analogous to the Christian idea. For them the grave means a timeless, endless separation from each other, a grimmer version of the lover's psychological state in the *chanson*. The cycle of separation and union has returned to something like its starting point.

From an Augustinian point of view, the *alba* and the *chanson* represent two different aspects of the grief produced by *cupiditas*. Both poems elevate the love for a creature of this world—whether the love is an unsatisfied longing or a consummated union—to the height of the most important thing in the universe. And such a love is doomed to failure. It is like the story of the brooch of Thebes, in Chaucer's *Compleynt of Mars* (a rumination on time and love closely connected to the themes of the *alba*). For the man who did not have the brooch, it was a source of suffering because he longed for it. For the man who had acquired it, it was a source of suffering because he feared to lose it. And for the man who had lost it, the memory of his loss was the source of still more suffering. Both the *chanson* and the *alba* are poems of grief: in one case, grief for what one does not have; and in the other, grief for what one has and now must lose. The exclusive love for anything less than God can never lead to anything but suffering.

From a naturalistic and Freudian point of view, too, the *alba* and the *chanson*, for all their differences, have a fundamental similarity. Both show the impossibility of reconciling the pleasure principle and the reality principle; both show that desire must give way before reality, but also that desire can never stop asserting itself. The optative subjunctive, the dream, the prayer, the outright defiance of reality—all continue in the service of *eros*, no matter how disdainful the *chanson* lady may be, no matter how urgent the *alba* watchman's warnings. The desire for sexual and emotional possession of the adored lady may be frustrated from the very beginning, or it may be briefly satisfied and then frustrated. The frustrating reality that the erotic desire comes up against may be the recalcitrant will of the lady, or the antierotic mores of society, or the impersonal forces of nature. The form the desire takes may be a longing to get within, or a longing to remain within; a hope that time will bring fulfillment, or a hope that time will cease. But both the desire and the frustration are always there. Their conflict lies at the heart of both the *chanson* and the *alba*.

CONCLUSION

IN ANALYZING the *alba*, we have noted a number of structural analogies to Christian thought and a number of contrasts with Christian values. The inside-outside structure is found frequently in Christian thought, but the notion that the inner world of value is a world of erotic, adulterous love is scarcely consonant with the Christian value system. The wish for an eternity of bliss, free from destructive time, is common to both Christianity and the *alba*; but what the *alba* considers bliss Christianity calls *cupiditas* and a mortal sin. In both Christian thought and the *alba* we find the idea of the soul making a free choice between two alternative sets of values and two alternative courses of action. But there is a considerable difference in the nature of the choice when it is between the pleasures of the flesh and the worship of God, as it is in Saint Augustine, and when it is between the pleasures of the flesh and a prudent escape from the cuckolded husband, as it is in the *alba*. The *alba* closely resembles the Christian dawn-hymn in its emphasis on the contrasting symbolic meanings of night and day; but it neatly—and perhaps intentionally—reverses the Christian symbolism.

The *alba* is very much of the Middle Ages in the various kinds of structure that go to make it up. But its ethics are not Christian. It shows, with approval, an excessive and exclusive love for a mortal creature; an obedience to the subjective desires of the heart, in preference to the objective commands of the Church; a devotion to the pleasures of this world, rather than to the eternal bliss of the soul in heaven; and a very unchristian enjoyment of sex, along with an idealization and spiritualization of sexual love that is, if anything, even more unchristian.

We spoke, in Chapter Two, of the various theories that have been used to explain the relationship between these quite unchristian ethical values and the ethics of medieval Christianity. These theories —the theory of gradualism, the "Sowohl-als-Auch" theory, the theory of conscious anti-Christianity—all suppose that the ethical values we see in medieval secular poetry are real values, really held by poets and audiences, that is, by persons outside the fictional worlds portrayed in the poems. In other words, the dramatic presentation of fictional characters, behaving according to certain ethical norms, is taken as a philosophical statement about the true and the good.

This assumption has been attacked by Jean Fourquet in a number of articles, and perhaps most persuasively in his review of Gottfried Weber's large book on *Tristan*.[1] He objects to the confusion, in the minds of those who have dealt with the problem of the ethics of medieval poetry, between fiction and philosophy. "Cette idée que la fonction du poéte est de révéler par l'art les suprêmes vérités, ne remonte pas, à notre sens, au-delà du XVIIIe siècle" (p. 38). That is, we cannot look in medieval secular poetry for any real ethical or metaphysical *ideas*. This would apply *a fortiori* to the *alba*, since we would hardly expect a medieval poet to try to reveal supreme truths about life, God, reality, and value in a small, vernacular, lyric form.

My own investigation of the *alba* has been based, as should be evident by now, on a very different attitude toward medieval poetry. I believe that every human expression carries with it a more or less formed ethical and metaphysical theory. A literary work that deals with objects or persons treated as real presents us, in however rudimentary a way, with a theory of reality; and a literary work that gives a positive or negative value-tone to the actions and feelings it portrays is communicating a theory as to what is good and what is not good. The *alba* is not philosophical in the sense of its being a discursive exposition of ideas; and it is not normative, in the sense of urging us to go out and do things. But it is filled with ideas, ideas which find expression not in abstract discourse but rather in concrete action and emotion. That there is a high value to the joys of erotic love, that joy in this world cannot last, that a man is free to choose, that the universe is composed of two opposed worlds of value, that desire and reality can never be reconciled—what are these, if not ideas? Since the ideas are not given to us explicitly and discursively, it has been necessary for me to extract them from the poems, using certain techniques of literary analysis: the isolation of various structures inherent in the poems; the study of symbols; and the comparison with the way these and analogous structures and symbols are used in other works of medieval literature, medieval art, and medieval (particularly Augustinian) thought—as well as in more modern literary works, and in universal psychological processes as they are described by psychoanalysis. Some readers may object to one or more of these techniques, or may feel that I have misused them. My defense must be that I have attempted to stay close to the actual literary texts and have exerted all my will power not to read anything into the texts but only to see what is really there. The results of this study seem to me to show decisively that, in spite of its being merely a small lyric form, the *alba* contains and communicates a number of real ideas—and also that these ideas touch on several of the supreme truths Fourquet referred to in the quotation above.

But if the *albas* contain, as all human expressions must, various notions of the real and the good, does that mean that the poets put these ideas there with the intention of making contributions to the study of ethics and metaphysics? Fourquet would answer no. According to him, "les problèmes derniers sont résolus [au moyen âge] par la foi; leur discussion technique appartient aux seuls clercs"

(p. 38). But surely a man does not have to be a scholar or a bishop to be able to think about ultimate questions. It is not a matter of making intentional philosophical statements. Any man, no matter how ignorant of the philosophy of his time or of philosophy in general, has a great many unreasoned, unexplicit, even unconscious, but nevertheless very real attitudes toward reality and value. Medieval man may have accepted—at least with part of his mind—the faith of the clerks, and he may have been able to repeat some of their phrases. But he may have had other ideas as well, ideas which found expression not in philosophical discourse but in his gestures, his life-style, his instinctive reactions. And if the man was a poet, these ideas may have found expression in his artistic creations as well. The fact that a man writes erotic secular poetry at all is already the expression of an idea about reality and value. A man who totally rejects this world, in the manner of Saint Jerome, will not write erotic *albas*. The fact that a poet does write such poems shows us at least one philosophical position of his: the world is *not* totally to be rejected.

To suppose that the only philosophical ideas that existed in the Middle Ages were those of the theologians and the philosophers— and only those *written down* by the theologians and philosophers— is to deprive the great majority of medieval people, including poets, of most of what constitutes human intellect: attitudes, concepts of reality, held values. And to say that poetry in the Middle Ages does not deal with ultimate questions is to say that medieval poetry, unlike all other poetry, does not have a way of depicting reality, that it does not portray moral attitudes and conflicts, that it has no conception of what a man is or ought to be—or that, if it does do these things, they have no relation to what anyone in the Middle Ages, poet or listener, really felt about reality, value, and man. But if the depiction of reality, value, and man in medieval poetry did not correspond to anyone's real values and beliefs, why did the way of depicting these things *change* throughout the Middle Ages? Why did it change in the Renaissance? Why did it go on changing, centuries before the rise of Romantic conceptions of poetry-as-expression? And how is it that a system of ethics with many of the elements we have found in the *alba* eventually came to be believed in as true by many real people in the real world? That sexual love is the highest source of value is one of the most widespread beliefs of our contemporary culture. That value is to be found only in this life, and not in any other, is a conviction of much of the modern world from the Renaissance on. That the only reasonable reaction to the destructive force of time is to get the most out of each passing moment is a notion equally characteristic of much Renaissance and post-Renaissance thought. And the idea that what is good lies within the subjective feelings and experiences of the individual, and not in any external, objective world-order, is a commonplace of Romantic belief.

When these philosophical notions appear in a modern novel we do not doubt that the author believes them and intends them to apply to the real world, not merely to a world of imaginative experience. There is no convincing reason for us to suppose that anything different obtained in medieval epics, romances, satires, and even lyrics. We may debate the exact degree of intention, but that after all is not the main point. I think it is true that we would make a mistake in trying to read medieval romances and lyrics as allegories expressing complex technical points of philosophy: this is what Fourquet reproaches Gottfried Weber for in Weber's reading of *Tristan*. But there are attitudes and ideas of a more general and more concretely human sort, and it is precisely these that we find expressed in works of imaginative literature. This must be considered a particularly important function of imaginative literature in the Middle Ages, when there was such a huge distance between the ideal Christian concept of things, expressed by philosophers and theologians, and the actualities of experience.

It would be methodologically incorrect, of course, to presume that there is a clear one-to-one relationship between the ideas we find in medieval poems and the attitudes and opinions of their particular authors. There is, there must be, some relation between the literary work and the mind that produced it, but in the case of much medieval literature there can be no way of saying which ideas in the poem are intentionally put there by the poet, which ideas occur there without his being aware that he has put them there, which ideas occur there that he is not even aware of ever having thought, and which ideas he merely copies, more or less mindlessly, from his predecessor in the genre. Medieval poems, just like modern poems, cannot be legitimately used *by themselves* to write the spiritual biographies of their poets. The *Kulturproblem des Minnesangs* will never be solved if it asks such specific questions as "What did Giraut de Bornelh *really* think about love, and God, and nature, and society?" Unless some old monastic library yields up a manuscript by Giraut entitled "My Secret Life," we will never know precisely what Giraut thought about the real world. A work of this sort from a vernacular poet of the twelfth or thirteenth century is a virtual impossibility. If anything, we might uncover a *De amore libri tres*— but there again we would probably have insuperable difficulties in getting at Giraut's real opinions. The difficulties of elucidating the complex relationship between author and work—difficulties inherent in the nature of literature—are compounded in the Middle Ages not only by the fact that the precise personal opinions of the authors of medieval poems are to a large extent undeterminable by outside documentation, but also by the fact that literary and rhetorical traditions play so strong a role in the composition of medieval literary works. Both the absence of personal self-revelations and the pervasiveness of imitation as an accepted literary procedure work against our having direct access to the poets' minds.

This does not mean, however, that the ideas that structural and symbolic analyses enable us to discover in such poems as the *alba* must be treated exclusively as "fictional" ideas, meaningful only within the autonomous imaginative worlds of the poems. If the individual poets are not accessible, their cultural environment is. And the cultural environment of the High Middle Ages—the period's peculiar "Sowohl-als-Auch" mixture of Christianity and secularism—is known to us from countless extra-literary sources. The meaning of the *alba*, with its Christian thought-forms and its thisworldly ideals, fits harmoniously into the pattern of high medieval culture that emerges from a study of the economic, social, and political history of the period. Thus, if the *alba* is an autonomous imaginative form, with its own inherent structures and meanings, it is also a reflector of thought-structures and human values that existed in the wider sphere of real medieval life. In fact, it may not be too much to claim that the medieval thought-structures and ideas we have uncovered in the *alba* are among the most important and most widespread in that fascinating and contradictory culture out of which the *alba* grew and in which it so brilliantly flourished.

APPENDIX A: THE *ALBA*-SCENE
IN CHAUCER'S *TROILUS*

Resoun wol nought that I speke of slep,
For it acordeth nought to my matere.
God woot, they took of that ful litel kep!
But lest this nyght, that was to hem so deere,
Ne sholde in veyn escape in no manere,
It was byset in joie and bisynesse
Of al that souneth into gentilesse.

But whan the cok, comune astrologer,
Gan on his brest to bete and after crowe,
And Lucyfer, the dayes messager,
Gan for to rise, and out hire bemes throwe,
And estward roos, to hym that koude it knowe,
Fortuna Major, that anoon Criseyde,
With herte soor, to Troilus thus seyde:

"Myn hertes lif, my trist, and my plesaunce,
That I was born, allas, what me is wo,
That day of us moot make disseveraunce!
For tyme it is to ryse and hennes go,
Or ellis I am lost for evere mo!
O nyght, allas! why nyltow over us hove,
As longe as whan Almena lay by Jove?

"O blake nyght, as folk in bokes rede,
That shapen art by God this world to hide
At certeyn tymes wyth thi derke wede,
That under that men myghte in reste abide,
Wel oughten bestes pleyne, and folk the chide,
That there as day wyth labour wolde us breste,
That thow thus fleest, and deynest us nought reste.

"Thow doost, allas, to shortly thyn office,
Thow rakle nyght, ther God, maker of kynde,
The, for thyn haste and thyn unkynde vice,
So faste ay to oure hemysperie bynde,
That nevere more under the ground thow wynde!
For now, for thow so hiest out of Troie,
Have I forgon thus hastili my joie!"

This Troilus, that with tho wordes felte,
As thoughte hym tho, for piëtous distresse,
The blody teris from his herte melte,
As he that nevere yet swich hevynesse
Assayed hadde, out of so gret gladnesse,
Gan therwithal Criseyde, his lady deere,
In armes streyne, and seyde in this manere:

"O cruel day, accusour of the joie
That nyght and love han stole and faste iwryen,
Acorsed be thi comyng into Troye,
For every bore hath oon of thi bryghte yën!
Envyous day, what list the so to spien?
What hastow lost, why sekestow this place,
Ther God thi light so quenche, for his grace?

"Allas! what have thise loveris the agylt,
Dispitous day? Thyn be the peyne of helle!
For many a lovere hastow slayn, and wilt;
Thy pourynge in wol nowher lat hem dwelle.
What profrestow thi light here for to selle?
Go selle it hem that smale selys grave;
We wol the nought, us nedeth no day have."

And ek the sonne, Titan, gan he chide,
And seyde, "O fool, wel may men the dispise,
That hast the dawyng al nyght by thi syde,
And suffrest hire so soone up fro the rise,
For to disese loveris in this wyse.
What! holde youre bed ther, thow, and ek thi Morwe!
I bidde God, so yeve yow bothe sorwe!"

Therwith ful soore he syghte, and thus he seyde:
"My lady right, and of my wele or wo
The welle and roote, O goodly myn, Criseyde,
And shal I rise, allas, and shal I so?
Now fele I that myn herte moot a-two.
For how sholde I my lif an houre save,
Syn that with yow is al the lyf ich have?

"What shal I don? For, certes, I not how,
Ne whan, allas! I shal the tyme see
That in this plit I may ben eft with yow.
And of my lif, God woot how that shal be,
Syn that desir right now so biteth me,
That I am ded anon, but I retourne.
How sholde I longe, allas, fro yow sojourne?

"But natheles, myn owen lady bright,
Yit were it so that I wiste outrely
That I, youre humble servant and youre knyght,
Were in youre herte iset as fermely
As ye in myn, the which thyng, trewely,
Me levere were than thise worldes tweyne,
Yet sholde I bet enduren al my peyne."

To that Criseyde answerde right anon,
And with a sik she seyde, "O herte deere,
The game, ywys, so ferforth now is gon,
That first shal Phebus fallen fro his spere,
And everich egle ben the dowves feere,
And everi roche out of his place sterte,
Er Troilus out of Criseydes herte.

"Ye ben so depe in-with myn herte grave,
That, though I wolde it torne out of my thought,
As wisly verray God my soule save,
To dyen in the peyne, I koude nought.
And, for the love of God that us hath wrought,
Lat in youre brayn non other fantasie
So crepe, that it cause me to dye!

"And that ye me wolde han as faste in mynde
As I have yow, that wolde I yow biseche;
And if I wiste sothly that to fynde,
God myghte nought a poynt my joies eche.
But herte myn, withouten more speche,
Beth to me trewe, or ellis were it routhe;
For I am thyn, by God and by my trouthe!

"Beth glad, forthy, and lyve in sikernesse!
Thus seyde I nevere er this, ne shal to mo;
And if to yow it were a gret gladnesse
To torne ayeyn soone after that ye go,
As fayn wolde I as ye that it were so,
As wisly God myn herte brynge at reste!"
And hym in armes tok, and ofte keste.

Agayns his wil, sith it mot nedes be,
This Troilus up ros, and faste hym cledde,
And in his armes took his lady free
An hondred tyme, and on his wey hym spedde;
And with swiche voys as though his herte bledde,
He seyde, "Farewel, dere herte swete,
Ther God us graunte sownde and soone to mete!"

To which no word for sorwe she answerde,
So soore gan his partyng hire distreyne;
And Troilus unto his paleys ferde,
As wo-bygon as she was, soth to seyne.
So harde hym wrong of sharp desir the peyne,
For to ben eft there he was in plesaunce,
That it may nevere out of his remembraunce.

(*Troilus*, iii.1408–1533.)

APPENDIX B: TEXTUAL PROBLEMS

IN THE *ALBA* OF GIRAUT DE BORNELH

The *alba* of Giraut de Bornelh, one of the chief examples analyzed in this study, presents certain textual problems that must be resolved before any close reading of the poem can be considered acceptable. Furthermore, these particular problems are representative of the more general problem of the uncertain accuracy of medieval texts and the uncertain legitimacy of treating such texts as aesthetic wholes capable of being analyzed in really close detail. I should like, in this appendix, to deal with the textual problems of Giraut's *alba* and also to explain my attitude toward the more general problem.

Strophes I–VI of Giraut's *alba* offer no difficulties—according to Giraut's editor, Kolsen—since I–V appear in all the manuscripts and VI is missing in only one of them.[1] The strophe I have treated as Strophe VII, however, has a less unanimous textual tradition, and for various reasons Kolsen rejects this strophe as not an authentic composition of Giraut de Bornelh. "So wäre es denn möglich," he suggests, "dass ein Joglar, der auch andere Tagelieder kannte und vortrug, die Str. VII hinzugefügt hätte" (II, 96).

Nevertheless, Strophe VII is of such high literary quality, and the *alba* is so much better with it, that several other students of Provençal lyric, both before and after Kolsen's edition, have accepted it as genuine. There is no unanimity on the question, some scholars taking one point of view and some the other. The following accept VII as authentic: Anglade, Appel, Bartsch, Bec, Bohn, Cassou, Crescini, Diez, Jeanroy, Lomatzsch, Nelli and Lavaud, Panvini, Riquer, and Scheunemann (with Ranke).[2] The following, along with Kolsen, reject it: Hill and Bergin, Hoepffner, Stengel, and Woledge.[3]

Let us consider, one by one, Kolsen's arguments against the authenticity of VII, in order to see how strong the case against this strophe really is.

Of the seven manuscripts containing the poem, only two, MSS. R and T, contain VII. The number of manuscripts containing a reading can offer no convincing proof for the authenticity of the reading. RT may represent a better tradition than the other five manuscripts in respect of this strophe. In any case, the proportion of manuscripts containing VII to those omitting it may be due to the accidents of manuscript preservation; there is certainly no way of showing that it is *not* due to this.

R and T, the only two manuscripts in which VII appears, are poor manuscripts. To understand what Kolsen means by this, we must consider his method of editing. He collects all the manuscripts for each particular poem, chooses one as the basis for his text, corrects its reading by means of the other manuscripts, and gives the variants from the final text in footnotes. His criterion for selecting the base manuscript is that it gives the best all-round reading of the poem. The choice, then, depends mainly on his personal judgment as to the artistic merits of any version of the poem. In certain cases, he takes several strophes from one base manuscript and several from another, because he finds the first manuscript artistically superior in certain strophes and artistically inferior to the second in other strophes.

There is certainly nothing objectionable in this method of editing, since he gives all variants in footnotes. But it is certainly wrong to suppose that the lines that appear in his printed text have any objective superiority over the variants that appear in the footnotes. And when this method of personal aesthetic preferences leads to the decision that certain manuscripts are objectively inferior, and that therefore whole strophes that appear in them (and nowhere else) are to be judged spurious, we find that what began as a more or less arbitrary choice of a base text has somehow developed into an objective criterion of textual authenticity.

In the present case, it is quite true that many of the readings in R and T will strike most readers as artistically inferior to the readings in Kolsen's base text, MS. C. On aesthetic grounds, then, we might be inclined to go along with Kolsen in declaring these manuscripts inferior. On the other hand, R and T are the only manuscripts to include VII, which many readers, including several of the greatest scholars of Provençal poetry, judge to be of high artistic merit and quite worthy of being placed along with I–VI. If it is personal aesthetic judgment that is to provide the criterion for whether we call a manuscript good or bad, why must our adverse aesthetic judgments of some R and T readings in I–VI outweigh our favorable aesthetic judgment of VII, as R and T give it to us? Note what Kolsen himself does, in Giraut's "Be for'oimais drechs el tems gen" (I, 314–20). In this seven-strophe poem, I–VI have as their base text MSS. RS^{g}a, whose readings in these strophes Kolsen judges as artistically superior to the readings in the other manuscripts. But for Strophe VII, he chooses as his base manuscript one of those that he had rejected as inferior for I–VI, viz., MS. C. For the readings in VII, it appears, C is now a superior manuscript and RS^{g}a are inferior! In short, whenever Kolsen wishes to he transforms a poor manuscript into a good one and a good manuscript into a poor one. Surely, when the quality of a manuscript can so easily vary with the winds of Kolsen's aesthetic preference, such a quality cannot be used as a firm ground for rejecting so excellent a piece of writing as VII of Giraut's *alba*.

I should like to make it clear that I am not criticizing Kolsen for using aesthetic judgments in editing these texts. If it is impossible to get back to the reading of the autograph, then there is no reason why we should not prefer Kolsen's tasteful eclecticism to the often less tasteful eclecticism of the scribes of the manuscripts we do possess. I reproach him with trying to give the impression that such a method of editing can provide objective criteria for declaring a manuscript to be good or to be poor. Even more fundamentally, I reproach him with not recognizing the artistic excellence of VII in Giraut's *alba*; for if he had recognized it, he would certainly have declared R and T to be *good* manuscripts, so far as VII was concerned, just as in his text of "Be for'oimais drechs el tems gen" he decided that MS. C, inferior for I–VI, had suddenly become superior for VII of that poem.

Since Giraut's alba is in coblas doblas, *that is, divided into pairs of strophes with each pair sharing a set of rhymes, VII would break this pattern, lacking, as it does, a VIII to share its rhymes with.* Both Jeanroy (*Origines*, p. 65) and Riquer (*Las albas provenzales*) reject this sort of argument, and with good cause.[4] Provençal lyrics in *coblas doblas* with an unpaired strophe at the end are not at all infrequent. This is the form of "Bel m'es can eu vei la brolha" by Bernart de Ventadorn, for example, although the existence of a *tornada* in Bernart's poem makes it somewhat different from Giraut's *alba*.[5] But there is more to be said about this structure in Giraut's *alba* than merely that it was not unique, i.e., that it was part of a tradition. Is it not possible that Giraut intentionally left VII unpaired, in order to set it off more strikingly from I–VI? I–VI are spoken by the friend, and VII by the lover; and our analyses of the poem (supposing VII to be part of it) have shown that the last strophe is opposed to the other six in many other important ways: in its type of space, in its notion of time, in its attitude toward the relationship of God and the world, and so on. If VII is the authentic production of Giraut, therefore, it would be an indication of artistic good sense for him to have made the final strophe break the *coblas doblas* pattern. It is an unfortunate characteristic of some scholars in the older literatures—now much less in evidence than formerly—that when they come upon something out of the ordinary in a literary work, whether it be in a medieval lyric or in a play of Shakespeare, they at once conclude that another hand than the author's must have written the offending passage. Sometimes another hand may indeed have been at work, but it seems to me that one ought to bring in the anonymous reviser only when a search for an *artistic* reason behind the change in style or form has failed.

The refrain of VII does not fit the melody of I–VI. Kolsen attributes this objection to Bohn ("Zwei Trobadorlieder"), but while Bohn does find some difficulty in the refrain of VII, he by no means says that this refrain cannot fit the music at all, nor does he suggest that VII is not authentic. Furthermore, even the slight difficulties Bohn encounters in setting the refrain of VII to the music are purely imaginary. According to Bohn's arrangement of the music, the refrain of I–VI, "et ades sera l'alba," has musical stresses falling on the syllables "ra" and "l'al." If the refrain of VII, "lo fol gilos ni l'alba," were to follow this same pattern, "würde die vorletzte Ligatur (auf die zweite Silbe des Wortes *sera* der beiden ersten Strophen [actually of Strophes I–VI]) . . . auf das unbetonte Wortchen *ni* fallen, was natürlich ganz undenkbar ist."[6] That is, the musical accents would fall on the syllables "ni" and "l'al," the fifth and sixth syllables of the line, as in the earlier refrains. Bohn's simple solution is to alter the way the syllables are set to the melody, so that the musical accents will now fall on "los" and "l'al." But none of this is necessary. On the same page Bohn had already remarked, "Die Strophen . . . 3 und 7 . . . lassen sich im allgemeinen den Noten ziemlich ungezwungen unterlegen; da, wo einmal eine betonte Note auf eine weniger betonte Silbe fällt, wird ein verständiger Sänger das Manco leicht durch den Vortrag ausgleichen können." In other words, the musical accents need *not* match the word accents, something quite evidently true in such melismatic music. (Besides, the bar lines are the invention of modern editors and do not indicate any real upbeat or downbeat; three scholars have notated this little song, and they all differ radically in their indication of the rhythm, the bar lines, and the accents.[7])

In any case, if it is unthinkable that a little word like "ni" should fall on a musical accent and be given a three-note melisma, why should not the same thing be true of a syllable like "ra," which hardly deserves a great emphasis? My own opinion is that "ni" in the refrain of VII is a very important word and deserves to be emphasized. "Lo fol gilos *ni* l'alba"— does not this express perfectly the lover's contempt for the dawn, for all the dawn symbolizes, and for the friend's repeated warnings that the dawn is so near? From this point of view, that is, the point of view of internal literary meaning rather than of external technical a priori judgments, the musical setting that gives a strong accent and a drawn-out melisma to "ni" would be reinforcing, in a very expressive way, exactly what the poet wanted to communicate.

The vocative "companh" in VII contrasts with the vocative "companho" in II–VI. This word, following the usual declension of imparisyllabics in Old Provençal, has a nominative form *compánh*, and an oblique form *companhó*. The vocative of nouns in Old Provençal varies between the two cases: sometimes it is identical with the nominative form, and sometimes with the oblique form (Crescini, *Manuale*, p. 63, with further bibliography). Hence, both *companh* and *companho* can properly be used as vocatives. But would Giraut have used both forms in the same poem? There is not the slightest reason to suppose that he would not have done so. The use of the substantive cases in this language is extremely flexible and often seems to be independent of any grammatical rules. Nominative and oblique forms are often interchanged, apparently without any offense to the grammatical sensibilities of poet or audience. Strophe I of Giraut's *alba* uses *companh*, the nominative form, as the object of a preposition ("al meu companh"). One finds this sort of thing everywhere in Old Provençal poetry. There is thus no reason not to suppose that *companh* and *companho* were often completely interchangeable forms, and that one or the other was often used merely for metrical consideratons. Wishing, for expressive reasons, to introduce the epithet "dous" in VII, Giraut could easily have changed the vocative *companho*, used in II–VI, to *companh*, just in order to leave room for the extra word. In any case, we are dealing in this poem with two different speakers: the friend, who speaks I–VI, and the lover who speaks VII. Since the two are utterly opposed in their attitudes toward reality and in the kind of action they believe to be advisable, could not Giraut have wished to contrast them in the kind of vocatives they use, as well? Either of these explanations, it seems to me, is sufficient to account for the variation in the vocative, without bringing in a second author as Kolsen wants to do.

A final objection to VII of Giraut's *alba* was voiced not by Kolsen but by Stengel ("Entwicklungsgang"). Stengel, as I have noted elsewhere in this study, believed (on no evidence whatsoever) that the *alba* was originally a watchman's song, to which the lovers and their dialog were subsequently added. It is necessary for his theory, therefore, that VII be unauthentic, since I–VI by themselves constitute a kind of watchman's song—the primitive stratum of the *alba*, as Stengel would call it. This, of course, is an example of nineteenth-century positivist criticism at its worst: first the "historical" theory, and then alteration of the poetic texts so that they can be used to prove the theory for whose sake they have been altered.[8]

None of my arguments here should be construed as attempts to prove that VII actually was by Giraut de Bornelh. There is surely no way of proving that. I have merely wished to show that there is no irrefutable evidence to the contrary. There is no objective scholarly reason, therefore, against our treating all seven strophes (I–VII) of Giraut's *alba* as a poetic unity, with a unified structure and a consistent meaning.

Let us suppose, however, that there *were* convincing arguments in favor of VII's having been written by someone other than Giraut—some "Joglar, der auch andere Tagelieder kannte und vortrug." Would we have to treat I–VI and VII as separate poetic entities, and confine our analyses to I–VI alone?

If our main interest were in the poetic personality of Giraut de Bornelh, there is no doubt that this is precisely what we would have to do. But if our interest is in poems rather than in poets, we have, it seems to me, a perfect right to treat a poem found in a medieval manuscript as a unified work of art, whether it is by one poet, or two, or six. Giraut de Bornelh, let us say, wrote six strophes of an *alba*. This was a complete poem, with a coherent structure and meaning, and it can legitimately be subjected to a close critical analysis. Later on, other poets, some good and some not so good, made changes in Giraut's text, altering a phrase, or even adding new strophes. Each of these later versions, as presented by the later poet (assuming that the later poets were, in fact, *joglars*), is a work of art in its own right, and has its own structure and meaning and poetic worth. The fact that such a version is a reworking of the original by Giraut de Bornelh does not make it any less of an artistic whole: many of the most brilliantly unified literary works of the Middle Ages are reworkings of earlier works by other authors.

In the case of the version of Giraut's *alba* found in MSS. R and T, then, we would be dealing with a reworking of the original by an excellent later poet, who had great insight into the implications of Giraut's I–VI, and who succeeded in giving them added force and point by the addition of a new strophe, VII. The addition of VII changed the structure of the poem and added to its meaning: it resulted in the creation of a new poem, similar in many ways to the original, but with its own new aesthetic properties and intellectual content. We may think of this new poem as the work of an anonymous *joglar* or as a collaboration between the *joglar* and Giraut, but it is most certainly a poem, not a collection of disparate elements. And, as a poem, it ought to be as capable of being read and analyzed closely as any other poem. There are several other versions of Giraut's *alba*, perhaps by other individual *joglars* or by the collaboration of several *joglars* at once. The various manuscripts give us a number of extra strophes in addition to VII, in various combinations. Each of these versions is a poem; each has a structure and a meaning; each is subject to analysis and critical judgment. Certainly, not all the versions are equal in poetic merit. The *joglar* who wrote VII (always assuming that it was a *joglar*, and not Giraut himself, who wrote it) was an excellent poet and made an excellent poem (I–VII), which many students, including myself, have judged to be superior to the version that appears in the manuscript group EPSg, that is, the version consisting of strophes I–VI alone. Some of the other later poets who revised Giraut's work were less talented, and their versions, with their extra strophes, were less good than the original. But good or bad, each of these versions is a poem—a collaborative poem if you will, but a poem nevertheless.

I have based this discussion on the hypothesis that I–VI was the original poem, and that VII and the other additional strophes were added later on. This hypothesis is a useful one for orienting ourselves in the problem, but it has no basis in fact, and at this point we may as well discard it. It is not impossible that the original poem consisted of I–VII, and that a later *joglar* altered the poem by omitting VII; and the same thing might be said of any of the other "extra" strophes. In fact, we do not possess any single poem that we can call "the" *alba* of Giraut de Bornelh. What we do possess is a group of *albas*, differing among themselves, yet sharing a large number of elements—and all associated with the name of Giraut de Bornelh. We are surely within our rights as critics and scholars if we select one of these poems for critical analysis; and there is nothing wrong with our selecting, among the group, the poem that we find to be the best. On the contrary, if we are interested in poetry for its own sake and in the possibilities offered by a poetic genre or subject, we would be wrong to select any but the best version for analysis, for the best version will inevitably tell us more about poetry and its possibilities than an inferior version would. Naturally, it would not be right to claim that the particular poem we have picked, on the basis of our judgment of its artistic worth, must be the original version by the poet to whom the whole set of versions is attributed. That, essentially, is what Kolsen does in his edition: the lines and strophes he likes best are asserted to be by Giraut; the others are asserted to be by *joglars*. If in this study I have referred to I–VII as "Giraut's *alba*," I have only done so for the sake of convenience. I make no claims to have contributed anything to our positive knowledge of Giraut de Bornelh (of which, by the way, there is virtually none). My concern has been with a particular poem —whether all by Giraut, or partially by him, or not by him at all.

In any case, the author of VII, whoever he may have been, had a great understanding of I–VI, as I have noted. Strophe VII adds to and deepens I–VI, but it does not distort them. It makes explicit what is already implicit in I–VI, and it is therefore of special usefulness in this sort of criticism, the purpose of which is to make everything in the poem explicit. And although he created a new poem, the *joglar* (if it was a *joglar*) at the same time retained everything that was in the old one. Consequently, almost everything I have said about the structure and meaning of I–VII could apply equally well to I–VI taken by themselves.

A final note: when I say that each addition or alteration of the original text results in a new poem, more or less worthy of being studied in its own right, I am referring to additions and alterations of a creative sort, made by poets. Changes demonstrably due to the stupidity of scribes do not fall into this category, of course. It would be absurd to assert that when a scribe accidentally omits a line, discovers the mistake some ten lines later, and then conscientiously inserts the missing line *there*, all of this results in the creation of a new poem. In cases when the scribe is more than an inefficient machine and yet less than a poet, that is, when he is one of those who make conscious alterations for ideological or stylistic reasons, the problem as to what rights his version of the poem has to serious critical attention becomes a knotty one, on which I am not prepared to offer an opinion.

APPENDIX C: THE *ALBA* OF HEINRICH VON MORUNGEN

Owê, sol aber mir iemer mê
geliuhten dur die naht
noch wîzer danne ein snê
ir lîp vil wol geslaht?
der trouc diu ougen mîn:
ich wânde, ez solde sîn
des liehten mânen schîn,
    dô taget ez.

Owê sol aber er immer mê
den morgen hie betagen?
als uns diu naht engê,
daz wir niht durfen klagen:
"owê, nu ist ez tac,"
als er mit klage pflac

do'r jungest bî mir lac.
  dô taget ez.

Owê, si kuste âne zal
in deme slâfe mich.
dô vielen hin ze tal
ir trêne nidersich,
iedoch getrôste ich sî,
daz si ir weinen lî,
und mich al ummevî.
  dô taget ez.

Owê, daz er sô dicke sich
bî mir ersêen hât!
als er endahte mich,
sô wolte er sunder wât
mich armen schouwen blôz.
ez was ein wunder grôz
daz in des nie verdrôz.
  dô taget ez.

Alas, shall it ever again
shine to me through the night,
whiter yet than snow—
her body, so well-formed?
It deceived my eyes:
I thought it must be
the gleaming of the bright moon.
  Then the dawn came.

Alas, shall he ever again
stay here in the morning?—
so that when the night leaves us
we shall not have to lament,
"Alas, now it is day,"
as he lamented
the last time he lay by me.
  Then the dawn came.

Alas, she kissed me numberless times
as I lay sleeping.

Then her tears fell
down and down.
But I comforted her
so that she left off weeping
and embraced me all around.
  Then the dawn came.

Alas, that he has so often
looked upon me!
When he took the covers off me
he wanted to look at poor me
naked, without clothing.
It was a great wonder
that he never grew bored with this.
  Then the dawn came.

(*MF*, pp. 189–90.)

KEY TO ABBREVIATIONS USED

IN THE NOTES AND BIBLIOGRAPHY

AfdA	Anzeiger für deutsches Altertum
AIEO	Annales de l'Institut d'Études Occitanes
AR	Archivum Romanicum
Archiv	Archiv für das Studium der neueren Sprachen und Literaturen
Beiträge	Beiträge zur Geschichte der deutschen Sprache und Literatur
CN	Cultura Neolatina
DL	*Deutsche Liederdichter des 13. Jahrhunderts*, ed. Carl von Kraus, 2 vols. (Tübingen, 1952–1958)
DVLG	Deutsche Vierteljahrsschrift für Literaturwissenschaft und Geistesgeschichte
EG	Études Germaniques
Freud, *GW*	Sigmund Freud, *Gesammelte Werke*, 18 vols., 4th ed. (Frankfurt am Main, 1964)
MF	*Des Minnesangs Frühling*, ed. Karl Lachmann, Moriz Haupt,

and Friedrich Vogt, 33rd ed., revised by Carl von Kraus (Stuttgart, 1965)

P. L.   *Patrologiae cursus completus . . . Series latina*, ed. J.-P. Migne

ZfdA   Zeitschrift für deutsches Altertum

ZfdPh   Zeitschrift für deutsche Philologie

ZfrPh   Zeitschrift für romanische Philologie

ZfSL   Zeitschrift für französische Sprache und Literatur

NOTES

PREFATORY MATERIAL

1. Abū Muḥammad ʿAlī Ibn Ḥazm, *A Book Containing the Risāla, known as The Dove's Neck-Ring, about Love and Lovers . . .* , trans. Alois Richard Nykl (Paris, 1931), pp. 127–28.

2. "Ich hört ein frewlein klagen," in Franz Magnus Böhme, *Altdeutsches Liederbuch* (Leipzig, 1877), p. 217.

3. *DL*, I, 597–98.

INTRODUCTION

1. The name "aubade" is usually applied to a waking song addressed to the beloved, and does not appear before the fifteenth century. See Jean Frappier, *La poésie lyrique française aux XIIᵉ et XIIIᵉ siècles: Les auteurs et les genres* (Paris: "Les cours de Sorbonne," n.d.), p. 41.

2. This is the French term. The Provençal equivalent is *canso*.

3. A full account of this theory, as well as of the other theories as to the origins of the *alba* and of troubadour poetry in general, will be found in André Moret, *Les débuts du lyrisme en Allemagne* (Lille, 1951).

4. Ludwig Fränkel, *Shakespeare und das Tagelied: Ein Beitrag zur vergleichenden Literaturgeschichte der germanischen Völker* (Hannover, 1893), p. 41.

5. Gaston Paris, "*Les origines de la poésie lyrique en France* ... par Alfred Jeanroy ..." [Review, part 3], *Journal des Savants* (1892), p. 163.

6. The chief debating point in the argument over the existence of an autochthonous German *Tagelied* is whether a word in the *Tagelied* ascribed to Dietmar von Aist is to be read "wan" or "man." A theory of literary history whose validity depends totally on the paleographical interpretation of three minims can hardly be said to rest on a firm foundation.

7. Arthur T. Hatto, ed. *Eos: An Enquiry into the Theme of Lovers' Meetings and Partings at Dawn in Poetry* (The Hague, 1965).

8. See Leo Spitzer, *L'amour lointain de Jaufré Rudel et le sens de la poésie des troubadours* (Chapel Hill, 1944), for an eloquent statement of this view. André Moret, "Le problème des Origines du Minnesang," *EG*, II (1947), 22–41, makes a similar point.

9. The most extensive treatment of the problem of origins, dealing mainly with the *chanson* but mentioning the other lyric types as well, is to be found in the series of articles by Dimitri Scheludko listed in the Bibliography. Shorter, but perhaps just as valuable, are the introductory section of Pierre Bec, *Petite Anthologie de la Lyrique Occitane du Moyen Age*, 4th ed. (Avignon, 1966), and a brief article by Gerald Gillespie, "Origins of Romance Lyrics: A Review of Research," *Yearbook of Comparative and General Literature*, XVI (1967), 16–32. For the theory of Arabic origins, there is a particularly good survey, with extensive bibliography, in Reto R. Bezzola, *Les origines et la formation de la littérature courtoise en Occident, 500–1200*, IIᵉ partie: *La société féodale et la transformation de la littérature de cour* (Paris, 1960), I, 186 ff.

10. Eugen Lerch, "Trobadorsprache und religiöse Sprache," *CN*, III (1943), 214–30; Myrrha Lot-Borodine, *De l'Amour profane à l'amour sacré: Études de psychologie sentimentale au Moyen Age* (Paris, 1961), especially Chapter Four; Julius Schwietering, "Der Tristan Gottfrieds von Strassburg und die Bernhardische Mystik," in his *Mystik und höfische Dichtung im Hochmittelalter* (Darmstadt, 1962), pp. 1–35.

11. As all of the above do, to a greater or lesser extent.

12. See the list of these particular variants in Friedrich Nicklas, *Untersuchungen über Stil und Geschichte des deutschen Tagelieds*, Germanische Studien, No. 72 (Berlin, 1929), pp. 33–34.

13. Alois Richard Nykl, "Leo Spitzer, *L'amour lointain de Jaufré Rudel* ..." [Review], *Speculum*, XX (1945), 252.

CHAPTER ONE: THE TWO WORLDS OF VALUE

1. For the analysis of spatial relations as a technique of literary criticism, see Gaston Bachelard, *La poétique de l'espace* (Paris, 1958); Roland Barthes, *Sur Racine* (Paris, 1965); K. von Dürckheim, "Untersuchungen zum gelebten Raum: Erlebniswirklichkeit und ihr Verständnis," *Neue psychologische Studien*, VI (1932), 383 ff.; George Wilson Knight, *The Shakespearian Tempest, with a Chart of Shakespeare's Dramatic Universe* (London, 1960); and Hans Furstner, *Studien zur Wesensbestimmung der höfischen Minne* (Groningen, 1956), which gives further references on p. 44.

2. Honorius Augustodunensis, *Expositio in Cantica canticorum, P. L.,* CLXXII, cols. 423–24.

3. See Friedrich Ranke, *Die Allegorie der Minnegrotte in Gottfrieds Tristan,* Schriften der Königsberger Gelehrten Gesellschaft, Geisteswissenschaftliche Klasse, II, Heft 2 (Berlin, 1925); and Joseph Sauer, *Die Symbolik des Kirchengebäudes* (Freiburg, 1902).

4. Bernard of Clairvaux, *Sermones de Diversis,* Sermo XLII, 4, *P. L.,* CLXXXIII, col. 663.

5. Richard of St. Victor, *Explicatio in cantica canticorum, P. L.,* CXCVI, cols. 405–524, quoted in Friedrich Wilhelm Wodtke, "Die Allegorie des 'Inneren Paradieses' bei Bernhard von Clairvaux, Honorius Augustodunensis, Gottfried von Strassburg und in der deutschen Mystik," *Festschrift Josef Quint . . . ,* ed. Hugo Moser (Bonn, 1964), p. 281. See also Friedrich Ohly, *Hohelied-Studien: Grundzüge einer Geschichte der Hoheliedauslegung des Abendlandes bis um 1200* (Wiesbaden, 1958), especially pp. 135–205.

6. *Sermones de Diversis,* Sermo CXVII, *P. L.,* CLXXXIII, cols. 741–42. The allegory goes back to Philo Judaeus. See Wodtke, "Die Allegorie des 'Inneren Paradieses'," for other medieval examples.

7. Hugo of Fouilly, *De claustro animae, P. L.,* CLXXVI, cols. 1017–182. See also Hugh of St. Victor, *De claustro animae,* in this same volume of the *Patrologia,* cols. 1019 ff.

8. Karl Strecker, ed. *Die Cambridger Lieder* (Berlin, 1926), p. 69. See also F. J. E. Raby, *A History of Secular Latin Poetry in the Middle Ages* (Oxford, 1934), I, 302–4, for the text and a commentary.

9. The same text from the Song of Songs is used by Saint Bernard to symbolize the mystical union of the soul with God. See Étienne Gilson, *La théologie mystique de saint Bernard* (Paris, 1947), pp. 123–29.

10. The poem, with all of its probably authentic and all of its probably unauthentic strophes, is in *Sämtliche Lieder des Troubadors Giraut de Bornelh,* ed. Adolf Kolsen (Halle, 1907–1935), I, 342–47. The present stanza appears only in MS. Mü.

11. In the poem "Quan lo rius de la fontana," Jaufré Rudel expresses the desire to be together with his beloved ". . . dinz vergier o sotz cortina . . . ." The poem can be found in *Les Chansons de Jaufré Rudel,* ed. Alfred Jeanroy, 2nd ed. (Paris, 1965), pp. 3–5. Carl Appel, "Wiederum zu Jaufré Rudel," *Archiv,* CVII (1901), 338–49, sees a reference in this phrase to the earthly or heavenly paradise, identified with the place of love-making. Such an identification would not be out of keeping with the conventional symbolism of some medieval erotic poetry, as we have seen, but in this particular text there is really not sufficient evidence for it. On the other hand, the enclosed love-space and the Garden of Eden do have the same topographical and moral structure (highly valued inside versus less valued outside), and they are related in that. See also Moshé Lazar, *Amour courtois et "Fin 'amors" dans la littérature du XIIᵉ siècle* (Paris, 1964), p. 99.

12. The standard monograph on this subject is Roberta Douglas Cornelius, *The Figurative Castle* (Bryn Mawr, 1930), which gives numerous examples.

13. Honorius Augustodunensis, *Speculum Ecclesiae: De assumptione Sanctae Mariae, P. L.* CLXXII, cols. 991–94.

14. Described by Cornelius, pp. 17 ff.

15. *Speculum Ecclesiae: In conventu populi, P. L.,* CLXXII, col. 1097.

16. See W. T. H. Jackson, "The Epic Center as Structural Determinant in Medieval Narrative Poetry," *New York University Department of German Studies in Germanic Languages and Literature,* ed. Robert A. Fowkes and Volkmar Sander (Reutlingen, 1967), pp. 79–95.

17. Guillamme de Lorris and Jean de Meun, *Le Roman de la Rose,* ed. Ernest Langlois, 5 vols. (Paris: Société des anciens textes français, 1914–1924), II, 7–66 (lines 129–1278).

18. V, 36–50 (lines 20279–624).

19. II, 189–98 (lines 3797–958).

20. V, 81–95 (lines 21346–730).

21. For these various analogies to the *Minnegrotte* and its structure see Ranke, *Die Allegorie der Minnegrotte,* and Wodtke, "Die Allegorie des 'Inneren Paradieses'," both already cited; also two articles by Rainer Gruenter, "Bauformen der Waldleben-Episode in Gotfrids Tristan und Isold," *Festschrift Günther Müller,* ed. Richard Alewyn (Bonn, 1957), pp. 21–48, and "Das *wunnecliche tal*," *Euphorion,* LV (1961), 341–404. Herbert Kolb, "*Der Minnen hus:* Zur Allegorie der Minnegrotte in Gottfried's *Tristan,*" *Euphorion,* LVI (1962), 229–47, denies the relation of the *Minnegrotte* to the allegorized church, but his arguments are much less convincing than those of Ranke, who first pointed out the analogy.

22. See Wystan Hugh Auden, *The Enchafèd Flood; or the Romantic Iconography of the Sea* (New York, 1950), especially pp. 23–39; also Northrop Frye, *Anatomy of Criticism* (Princeton, 1957), pp. 141–58.

23. From "Trilogie der Leidenschaft: An Werther." I quote from Johann Wolfgang von Goethe, *Gedenkausgabe der Werke, Briefe und Gespräche,* ed. Ernst Beutler (Zürich and Stuttgart, 1949), I, 474. See Furstner, *Studien,* p. 47. This poem has numerous analogies with the *alba,* often with interesting variations on its characteristic images. Here, for example, are words that could easily have been spoken by one of the lamenting heroes or heroines of a medieval *Tagelied*:

Das Wiedersehn ist froh, das Scheiden schwer,
Das Wieder-Wiedersehn beglückt noch mehr,
Und Jahre sind im Augenblick ersetzt . . . .

Meeting again is joyous; separation is painful;
Meeting once again after a separation makes one even more joyful,
And years are compensated for by a minute . . . .

On the Romantic variations of the inside-outside topography, see Georges Poulet, *Les métamorphoses du cercle* (Paris, 1961), especially Chapter Five on Rousseau.

CHAPTER TWO: THE ENEMIES OF LOVE

1. See Wolfgang Mohr, "Minnesang als Gesellschaftskunst," *Der Deutschunterricht,* VI (1954), No. 5, pp. 83–107.

2. For a list of these epithets in the German *alba* see Nicklas, *Untersuchungen,* pp. 62 ff.

3. See Saint Bernard's treatment of the Gospel passage, "A man shall leave his father and his mother and shall become one with his wife," cited and discussed in Gilson, *La théologie mystique de saint Bernard*, pp. 156–63.

4. *L'amour lointain de Jaufré Rudel*, p. 29.

5. First lines of an alba by Von Wissenlo, in *DL*, I, 595. I depart from von Kraus's text by substituting for his "het" in the first line the reading of MS. C, "hat," which makes more sense in the context.

6. *Der Trobador Cadenet*, ed. Carl Appel (Halle, 1920), pp. 80–81.

7. Cf. the quite different attitude of Arnold Hauser, *The Social History of Art* (New York: Vintage Books, n.d.), I, 218. However, Hauser's description of a medieval childhood depends ultimately on literary (fictional) sources and modern fantasies about them.

8. *DL*, I, 598–99. A characteristic of Wolfram's style, here and elsewhere in his work, is his unwillingness to allow the demands of logical syntax to interfere with the expression of his thought. In my translation, the only effort I have made to clear up the syntactical confusion of the original has been the addition of some punctuation.

9. See Georg Keferstein, "Zur Liebesauffassung in Wolframs 'Parzival'," *Festschrift Albert Leitzmann* (Jena, 1937), pp. 15–32; Kurt Boestfleisch, *Studien zum Minnegedanken bei Wolfram von Eschenbach*, Königsberger Deutsche Forschungen, No. 8 (Königsberg, 1930); Hans-Joachim Koppitz, *Wolframs Religiosität: Beobachtung über das Verhältnis Wolframs von Eschenbach zur religiösen Tradition des Mittelalters* (Bonn, 1959), especially pp. 141–44.

10. For example: Jan Hendrik Scholte, "Wolframs Lyrik," *Beiträge*, LXIX (1947), 409–19; Helmut de Boor, *Die höfische Literatur: Vorbereitung, Blüte, Ausklang, 1170–1250* (*Geschichte der deutschen Literatur*, ed. Helmut de Boor and Richard Newald, Vol. II [Munich, 1953]), 328–31; Wolfgang Mohr, "Wolframs Tagelieder," *Festschrift für Paul Kluckhohn und Hermann Schneider* (Tübingen, 1948), 148–65; *DL*, II (ed. Hugo Kuhn), 646–707, especially p. 684.

11. *DL*, I, 596.

12. *Aeneid* iv.522–32. Translation: *The Aeneid of Virgil*, trans. Rolfe Humphries (New York and London, 1951), p. 106.

13. "Verna feminae suspiria," in Strecker, *Die Cambridger Lieder*, p. 95.

14. Karl Strecker, ed. *Die Lieder Walters von Chatillon in der Handschrift 351 von St. Omer* (Berlin, 1925), p. 31.

15. *Bernart von Ventadorn: Seine Lieder*, ed. Carl Appel (Halle, 1915), p. 260.

16. Appel takes this verb as transitive, and translates: "So habe ich mein Herz von Freude voll, sie will mein Wesen ganz verrücken" (ibid., p. 268). But the poem is not about how love transforms the nature of the lover but rather about how nature itself seems transformed to the lover's senses. Kurt Lewent, "Weitere textkritische Bemerkungen zu den Liedern des Bernart von Ventadorn," *ZfrPh*, XLIII (1923), 674, suggests that "desnatura" be taken as intransitive and "me" be considered a dative rather than an accusative, and I follow this suggestion.

17. Other Provençal poets play on these paradoxes with much verve, but the emphasis on the distinction between the lover and nature is never lost. See,

for example, "Er resplan la flors enversa" of Raimbaut d'Aurenga, in Raymond Thompson Hill and Thomas Goddard Bergin, eds. *Anthology of the Provençal Troubadours* (New Haven, 1941), p. 50.

18. iii.1450–54. Citations from Chaucer are from *The Works of Geoffrey Chaucer*, ed. Fred N. Robinson, 2nd ed. (Boston, 1957). See Appendix A, below.

19. *DL*, I, 597–98, first lines of Strophe 5.

20. First lines of Strophe 1.

21. Joachim Bumke, *Wolfram von Eschenbach* (Stuttgart: Sammlung Metzler, 1964), p. 22.

22. From the *Middle English Bestiary*; text in Oliver Farrar Emerson, ed. *A Middle English Reader* (New York, 1905), p. 15. I have substituted "th" for eth and thorn and have eliminated the diacritical marks.

23. T. H. White, trans. *The Bestiary, A Book of Beasts: Being a Translation from a Latin Bestiary of the Twelfth Century* (New York: Capricorn Books, 1960), p. 107.

24. F. R. Schröder points out an analogous instance in Arabic poetry, where the day is metaphorized as a lion, chasing the shy gazelle of the night. See *DL*, II, 663–64. Like the eagle, of course, the lion is thought of as ferocious and kingly.

25. From "Den morgenblic bî wahters sange erkôs," Strophe 2, in *DL*, I, 596.

26. Cornelius, *The Figurative Castle*, p. 18.

27. Cornelius summarizes this sermon on pp. 52 ff. The quotation is from pp. 53–54.

28. On these dawn-hymns, see Samuel Singer, *Die religiöse Lyrik des Mittelalters* (Bern, 1933); Jole M. Scudieri Ruggieri, "Per le origini dell'alba," *CN*, III (1943), 191–202; and three articles by Philipp August Becker, "Vom geistlichen Tagelied," *Volkstum und Kultur der Romanen*, II (1929), 293–302; "Vom christlichen Hymnus zum Minnesang," *Historisches Jahrbuch im Auftrage der Görres-Gesellschaft*, LII (1932), 1–39 and 145–77, reprinted in Becker's *Zur romanischen Literaturgeschichte: Ausgewählte Studien und Aufsätze* (Munich, 1967), pp. 14–77; and "Vom Morgenhymnus zum Tagelied," in this same collection, pp. 149–73.

29. Text in Hatto, *Eos*, pp. 277–78.

30. See Clemens Blume and Guido Maria Dreves, eds. *Analecta hymnica medii aevi*, II (Leipzig, 1888), Nos. 1, 4, 7, 10, 13, 16, 20, 23, 26, 33, 35, 36, 46, 113; XXVII (Leipzig, 1897), Nos. 30, 51, 65; XLVI (Leipzig, 1905), Nos. 3, 4; L (Leipzig, 1907), Nos. 4, 5, 22, 23, 24; LI (Leipzig, 1908), Nos. 5, 6, 7, 8, 9, 10, 11, 33, 49, 58, 59, 89, 92. A few of these are duplicate versions, in different hymnals, of the same hymns.

31. For example, Alfred Jeanroy, *Les origines de la poésie lyrique en France au moyen-âge* (Paris, 1889), p. 74; Dimitri Scheludko, "Beiträge zur Entstehungsgeschichte der altprovenzalischen Lyrik [Die mittellateinische Theorie]," *AR*, XV (1931), 203; Karl Bartsch, "Die romanischen und deutschen Tagelieder," in his *Gesammelte Vorträge und Aufsätze* (Freiburg i.B. and Tübingen, 1883), p. 260; and Theodor Kochs, *Das deutsche geistliche Tagelied* (Munster i.W., 1928), p. 30.

32. Alanus de Insulis, *Liber in distinctionibus dictionum theologicalium, P. L.*, CCX, cols. 685–1012. Any of the numerous symbol dictionaries would provide much the same information.

33. S.v. "nox": "caecitas materialis," "caecitas mentis," "ignorantia," "culpa," "adversitas," "tempus ante adventum Christi," "Vetus Testamentum," "mors temporalis," "vita praesens," "miseria temporis," "diabolus," "captivitas," "peccator."

34. S.v. "dies": "tempus gratiae," "tempus judicii," "lux gratiae," "vita aeterna," "prosperitas," "intellectus humanus," "judaei ad fidam conversi," "spiritualis doctor," "animae electorum," "aeternitatis longitudo," "status angelicae naturae."

35. S.v. "sol": "Christus," "sanctus," "claritas boni operis," "lumen veritatis," "praedicatorum claritas," "manifestatio," "donum sapientiae," "divina Christi natura."

36. S.v. "nox": "hora in qua Christus veniet ad judicium," "praedicator qui minoribus praedicat." S.v. "dies": "tempus praesentis vitae," "prava conscientia," "miseria temporis vel peccati delectatio." S.v. "sol": "tribulatio," "tentatio," "Antichristus."

37. From *De S. Guthlaco presbytero*, in *Acta Sanctorum*, Aprilis, Vol. II (Antwerp, 1675), pp. 37-50. The passage quoted is on p. 42. The author of this baroque extravaganza is Bishop Felix of Crowland.

38. See Millard Meiss, "Light as Form and Symbol in Some Fifteenth-Century Paintings," *Art Bulletin*, XXVII (1945), 175-81; Erwin Panofsky, *Early Netherlandish Painting, its Origins and Character*, 2 vols. (Cambridge, Mass., 1958), especially I, 147-48.

39. Quoted in Meiss, "Light as Form and Symbol," p. 176. Meiss's source is Anselm Salzer, *Die Sinnbilder und Beiworte Mariens in der deutschen Literatur und lateinischen Hymnenpoesie des Mittelalters* (Linz, 1893), p. 74. I have given Meiss's translation here.

40. The structure of this iconographic representation presents some interesting analogies with the allegory of the cave in Plato's *Republic* (vii.514A-521B). There is no doubt a real connection, in the history of ideas, between the two representations, with Neoplatonic light imagery providing the main connecting stage. For further material on light symbolism in medieval art and thought, see Edgar de Bruyne, *Études d'esthétique médiévale* (Bruges, 1946), III, 9 ff.; Joseph Antony Mazzeo, *Medieval Cultural Tradition in Dante's Comedy* (Ithaca, 1960), pp. 56-90; and Erwin Panofsky, *Abbot Suger on the Abbey Church of St.-Denis and its Art Treasures* (Princeton, 1946).

41. Wolfram von Eschenbach, *Parzival*, ed. Karl Lachmann, 6th ed. (Berlin and Leipzig, 1926), p. 224 (ix.446.1-4).

42. *Parzival*, pp. 224-25 (ix.466.15-467.4, with several lines omitted).

43. Koppitz, *Wolframs Religiosität*, p. 293, sees a background of mysticism in this passage. But the light imagery that suggests this to him is traditional in medieval Christian thought in no way connected with mysticism, and the moral ideas expressed by the imagery are equally nonmystical. Compare, for example, the following, in which one can hardly suspect the influence of mysticism:

Lo solelhs clars fai lo jorn clar;
mais sa clardatz enluminar

276 NOTES

non pot lo jorn per sa clardor
si com tu·l cor de peccador.

The bright sun makes the day bright;
but its brightness cannot illuminate
the day by its brightness
as You [illuminate] the heart of the sinner.

(Daude de Pradas, "Qui finamen sab cossirar," Strophe 6, in *Poésies du Trouba-dour Daude de Pradas*, ed. Alexander Schutz [Paris, 1933], p. 62).

44. John Donne, *The Poems*, ed. Herbert J. C. Grierson (Oxford, 1912), I, 11–12.

45. See Jacques Wettstein, "*Mezura*": *L'Idéal des troubadours* (Zürich, 1945), pp. 17–18.

46. The genre, if it can really be called that, was invented by Guiraut Riquier. See Hill and Bergin, *Anthology*, p. 212.

47. *L'amour lointain de Jaufré Rudel*, p. 69. The italics are Spitzer's.

48. See Dimitri Scheludko, "Religiöse Elemente im weltlichen Liebeslied der Trobadors," *ZfSL*, LIX (1935), 402–21, and LX (1937), 18–35; Lerch, "Troba-dorsprache und religiöse Sprache."

49. Bruno Panvini, "Giraldo di Bornelh, Trovatore del Sec. XII," *Siculorum Gymnasium* (Catania), Gennaio-Giugno 1949, p. 88.

50. Anonymous, "Flor de Paradis," in Karl Bartsch, ed. *Denkmäler der provenzalischen Literatur* (Stuttgart, 1856), p. 68.

51. "Vida" of St. Mary Magdalene, in Camille Chabaneau, *Sainte Marie Madeleine dans la littérature provençale* (Paris, 1887), p. 95.

52. Matfré Ermengaud, *Le Breviari d'Amor de Matfre Ermengaud*, ed. Gabriel Azaïs (Béziers, 1862–1866), line 11183.

53. Louis Alibert and René Nelli, eds. *VII Troubadours des Pays d'Aude* (Carcassonne, 1948), p. 27.

54. Guilhem Figueira, "Totz hom qui ben comensa e ben fenis," in *Guilhem Figueira, ein provenzalischer Troubadour*, ed. Emil Lévy (Berlin, 1880), p. 52.

55. Ed. Kolsen, I, 472 ("Be vei e conosc e sai," Strophe 2).

56. Denis de Rougemont, *L'Amour et l'Occident*, 2nd ed. (Paris, 1956), p. 72, maintains that the use of the adjective "verais" in connection with "lums," as we see it in the first line of Giraut's *alba*, probably indicates that the poet was a Catharist. This is preposterous.

57. Diego Zorzi, *Valori religiosi nella letteratura provenzale: La spiritualità trinitaria*, Pubblicazioni dell' Università Cattolica del S. Cuore, N.S., No. 44 (Milan, 1954), p. 112, quoting from Amédée Gastoué, *Le Cantique populaire en France* (Lyon, 1924), p. 34. The same melody was used for Adam of St. Victor's "O Maria stella maris," and Folquet de Marselha's "Bem platz longua."

58. This is the opinion of Becker, "Vom Morgenhymnus zum Tagelied," as the title of his article indicates; of Scudieri Ruggieri, "Per le origini dell'alba"; of Dimitri Scheludko, "Beiträge zur Entstehungsgeschichte der altprovenzalischen Lyrik [Die mittellateinische Theorie]," *AR*, XV (1931), 137–206; of Samuel Singer, *Die religiöse Lyrik des Mittelalters* (Bern, 1933), who thinks the *alba* is a "Mischung" of the religious dawn-hymn and popular love poetry (p. 50); and

of Manuel Rodrigues Lapa, *Das origens da poesia lírica em Portugal na idade-média* (Lisbon, 1929): "Todo o que constitui a substância dêsse género se encontrava na liturgia e no simbolismo cristãos" (p. 139). On the other hand, Kochs, *Das deutsche geistliche Tagelied*, p. 29, was of the opinion that the erotic *alba* "nicht aus der geistlichen Weckhymne entstanden sein kann." Alfred Jeanroy was of two minds on the subject. In *Les origines de la poésie lyrique en France au moyen-âge* (Paris, 1889), p. 74, he suggested that the religious dawn-hymns may have aided in the development of the erotic *alba*. But in *La Poésie lyrique des Troubadours* (Toulouse and Paris, 1934), II, 293, he declared that "les hymnes de ce genre, qui, sous des plumes savantes, celles de saint Ambroise et de Prudence, par exemple, s'amplifiaient en développements mystiques et allégoriques, n'exercèrent naturellement aucune influence sur les aubes profanes . . . ." Phrased in terms of "influences" and "origins," the problem of the relationship between the dawn-hymns and the erotic *albas* is essentially insoluble.

59. See, for example, Nicklas, *Untersuchungen*, p. 76: "Die eigenartige Erscheinung, dass man hier Gott zum Schützer des Ehebruchs anruft, darf wohl als Naivität der Minnesänger ausgelegt werden."

60. Ed. Kolsen, I, 346. This is the last strophe of Giraut's *alba* as the poem is given to us in MSS. R and T. For a discussion as to the authenticity of this strophe, and as to the legitimacy of analyzing the poem as though the strophe were authentic, see Appendix B.

61. "En un vergier," in Hatto, *Eos*, p. 358.

62. Kristan von Hamle, "Ich bin der der lieben liebiu maere singet," in *DL*, I, 224.

63. Bruno von Hornberg, "Swer tougenlicher minne pflege," in *DL*, I, 24.

64. See Günther Müller, "Gradualismus: Eine Vorstudie zur altdeutschen Literaturgeschichte," *DVLG*, II (1924), 681–720; Friedrich Ranke, *Gott, Welt und Humanität in der deutschen Dichtung des Mittelalters* (Basel, 1952); Gottfried Weber, *Parzival: Ringen und Vollendung* (Oberursel, 1948); Koppitz, *Wolframs Religiosität*, especially pp. 280–88.

65. *MF*, p. 47.

66. *MF*, p. 116. See Ranke, *Gott, Welt und Humanität*, pp. 22 ff., for his discussion of these citations.

67. Felix Schlösser, *Andreas Capellanus: seine Minnelehre und das christliche Weltbild um 1200* (Bonn, 1960), pp. 383 ff.

68. For two quite different explanations of the structure of Andreas's treatise, see W. T. H. Jackson, "The *De Amore* of Andreas Capellanus and the Practice of Love at Court," *Romanic Review*, XLIX (1958), pp. 243–51; and Durant W. Robertson, Jr., "The subject of the *De amore* of Andreas Capellanus," *Modern Philology*, L (1952–1953), 145–61. Schlösser fails to take into account Andreas's witty relationship to literary traditions, both in the first two books, where Andreas is imitating Ovid, and in the third, where he is retailing the conventional rhetorical wares of medieval antifeminism.

69. See Luigi Barzini, *The Italians* (New York, 1964).

70. Schlösser, *Andreas Capellanus*, p. 385. One of the sources of Schlösser's interpretation is Alexander J. Denomy, *The Heresy of Courtly Love* (New York, 1947), who extends these ideas to troubadour lyric in general. "There is no

indication, implied or explicit, that the troubadours were conscious of anything shocking, irreverent or disrespectful in invoking the divine assistance and the aid of holy persons and holy things to further their quest for what, in Christian eyes, is sinful and immoral. Likewise there is no indication that they were conscious of the sinfulness or the immorality of their conception of love, even of their pure love. On the contrary. As a matter of fact, they were not at all concerned with the Christian concept of the morality of human love, at least in their poems. They simply did not advert to it, or, if they did, they ignored it. Courtly love is neither moral nor immoral. It is amoral in the sense that it is wholly divorced from Christian morality" (Denomy, pp. 27–28). Denomy sees the source of this attitude in the so-called Latin Averroist tradition, a theory in which Schlösser does not set great stock. As for Denomy's analysis of the attitudes in troubadour poetry, I think it is applicable to a certain extent to the *alba*, but it does not tell the whole story, as I hope to indicate.

71. Eduard Wechssler, *Das Kulturproblem des Minnesangs* (Halle, 1909), p. 321: "Eben damals hatten die Troubadours, als die Sprecher der Hofkreise, eine neue Anschauung vom Leben gewonnen. Es war eine Umwertung der Werte vollzogen, eine neue Weltanschauung verkündigt worden, im offenen Gegensatz zur Kirche. . . . Statt der Askese wurde die Lebensfreude nicht nur als Recht, sondern als vornehmste Pflicht des gebildeten Mannes und der gebildeten Frau hingestellt. . . . Damals zuerst gab man der sexuellen Liebe ihre Rechte wieder und liess die geschmähte Natur an ihren Platz zurückkehren. . . . Einst war den Vätern der Kirche die *concupiscentia carnis* als das Brandmal der menschlichen *natura vitiata* erschienen; jetzt erklang aus der heiteren Provence eine neue Heilsbotschaft, dass edle Liebe von Mann und Weib der Quell und Ursprung alles Guten sei."

72. Julius Schwietering, "Der Tristan Gottfrieds von Strassburg und die Bernhardische Mystik," and the relevant section in his *Die deutsche Dichtung des Mittelalters*, 2nd ed. (Darmstadt, 1957).

73. In *Die Allegorie der Minnegrotte* and *Gott, Welt und Humanität*. In the latter, Ranke declares that Gottfried von Strassburg is no longer a medieval Christian.

74. Gottfried Weber, *Gottfrieds von Strassburg Tristan und die Krise des hochmittelalterlichen Weltbildes um 1200* (Stuttgart, 1953), I, 301.

75. For a critique of Wechssler, see Gilson, *La théologie mystique de saint Bernard*, pp. 193–215. For critiques of Weber: Max Wehrli, "Der Tristan Gottfrieds von Strassburg," *Trivium*, IV (1946), 81–117; Jean Fourquet, "Littérature courtoise et théologie," *EG*, XII (1957), 34–39; Hans Eggers, "Grundriss und Aufbau von Gottfried Webers Tristanwerk," *Euphorion*, XLVIII (1954), 473–84; Eduard Neumann, "Zum Problem einer mittelaltergemässen Tristan-Interpretation," *Euphorion*, XLVIII (1954), 484–90; Rainer Gruenter, "Gottfried Weber, *Gottfrieds von Strassburg Tristan* . . ." [Review], *Deutsche Literaturzeitung*, LXXV (1954), 267–83. The difficulty of Weber's style has made the controversy over his ideas that much the more acute.

D. W. Robertson, Jr., in a number of writings of which *A Preface to Chaucer: Studies in Medieval Perspectives* (Princeton, 1963) is the most comprehensive, has sought to prove that a serious medieval poem expressing opposition to

Christian doctrine is a logical impossibility; but his arguments do not relate directly to the poems Wechssler, Schwietering, and Weber were concerned with.

76. "Ode to a Nightingale," lines 51–56.

77. The immediate sources seem to be Novalis and Schopenhauer.

78. Richard Wagner, *Tristan und Isolde* (London, Mainz, Zürich, and New York: Edition Eulenburg, n.d.), pp. 535–47.

79. Charles Baudelaire, *Les Fleurs du Mal*, ed. Ernest Raynaud (Paris: Garnier, 1954), p. 270.

CHAPTER THREE: THE WATCHMAN AND THE LADY

1. For example, E. Stengel, "Der Entwicklungsgang der provenzalischen Alba," *ZfrPh*, IX (1885), 407–12.

2. For example, Gaston Paris, in his review (part 3) of Jeanroy's *Origines*; Leo Spitzer, "The Mozarabic Lyric and Theodor Frings' Theories," *Comparative Literature*, IV (1952), 1–22.

For the theory that the genre of women's laments is of folk origin, see Eugenio Asencio, *Poética y realidad en el cancionero peninsular* . . . (Madrid, 1957); Erich Auerbach, "Frings, Theodor. Minnesinger und Troubadours" [Review], *Romance Philology*, IV (1950–1951), 65–67; Friedrich Brachmann, "Zu den Minnesängern," *Germania*, XXXI (1886), 443–86; Irénée M. Cluzel, "Les jarŷas et l'*amour courtois*," *CN*, XX (1960), 233–50; Theodor Frings, "Frauenstrophe und Frauenlied in der frühen deutschen Lyrik," *Festschrift Hermann August Korff* (Leipzig, 1957), pp. 13–28; Manuel Rodrigues Lapa, *Lições de Literatura Portuguesa, Época Medieval* (Lisbon, 1934), pp. 111–32; Dimitri Scheludko, "Beiträge zur Volksliedertheorie," *ZfSL*, LII (1929), 1–38 and 201–66.

3. For example, Jeanroy, *Origines*, pp. 61–83.

4. *Der Trobador Cadenet*, ed. Appel, pp. 76–83 and 113. The text of the poem is on pp. 80–81. (Part of the fifth strophe was quoted earlier, in my Chapter Two.)

5. See, aside from Appel's notes, the somewhat fuller treatment in Brian Woledge's section of Hatto's *Eos*, pp. 383–84.

6. *The Castell of Perseverance*, in F. J. Furnivall and A. W. Pollard, eds. *The Macro Plays*, Early English Text Society, Extra Series, No. 91 (London, 1904), pp. 75–186. The speeches of Mundus, Belyal, and Caro are on pp. 82–85.

7. Gaston Paris, in his review of Jeanroy's *Origines*.

8. Alwin Schultz, *Das höfische Leben zur Zeit der Minnesinger* (Leipzig, 1889), I, 608 ff., assumed that such night visits were a common occurrence in the twelfth and thirteenth centuries, and he took each *alba* as autobiographical and true. When he says, "Der Burggraf von Lüenz besticht ihn [den Wächter] durch Vermittelung einer Jungfrau seiner Geliebten und wird von ihm des Abends eingelassen" (p. 609), he is not speaking figuratively, but is describing what he believes to have been a real event in the life of this poet. Eduard Kück, "Zu Wolframs Liedern," *Beiträge*, XXII (1897), 94–114, considered all of Wolfram's lyrics to be autobiographical records, including the five *albas*. Friedrich Diez, *Die Poesie der Troubadours* (Leipzig, 1883), p. 133, believed that either the *alba* sprang from actual night visits and dawn-partings, involving actual watchmen, or, if it did

not, it became such a popular literary genre as actually *to give rise* to such visits and separations!

9. Nicklas, *Untersuchungen*, pp. 71–72: "Da kann man zur Erklärung wohl mit Recht annehmen, dass der Sänger, dem eine Erfüllung seiner ständigen Bitten, eine Verwirklichung seiner glühendsten Träume niemals zur Wirklichkeit werden konnte, nun sich diese Befriedigung einfach in diesem erträumten Erlebnis verschaffte. . . . Gerade weil die Dame nicht so war, wird ihr hier das Wunschlied des Sängers vorgehalten."

10. Hugo Kuhn, "Soziale Realität und dichterische Fiktion am Beispiel der höfischen Ritterdichtung Deutschlands," in Carl Brinkmann, ed. *Soziologie und Leben* (Tübingen, 1952), pp. 195–219, reprinted in Kuhn's *Dichtung und Welt im Mittelalter* (Stuttgart, 1959), pp. 22–40, emphasizes the fictional character of medieval lyric and romance. Leo Spitzer, "Salvatore Santangelo, *L'amore lontano di Jaufre Rudel* . . . ." [Review], *Romania*, LXXV (1954), 396–402, and Stanislaw Stronski, *La Poésie et la réalité aux temps des troubadours* (Oxford, 1943), oppose the autobiographical interpretation of troubadour poetry. Jean Fourquet, "Thèses sur le Minnesang," *EG*, IX (1954), 1–15, suggests the analogy with opera.

11. Georg Schlaeger, *Studien über das Tagelied* (Jena, 1895), first pointed to this poem as a source for the *alba*, and especially for the watchman. Julius Schwietering, "Einwürkung der Antike auf die Entstehung des frühen deutschen Minnesangs," *ZfdA*, LXI (1924), 61–82, agreed with him. Alfred Jeanroy, "Studien über das Tagelied . . . von G. Schlaeger" [Review], *Romania*, XXIV (1895), 287–89, rejected Schaeger's thesis.

12. Ovid, *Heroides and Amores*, ed. Grant Showerman, Loeb Classical Library (London and Cambridge, Mass., 1914), p. 252 (*Heroides* xviii.115–17). There is a charming Middle High German version of Ovid's poem, which follows the original closely and does not elaborate on the *alba*-like moment. See Friedrich Heinrich von der Hagen, ed. *Gesamtabenteuer: Hundert altdeutsche Erzählungen* (Stuttgart and Tübingen, 1850; reprinted Darmstadt, 1961), I, 324. In another narrative in this collection, "Irregang und Girregar" (III, 124), there is a real medieval *alba* embedded in the story.

13. Compare Habakkuk ii.1–3.

14. English *to watch* derives from a variant form of Old English *wacian* 'to wake'. 'To be awake', 'to be on the watch', 'to look', and 'to guard', are the meanings associated in this word. The expression *watch and ward* redoubles all these meanings. Related meanings derived from *wardôn* can been seen in French *garder* 'to keep' and German *warten* 'to wait'. Latin *vigil* and *vigilia* also associated the ideas of wakefulness, watchfulness, and protection; as a substantive, *vigil* means 'watchman', and *vigilia* is the collective 'the watch, watchmen'. *Vigilare* and *custodire* have very similar meanings, as the quotation from Psalm cxxvi shows, although in *vigilare* the main emphasis seems to be on the "wakefulness" aspect of standing on watch, while *custodire* seems rather to emphasize the "protection" aspect. Old Provençal *guaita, gaita* 'watchman' (< *wahtôn*, cf. Old English *wacian*, etc.) and Middle High German *wahter* (of the same meaning and the same word family) both contain all of the associated ideas we have been speaking of.

15. *Analecta hymnica*, L, No. 24, Strophe 4.

16. Valency, *In Praise of Love*, p. 172.

17. Hatto, *Eos*, p. 277.

18. It is seemingly these same ideas and metaphors that we find in the some-what mysterious tenth-century (?) poem, "Phoebi claro," often referred to as the "bi-lingual *alba*." The important line, for our purposes, is "spiculator pigris clamat 'surgite'," which seems to reiterate the notion we have seen in Prudentius of Christ as watchman calling upon sinners to awake out of their sleep of sin. That this is a religious dawn-song, in the fourth-century tradition, is the opinion of Becker, "Vom geistlichen Tagelied," p. 300; Singer, *Die religiöse Lyrik des Mittelalters*, p. 50; Scheludko, "Beiträge . . . [Die mittellateinische Theorie]," p. 203; and many others. Johannes Schmidt, "Die älteste Alba," *ZfdPh*, XII (1881), 333–41, claimed that "Phoebi claro," which he had discovered in a Vatican manuscript, was the first erotic *alba*, but this interpretation has been generally rejected by later scholars. See the discussion, with further bibliography, in Hatto, *Eos*, pp. 77–78. The text of the poem can be most conveniently found in *Eos*, p. 280.

19. Cornelius, *Figurative Castle*, pp. 52–54.

20. Mechthild von Magdeburg, to give another example, depicts a spiritual cloister whose doorkeeper is "die huote," a word which combines the meanings of watchfulness and protection. Mechthild's allegory can be found in *Offenbarung der Schwester Mechthild von Magdeburg, oder Das fliessende Licht der Gottheit*, ed. P. Gall Morel (Regensburg, 1869; reprinted Darmstadt, 1963), p. 251 (Siebenter Theil, Cap. XXXVI).

21. Sometimes, however, a watchman stationed on the walls may also take on the function of a doorkeeper, in charge of admitting visitors to the town or castle. See Chrétien de Troyes, *Le chevalier au lion* (*Yvain*), ed. Mario Roques (Paris, 1965), lines 4875–81, where a "guete" who has been blowing his horn from atop the walls comes down to open the gate for a young lady. The fact that he must leave his watchman's post in order to open the gate shows that the two functions, while compatible, are nevertheless quite distinct.

22. *De anima, Liber Quartus*, P. L., CLXXVII, cols. 165–90. The allegory is in Cap. XIII–XVI (cols. 185–90).

23. *De anima*, col. 185.

24. For the medieval *topos* of *sapientia et fortitudo*, which resembles closely this combination of qualities in the watchman, see Ernst Robert Curtius, *European Literature and the Latin Middle Ages*, trans. Willard R. Trask (New York: Harper Torchbooks, 1963), pp. 173–78. We should note that the relation of this *topos*, and of the watchman's twofold function, to Hugh's allegory is not clear-cut, since Hugh also associates Justitia with the guard at the door. On the allegorical level, justice may understandably have a part in the proper operation of conscience; but how this figure functions in the defense of the house—on the literal level—is not clear.

25. J. A. W. Bennett and G. V. Smithers, eds. *Early Middle English Verse and Prose* (Oxford, 1966), p. 249.

26. Text in Raby, *Secular Latin Poetry*, I, 289.

27. For information on the historical circumstances, the question of date, and

various textual matters, see Aurelio Roncaglia, "Il 'Canto delle scolte modanesi'," *CN*, VIII (1948), 5–46.

28. *Der Münchener Oswald*, ed. Georg Baesecke (Breslau, 1907), lines 1643–45.

29. Herbort von Fritzlar, *Liet von Troye*, ed. G. K. Frommann (Quedlinburg and Leipzig, 1837), p. 77 (lines 6655–62). I have expanded the contractions and changed the orthography slightly.

30. *Liet von Troye*, pp. 48–49 (lines 4175–202).

31. Herbort's poem cannot be dated more precisely than between 1190 and 1217. See de Boor, *Die höfische Literatur* (*Geschichte der deutschen Literatur*, II), pp. 49–50, where a date quite early in this period is suggested. If Herbort was drawing on the *Tagelied*, which of course is much more likely than the reverse possibility, his familiarity with the *Tagelied* style would suggest a later rather than an earlier date. Herbort's source, the *Roman de Troie* of Benoît de Sainte-Maure, has nothing equivalent to this watchman and his "tageliet," although Benoît does mention "gaites" elsewhere. See Bartsch, "Die romanischen und deutschen Tagelieder," pp. 250–317.

32. Heinrich von dem Türlin, *Diu crône*, ed. G. H. F. Scholl (Stuttgart, 1852), lines 5379–86.

33. *Diu crône*, lines 20738–42.

34. For example, in the collection of texts by Ernst Scheunemann and Friedrich Ranke, eds. *Texte zur Geschichte des deutschen Tagelieds* (Bern, 1947), the watchman is specifically placed on the *zinne* in Nos. 15, 31, 33, 34, 38, 43, 44. Numerous other examples, particularly from the later Middle Ages, could be cited.

35. Opening lines of the *Tagelied* by the Margrave von Hohenburg, in *DL*, I, 177.

36. *Liederbuch der Clara Hätzlerin*, ed. Carl Haltaus (Quedlinburg and Leipzig, 1840), Part Two, p. 17 ("Ich wachter will nun singen," lines 43–44).

37. Cf. Gaston Paris, in his review (part 3) of Jeanroy's *Origines*, p. 167: "Le petit drame à trois personnages où le veilleur joue son étrange rôle n'est là qu'un pur symbolisme exprimant la douceur des amours furtives et les amertumes qui en sont inséparables." I am trying to be more specific about the watchman's symbolic function than Gaston Paris was; but his insights into the meaning of this genre are not to be slighted.

38. "Swer tougenlîche minne hât," in Karl Bartsch, ed. *Die Schweizer Minnesänger* (Frauenfeld, 1886; reprinted Darmstadt, 1964), p. 176.

39. The relevant passage from the *Frauendienst*, along with Ulrich's *alba*, is reprinted in Scheunemann and Ranke, *Texte*, pp. 15–19.

40. For an account of other "realistic" treatments of the watchman, see Helmut de Boor, *Die deutsche Literatur im späten Mittelalter, Zerfall und Neubeginn, Erster Teil: 1250–1350* (*Geschichte der deutschen Literatur*, ed. Helmut de Boor and Richard Newald, Vol. III, Part I [Munich, 1964]), p. 347.

41. Jeanroy, *Origines*, p. 74, and Gaston Paris in his review of Jeanroy's book (part 3), pp. 161–64, were convinced that the bird-*albas* were the earliest, and that the watchman was a later addition. This notion, and the kind of reasoning that led to it, were severely criticized by Charles Read Baskerville, "English Songs on the Night Visit," *PMLA*, XXXVI (1921), 565–614.

42. Text in Hatto, *Eos*, p. 370. See also Victor Smith, "Vieilles chansons

recueillies en Velay et en Forez," *Romania*, VII (1878), 52–84; Smith suggests (p. 57) that this poem is the source of Juliet's *alba* (*Romeo and Juliet* III.v).

43. *Eos*, p. 370. I have changed the punctuation slightly.

44. Richard M. Meyer, "Walthers zweites Tagelied," *ZfdA*, XLIX [= Neue Folge, XXXVII] (1908), 385–94, goes so far as to class "Under der linden" as an *alba*; but the poem lacks almost all of the crucial ingredients of the *alba*: night, dawn, and the grief of parting.

45. *DL*, I, 596.

46. Hatto, *Eos*, p. 358.

47. The text of this anonymous poem is edited by Johannes Bolte, "Zum deutschen Volksliede: 36–42," *Zeitschrift des Vereins für Volkskunde*, XXI (1911), 76–79 (Poem No. 38).

48. Text in Max Wehrli, ed. *Deutsche Lyrik de Mittelalters* (Zürich, 1955), pp. 44–48.

49. See Franz Magnus Böhme, ed. *Altdeutsches Liederbuch* (Leipzig, 1877), p. 223.

50. "En un vergier," in Hatto, *Eos*, p. 358. (Previously quoted in my Chapter Two.)

51. *Hätzlerin*, p. 3 ("Ich Tummer wachter tritt daher," lines 76–78).

52. Böhme, *Altdeutsches Liederbuch*, p. 220 (Poem No. 120, lines 3–4).

53. See the lists in De Gruyter, *Das deutsche Tagelied*, pp. 35, 63, 107.

54. See Valency, *In Praise of Love*, pp. 67–68; Andreas Capellanus, *The Art of Courtly Love*, trans. John Jay Parry (New York, 1941), pp. 200–209; Francis Lee Utley, *The Crooked Rib: An Analytical Index to the Argument about Women in English and Scots Literature to the End of the Year 1568* (Columbus, Ohio, 1944); August Wulff, *Die frauenfeindlichen Dichtungen in den romanischen Literaturen des Mittelalters* . . . (Halle, 1914).

55. See above, Chapter Three, Note 2.

56. "Gegen dem morgen suoze ein wahter lûte sanc," in Bartsch, *Schweizer Minnesänger*, pp. 132–33.

57. Sigmund Freud, "Formulierungen über die zwei Prinzipien des psychischen Geschehens," *GW*, VIII, 230–38; see also the remarks on the two principles in "Jenseits des Lustprinzips," *GW*, XIII, 3–6.

58. *DL*, I, 177–78. I have slightly altered the punctuation, following Hatto, *Eos*, pp. 457–58.

59. See Hans Walther, *Das Streitgedicht in der lateinischen Literatur des Mittelalters* (Munich, 1920); also Max Manitius, *Geschichte der lateinischen Literatur des Mittelalters*, III (Munich, 1931; reprinted 1964), 944–63; and Raby, *Secular Latin Poetry*, II, 282–308.

60. For some brilliantly frivolous examples, see Milton's prolusions, especially the first (which is pertinent to some of the subjects we discussed in Chapter Two): "Whether Day or Night is the More Excellent." Of course, the ultimate purpose of these exercises is education in eloquence, which may eventually be put to public use.

61. Note the close resemblances in structure between Rabelais's parody of a judicial process (*Pantagruel*, Chapters 11–13) and his parody of a Humanistic philosophical debate (*Pantagruel*, Chapters 18–20).

62. Text in Charles H. Beeson, ed. *A Primer of Medieval Latin* (New York, 1925), pp. 320–22.

63. Text edited by A. Bömer, "Das Vagantenlied von Phyllis und Flora nach einer Niederschrift des ausgehenden 12. Jahrhunderts," *ZfdA*, Neue Folge, LVI (1919), pp. 217 ff.

64. Ed. Eric Gerald Stanley (London, 1960).

65. Ed. Israel Gollancz (London, 1920).

66. Text in Emerson, *Middle English Reader*, pp. 47–64.

67. William Roy Mackenzie, *The English Moralities from the Point of View of Allegory* (Boston, 1914), distinguishes between two kinds of structure in Christian allegory. The first, the structure of Prudentius's *Psychomachia*, simply opposes the virtues and the vices, who combat with each other for supremacy. The second kind of structure, which is the one found in most of the English moralities, is of the more complex sort we have been speaking of: the conflict of virtues and vices for the possession of man, who is a central character between the two opposing groups. See Mackenzie, pp. 57–179.

68. Furnivall, *Macro Plays*, p. 87. The emendation is mine.

69. *Macro Plays*, p. 90.

70. *The Merchant of Venice*, II.ii.1 ff.

71. Wenzel von Behein, "Ez taget unmâzen schône," in *DL*, I, 586–87.

72. Latin text: Saint Augustine, *Confessions*, ed. Pierre de Labriolle (Paris, 1944), I, 184–86 (Lib. VIII, Cap. v, 10 and 12). Translation: *The Confessions of St. Augustine*, trans. John K. Ryan (New York: Image Books, 1960), pp. 188–90.

73. Augustine's direct source for this image is Ephesians v.8–14, another of the numerous New Testament passages employing the darkness-light metaphor.

74. The idea is Saint Paul's:

. . . non enim quod volo bonum, hoc ago: sed quod odi malum, illud facio.

. . . for it is not what I wish that I do, but what I hate, that I do.

(Romans vii.15)

No notion could be more quintessentially Pauline and Augustinian than this concept of the divided will. Yet is appears in classical literature as well, for example in Ovid:

. . . aliudque cupido,
mens aliud suadet: video meliora proboque,
deteriora sequor. . . .

. . . I desire one thing;
my mind urges me toward another. I see the better things and approve of them;
I follow the worse things. . . .

(*Metamorphoses* vii.19–21)

This is Medea speaking, and her problem is that she cannot resist her love for Jason. The psychological structure is the same in both of these quotations. The crucial difference between the two is the fact that while, for Medea, the cause of her divided will lies in the opposition of some god ("nescio quis deus obstat"), for Paul and Augustine the cause lies in the innate sinfulness of fallen mankind. The ultimate source of both Augustine's and Ovid's notion of the divided will may be Plato's *Phaedrus*, with its image of the charioteer and the two contrary-minded horses. (Ovid may also have been influenced by Euripides's *Medea*, where, however, Medea's division of will relates to her taking revenge on Jason, rather than to her falling in love with him.)

75. The dangers of allegorizing secular works on the basis of a supposed relation to some theological system could not be more effectively demonstrated than by Denis de Rougemont, who suggests that the *alba* is a Catharist poem, and that the knight represents the soul, the friend or watchman represents the flesh, and the lady represents the spirit (*L'Amour et l'Occident*, p. 72).

76. Nevertheless, its thematic resemblances to the medieval *albas* have inclined some scholars to consider it the source of the medieval *alba*. For a discussion of Ovidian influences on troubadour poetry in general, see two articles by Dimitri Scheludko, "Beiträge zur Entstehungsgeschichte der altprovenzalischen Lyrik: klassisch-lateinische Theorie," *AR*, XI (1927), 273–312, and "Ovid und die Troubadours," *ZfrPh*, LIV (1934), 129–74. My own interest, as usual, is in assessing the difference in the treatment of similar motifs and in pointing out the meanings conveyed by the individual poems, rather than in positing genetic relationships.

77. *Heroides and Amores*, Loeb Classical Library, pp. 368–72.

78. The irony is all the greater if we consider the poet's situation here in the light of the Amphitryon myth, which no doubt lies in the back of his mind. What a man desires to do, a god *can* do: prolong the night for his own erotic enjoyment. But this magical act, which turns the optative subjunctive (contrary to fact) into a jussive subjunctive ("Let the night be longer!") *which is obeyed*, is possible only to a god. A mere mortal can only make the wish; he cannot make it come true. See Walter Muschg, *Tragische Literaturgeschichte*, 3rd ed. (Bern, 1957), pp. 445–46. (We may note that once Jupiter has had his fill of pleasure with Alcmena he permits the night to give way, at last, to the day; so that the first part of Plautus's play ends with a mock-pathetic parting at dawn [lines 500–50].)

79. I do not mean to imply that the kind of "Christian" thought structure we have been speaking of is entirely absent from classical literature. *Aeneid* iv shows us a very similar kind of structure, with a sensual lady opposed by the voice of duty, and a rather passive man forced to choose between them. Vergil's sense of historical destiny supplies the dynamic element which is absent in Ovid's ironic view of the world. The structure also appears, to a greater or lesser degree, in other works of Ovid, in Euripides, and in Plato, as I pointed out earlier.

CHAPTER FOUR: TIME

1. For Augustine's philosophy of time see Frank Herbert Brabant, *Time and Eternity in Christian Thought* (London, 1937); John Francis Callahan, *Four Views of Time in Ancient Philosophy* (Cambridge, Mass., 1948); J. Chaix-Ruy, "Le problème du temps dans les *Confessions* et dans *La Cité de Dieu*," *Giornale di Metafisica*, IX (1954), 464–77; Jean Guitton, *Le temps et l'éternité chez Plotin*

et Saint Augustin, 3rd ed. (Paris, 1959); Erich Lampey, *Das Zeitproblem nach den Bekenntnissen Augustins* (Regensburg, 1960). Important works on the philosophy of time in general are Ferdinand Alquié, *Le désir d'éternité*, 3rd ed. (Paris, 1960); G. Boas, *The Acceptance of Time*, University of California Publications in Philosophy, XVI, No. 12 (Berkeley, 1950), pp. 249–70; Hedwig Conrad-Curtius, *Die Zeit* (Munich, 1954); Werner Gent, *Das Problem der Zeit* (Frankfurt a. M., 1934; reprinted Hildesheim, 1965); idem, *Die Philosophie des Raumes und der Zeit*, 2nd ed. (Hildesheim, 1962); Jean Guitton, *Man in Time*, trans. Adrienne Foulke (Notre Dame, 1966); Louis Lavelle, *Du temps et de l'éternité* (Paris, 1945). See also the brilliant studies of Georges Poulet, *Études sur le temps humain* (Paris, 1952.)

2. Saint Augustine, *De civitate dei*, P. L., XLI, col. 394 (Lib. XIII, Cap. xx). Translation: *The City of God*, trans. Marcus Dods (New York, 1950), p. 430.

3. *De civitate dei*, col. 396 (Lib. XIII, Cap. xxiii). Trans. Dods, p. 433.

4. Ibid.

5. Augustine offers an allegorical interpretation of Adam's choice which sees the various characters as psychological faculties. Adam is superior reason, which has access to the eternal truths symbolized by God's warning ("Rationis autem pars superior aeternis rationibus conspiciendis vel consulendis adhaerescit . . ."). Eve is the lower reason, which interprets the things of this world. The serpent is sensuality, distinct from the lower reason (Eve) but closely allied with it. The higher reason, forced to choose between the word of God and the temptations of sensuality as relayed by the lower reason, succumbs to temptation and falls. See *De trinitate*, Lib. XII, Cap. xii, *P. L.*, XLII, cols. 1007–1008. The quotation is from the summary of Augustine's allegorization in Peter Lombard, *Sententiarum libri quattuor*, ed. J.-P. Migne (Paris, 1841), cols. 192–96 (Lib. II, Dist. xxiv, Cap. 5–11). The structure of this allegory naturally resembles that of Augustine's portrayal of the divided will, in the *Confessions*, as well as that of the *alba* seen as a dramatization of the problem of choice. The resemblance is not exact, however, because the Eden story contains four characters (Adam, Eve, God, and the serpent) while the passage in the *Confessions* and the *alba* each contain only three ("I," the spiritual will, and the carnal will—or the knight, the watchman, and the lady). In the Eden story, Adam, God, and the serpent are interrelated much in the manner of the other trios; Eve occupies an intermediate position between Adam, out of whose body she has been made, and the serpent (sensuality), who is "close" to her. See Augustine's own discussion of the difficulties in allegorization this fourth character causes, in *De trinitate*, Lib. XII, Cap. xiii (cols. 1008–9).

6. There is an equivalent to the exile from Eden in the spiritual life of every sinful man. The world of concupiscence is thought of as a place of exile from God, man's true home; to love the things of this world for their own sake is to exile oneself from one's true identity. Augustine (*Confessions* VII.x.16) and Saint Bernard (*De diversis*, Sermo XLII, 2, *P. L.*, CLXXXIII, col. 662) call this place of spiritual and moral exile the "regio dissimilitudinis." See Gilson, *La théologie mystique de saint Bernard*, p. 63. In the *alba*, the love chamber is the knight's true home, where he finds his identity as a lover; his exile from it constitutes a loss of spiritual identity.

7. *De civitate dei*, Lib. XIV, Cap. x, xvii, xxiii, xxiv.

8. "Pudet igitur hujus libidinis humanam sine ulla dubitatione naturam, et merito pudet. In eius quippe inobedientia, quae genitalia corporis membra solis suis motibus subdidit, et potestati voluntatis eripuit, satis ostenditur quid sit hominis illi primae inobedientiae retributum." *De civitate dei*, Lib. XIV, Cap. xx (col. 428).

9. And not only in sexual activity, but in all experiences of passionate love. Cf. Karl Jaspers, *Von der Wahrheit: Philosophische Logik*, I (Munich, 1947), 991: "In jeder Weise der Liebe erwacht ein Bewusstsein der Ewigkeit oder doch der Tilgung der Zeit" (quoted in Furstner, *Studien zur Wesensbestimmung der höfischen Minne*, p. 49). For literary examples of this subjective time-sense of persons in love, see Furstner, pp. 158 ff.

10. Cf. Guitton, *Man in Time*, p. 25: the separation of lovers is a shock "as if eternity had been rent asunder." The shock, and the sense of time suddenly intruding itself into a subjective experience of timelessness, are both characteristic of interrupted orgasm.

11. Freud, "Das Unbehagen in der Kultur," *GW*, XIV, 424–25.

12. Freud, "Das Ich und das Es," *GW*, XIII, 288–89.

13. *De vera religione*, in *Corpus Christianorum, Series Latina*, XXXII (Turnhout, 1962), p. 230 (Cap. xxxv, 65).

14. *In Joannis Evangelium, P. L.*, XXXV, col. 1680 (Tractatus XXXVIII, Cap. 10). The source of these notions is Plato's *Timaeus* (38).

15. *De trinitate, P. L.*, XLII, col. 1022 (Lib. XIII, Cap. viii, N. 11). The idea goes back to Plato's *Symposium*.

16. *Confessions*, ed. Pierre de Labriolle, II, 305–6 (Lib. XI, Cap. xi, 13). Trans. Ryan, p. 285.

17. *Roman de la Rose*, ed. Langlois, V, 25–26 (lines 20002–26). Compare Guillaume de Lorris's eloquent lines on the depredations of tragic time in the world of nature, II, 20–21 (lines 361–91). The contrast of these two passages and of the differing concepts of time they present is intentional on Jean's part.

18. Horace, *Odes* II.xiv.

19. Shakespeare, *Sonnet* lx.

20. Ronsard, "Je vous envoye un bouquet," in *Oeuvres complètes*, ed. Gustave Cohen (Paris, 1950), II, 814.

21. Iacopo Sannazaro, "Ad ruinas Cumarum, urbis vetustissimae," in Francesco Arnaldi et al., eds. *Poeti latini del Quattrocento* (Milan and Naples, 1964), pp. 1138–40.

22. Tasso, *Gerusalemme liberata* XV.xx.

23. Ronsard, "Mignonne, allons voir si la rose," in *Oeuvres complètes*, ed. Cohen, I, 419–20.

24. Lorenzo de' Medici. Text in Augusto Sainati, ed. *Le opere degli scrittori italiani*, I (Florence, 1964), 945.

25. Horace, *Odes* I.xi.

26. Horace, *Odes* III.xxx.

27. Shakespeare, *Sonnet* lv.

28. Ronsard, "Élégie II: A Philippes Des-Portes, Chartrain." in *Oeuvres complètes*, ed. Cohen, II, 647–49. Cf. Horace, *Ars poetica*, lines 63 ff.

29. Ibid.

30. See Appendix B for a discussion of the textual problems of this poem.

31. Ed. Kolsen, I, 342–46. I have slightly changed the punctuation.

32. Freud, *Neue Folge der Vorlesungen zur Einführung in die Psychoanalyse*, *GW*, XV, 80–81.

33. See Guitton, *Man in Time*, pp. 23–25.

34. See Mohr, "Wolframs Tagelieder."

35. This latter possibility suggests an additional meaning. "Lôn" is the word used in the usual love song to designate the reward the lover hopes to receive from his lady: her greeting, her affection, her kiss, and perhaps "anders." Here love would be personified as a lady, as in Gottfried's "gottinne Minne" (*Tristan*, line 16723), Walther von der Vogelweide's "frowe Minne" (Lachmann 40,19), and Wolfram's own "frou minne" (*Parzival* 291.1); both the lovers would be the recipients of her "lôn"; and the "lôn" would consist of their sexual joy together. Even if "minne" is not the subject of the sentence, "lôn" probably refers ironically to the reward longed for by unhappy lovers in the *chanson*.

36. "Slâfst du, friedel ziere?" in *MF*, p. 39.

37. "Ez gienc ein juncfrou minneclîch," in *DL*, I, 251.

38. See Saint Augustine, *De diversis questionibus*, Cap. xxxv: "Quid amandum sit," *P. L.*, XL, cols. 23–25.

39. See Robert E. Kaske, "The Aube in Chaucer's *Troilus*," in Richard J. Schoeck and Jerome Taylor, eds. *Chaucer Criticism*, II (Notre Dame, 1961), 167–79.

40. *Troilus* v.1838–41.

CHAPTER FIVE: THE *ALBA* AND THE *CHANSON*

1. Bernart de Ventadorn, "Be m'an perdut lai enves Ventadorn," ed. Appel, p. 69, lines 22–23.

2. Bernart de Ventadorn, "Lo gens tems de pascor," lines 43–46 (p. 168).

3. Peire Vidal, "Ges del joi que ai no·m rancur," *Les poésies de Peire Vidal*, ed. Joseph Anglade, 2nd ed. (Paris, 1965), p. 6, lines 9–12.

4. Gottfried von Strassburg, *Tristan und Isold*, ed. Friedrich Ranke, 9th printing (Zürich and Berlin, 1965), lines 129–30.

5. See, for example, "Bin ich dir unmaere" (Lachmann 50,19), and "Herzeliebez frowelîn" (Lachmann 49,25), in *Die Gedichte Walthers von der Vogelweide*, ed. Carl von Kraus, 12th ed. (Berlin, 1959), pp. 70–71 and 69–70. See also the commentary in Walther von der Vogelweide, *Sprüche und Lieder: Gesamtausgabe*, ed. Helmut Protze (Halle, 1963), pp. 201 and 203.

6. See the interesting combination of *alba* and crusade song by the Burggrave of Lüenz, in *DL*, I, 250–51. This poem demonstrates the close similarity between the love relationships portrayed in the two genres.

7. See Oskar Streicher, "Verhältnis zwischen Mann und Frau und dichterische Anschauung in der mhd. Lyrik," *ZfdPh*, XXIV (1892), 171–86.

8. See above, Chapter Three, Note 2.

9. See Streicher, "Verhältnis zwischen Mann und Frau," and G. Roethe, "Das deutsche Tagelied von Walter de Gruyter" [Review], *AfdA*, XVI (1890), 75–97.

10. A typical example of the fanciful thinking the theory of folk origins gives rise to is to be found in Friedrich Diez, *Leben und Werke der Troubadours*, 2nd ed., ed. Karl Bartsch (Leipzig, 1882), p. 119, where it is averred that the *alba* of Giraut de Bornelh "etwas von dem Zauber der Volkspoesie an sich trägt." Cannot courtly poetry have had a "Zauber" of its own?

For an interesting and suggestive refinement of the notion of "natural" love, free from the dogmatism of these Romantic scholars, see Alan W. Watts, *Nature, Man, and Woman* (New York, 1958).

11. Pierre Belperron, *La Joie d'Amour: Contribution à l'étude des troubadours et de l'amour courtois* (Paris, 1948), pp. 137 ff., believes that the love felt by the man in the *chanson* may come from an unconscious imitation of the Christian idea of love for God. In my own discussion, as usual, I am concerned with analogies rather than with imitations.

12. For the distinction between these terms, see Anders Nygren, *Agape and Eros: A study of the Christian Idea of Love*, trans. Philip S. Watson (Philadelphia, 1953).

13. Among the numerous studies of this problem we might mention Belperron, *La Joie d'Amour*; Herbert Kolb, *Der Begriff der Minne und das Entstehen der höfischen Lyrik* (Tübingen, 1958); and René Nelli, *L'Érotique des troubadours* (Toulouse, 1963).

14. See Belperron, *La Joie d'Amour*, p. 49; Denomy, *The Heresy of Courtly Love*, p. 26.

15. Bernart de Ventadorn, "Pois preyatz me, senhor," lines 30–36 (ed. Appel, pp. 206–7).

16. "Quan lo rius de la fontana," line 13 (ed. Jeanroy, p. 4).

17. *L'Amour lointain de Jaufré Rudel*, pp. 2, 9, 10, 19, etc. A similar analysis of "courtly love" is to be found in Schlösser, *Andreas Capellanus*, pp. 161 ff. See also K. Rob. V. Wikman, "Dis Einleitung der Ehe," *Acta Academiae Aboensis: Humaniora*, XI (1937), 331: "Die höfische Minne lebte in einer polaren Spannung zwischen Liebe und Entsagung." The implication is that the lover wishes to possess and at the same time wishes to be denied.

18. Emil Nickel, *Studien zum Liebesproblem bei Gottfried von Strassburg*, Königsberger deutsche Forschungen, No. 1 (Königsberg, 1927), p. 68.

19. Wolfram von Eschenbach, "Den morgenblic bî wahters sange erkôs," in *DL*, I, 596.

20. Wolfram, "Ez ist nu tac," in *DL*, I, 601–2.

21. *Canterbury Tales* I. 4234–37. For a delightful article on this parody see Robert E. Kaske, "An Aube in the Reeve's Tale," *ELH*, XXVI (1959), 295–310. Some other parodies of the *alba*: Steinmar, "Ein kneht der lac verborgen," in Bartsch, *Die Schweizer Minnesänger*, pp. 179–80; "Graserin," in Adelbert von Keller, ed. *Altdeutsche Gedichte* (Tübingen, 1846), pp. 4–10; Heinrich Wittenweiler, *Der Ring*, ed. Ludwig Bechstein (Stuttgart, 1851), pp. 189–90; Der Mönch von Salzburg, "Das Kchühorn," in Scheunemann-Ranke, *Texte*, pp. 30–31; "Ain tagweis von lewsen," in Hätzlerin, *Liederbuch*, Part Two, p. 25.

22. "Pro ai del chan essenhadors," lines 17–18 (ed. Jeanroy, p. 7).

23. See Diego Zorzi, "*L'Amor de lonh* di Jaufre Rudel," *Aevum*, XXIX (1955), 124–44. Leo Spitzer, *L'amour lointain de Jaufré Rudel*, deals with the problem as

to whether Jaufré's poems on the "amor de lonh" can be interpreted allegorically as crusade songs. For the present discussion it makes no difference whether the distant lady Jaufré longs for is literal or metaphorical. Jaufré conceives of the relationship between lover and unloving lady in terms of spatial distance, which is all that concerns us here.

24. Valency, *In Praise of Love*, p. 139.

25. Spitzer, *L'amour lointain*, p. 48.

26. Bernart de Ventadorn, ed. Appel, p. 181, lines 1–7.

27. Ed. Jeanroy, pp. 3–5.

28. Ed. Jeanroy, pp. 12–15.

29. Bernart de Ventadorn, ed. Appel, p. 15, lines 1–2.

30. Jaufré Rudel, "Lanquan li jorn son lonc en may," lines 12–14.

31. Bernart de Ventadorn, "Tant ai mo cor ple de joya," lines 49–52 (ed. Appel, p. 262).

32. Heinrich von Morungen, "Mirst geschên als eime kindelîne," in *MF*, pp. 191–2. Here, it is the lady who enters into the lover's world, not the lover who enters into the lady's world (as in the quotation from Bernart de Ventadorn, above). The dream in this poem is not a pure product of the pleasure principle, as it carries with it (in lines not quoted) a sense of imperfection and pain.

33. Jaufré Rudel, "No sap chanter qui so non di," lines 19–20 and 23–24 (ed. Jeanroy, p. 17).

34. Walther von der Vogelweide, "Nemt, frowe, disen kranz," ed. von Kraus, pp. 106–8 (Lachmann 74,20). Note the similarity in the last line to the refrain of Morungen's *alba* (Appendix C). In the *alba*, the dawn interrupts a real night of pleasure, while in these *chansons* it interrupts a night of imagined pleasure.

35. John Milton, *Sonnet* xxiii.

36. Friedrich Hölderlin, *Sämtliche Werke*, ed. Friedrich Beissner (Stuttgart, 1946–1961), III, 73–74.

CONCLUSION

1. "Littérature courtoise et théologie."

APPENDIX B

1. *Sämtliche Lieder des Trobadors Giraut de Bornelh*, ed. Adolf Kolsen, I (Halle, 1910), 342–47, and II (Halle, 1935), 95–96.

2. Joseph Anglade, ed. *Anthologie des Troubadours* (Paris, 1927), pp. 81–82; Carl Appel, ed. *Provenzalische Chrestomathie*, 6th ed. (Leipzig, 1930), pp. 91–92; Karl Bartsch, ed. *Chrestomathie provençale*, 2nd ed. (Elberfeld, 1868), pp. 98–99; Pierre Bec, ed. *Petite Anthologie de la Lyrique Occitane du Moyen Age*, 4th ed. (Avignon, 1966), pp. 152–54; Emil Bohn, "Zwei Trobadorlieder," *Archiv*, CX (1903), 110–24; Jean Cassou, "Le message spirituel des troubadours," *AIEO*, Fasc. 2 (1949), 115–20; Vincenzo Crescini, *Manuale per l'avviamento agli studi provenzali*, 3rd ed. (Milan, 1926), pp. 212–13; Friedrich Diez, *Leben und Werke der Troubadours*, 2nd ed., ed. Karl Bartsch (Leipzig, 1882), p. 119; Alfred Jeanroy, *Les origines de la poésie lyrique en France au moyen-âge* (Paris, 1889), p. 65; Erhard Lommatzsch, ed. *Provenzalisches Liederbuch* (Berlin, 1917), p. 79; René

Nelli and René Lavaud, eds. *Les troubadours*, II: *Le trésor poétique de l'occitanie* (Bruges, 1966), pp. 92–95; Bruno Panvini, "Giraldo di Bornelh; Trovatore del Sec. XII," *Siculorum Gymnasium* (Catania), Gennaio-Giugno 1949, pp. 88–89; Martin de Riquer, ed. *Las albas provenzales* (Barcelona, 1944), not paginated; Ernst Scheunemann and Friedrich Ranke, eds. *Texte zur Geschichte des deutschen Tagelieds* (Bern, 1947), pp. 5–6.

3. Raymond Thompson Hill and Thomas Goddard Bergin, eds. *Anthology of the Provençal Troubadours* (New Haven, 1941), pp. 59–60; Ernest Hoepffner, *Les Troubadours dans leur Vie et dans leurs Oeuvres* (Paris, 1955), pp. 92–93; E. Stengel, "Der Entwicklungsgang der provenzalischen Alba," *ZfrPh*, IX (1885), 407–12; Brian Woledge, "Old Provençal and Old French [*Albas*]," in Arthur T. Hatto, ed. *Eos: An Enquiry into the Theme of Lovers' Meetings and Partings at Dawn in Poetry* (The Hague, 1965), pp. 359 and 381–83.

4. Jeanroy is replying to Stengel, "Entwicklungsgang," who anticipated this argument of Kolsen's by many years.

5. Ed. Appel, pp. 55–56. For other examples of unpaired final strophes in *coblas doblas*, see the table of metrical structures in Appel's introduction to this edition of Bernart, pp. lxxxix-xcvi. The table includes the poems of several troubadours.

6. Bohn, p. 121.

7. The music for the three settings, by Antonio Restori, Bohn, and Pierre Aubry, is printed in Lommatzsch, *Provenzalisches Liederbuch*, pp. 431–33. An example of the differences in setting: for the phrase "Al meu companh siatz fizels ajuda," Restori accents "Al," "panh," "si," "zels," and "da." Bohn accents "Al," "panh," "zels," and "ju." Aubry accents "Al," "panh," "fi," and "ju."

8. See Jeanroy, *Origines*, pp. 63–65, for some adverse comments on Stengel's critical methods.

WORKS CONSULTED

The following list contains only those works bearing directly on the material and methods used in this book. More extensive bibliographies on medieval lyric will be found in the two volumes by de Boor, Kolb's *Der Begriff der Minne*, and Moret's *Les débuts du lyrisme en Allemagne*—all cited below. I have not taken note, here or in the book itself, of anything published after 1968.

Alanus de Insulis. *Liber in distinctionibus dictionum theologicalium.* P. L., CCX, cols. 685–1012.
Alibert, Louis, and René Nelli, eds. *VII Troubadours des Pays d'Aude.* Carcassonne, 1948.
Alquié, Ferdinand. *Le désir d'éternité.* 3rd ed. Paris, 1960.
Das Ambraser Liederbuch vom Jahre 1582, ed. Joseph Bergmann. Stuttgart, 1845.
Analecta hymnica medii aevi, eds. Clemens Blume and Guido Maria Dreves. 55 vols. Leipzig, 1886–1922.
Andreas Capellanus. *The Art of Courtly Love*, trans. John Jay Parry. New York, 1941.
Anglade, Joseph, ed. *Anthologie des Troubadours.* Paris, 1927.
Appel, Carl, ed. *Provenzalische Chrestomathie.* 6th ed. Leipzig, 1930.

——. "Wiederum zu Jaufré Rudel," *Archiv*, CVII (1901), 338–49.

Asencio, Eugenio. *Poética y realidad en el cancionero peninsular*. Madrid, 1957.

Auden, Wystan Hugh. *The Enchafèd Flood; or the Romantic Iconography of the Sea*. New York, 1950.

Auerbach, Erich. "Frings, Theodor. Minnesinger und Troubadours" [Review], *Romance Philology*, IV (1950–1951), 65–67.

Augustine. *Confessions*, ed. Pierre de Labriolle. 2 vols. Paris, 1944.

——. *The Confessions of St. Augustine*, trans. John K. Ryan. New York: Image Books, 1960.

——. *De civitate dei. P. L.*, XLI, cols. 13–804.

——. *The City of God*, trans. Marcus Dods. New York, 1950.

——. *De diversis questionibus. P. L.*, XL, cols. 11–100.

——. *De trinitate. P. L.*, XLII, cols. 819–1098.

——. *De vera religione. Corpus Christianorum, Series Latina*, XXXII (Turnhout, 1962), 169–260.

——. *In Joannis Evangelium. P. L.*, XXXV, cols. 1379–1976.

Bachelard, Gaston. *La poétique de l'espace*. Paris, 1958.

Barthes, Roland. *Sur Racine*. Paris, 1965.

Bartsch, Karl, ed. *Chrestomathie provençale*. 2nd ed. Elberfeld, 1868.

——, ed. *Denkmäler der provenzalischen Literatur*. Stuttgart, 1856.

——, ed. *Romances et pastourelles françaises des XIIe et XIIIe siècles*. Leipzig, 1870.

——. "Die romanischen und deutschen Tagelieder," in his *Gesammelte Vorträge und Aufsätze* (Freiburg i.B. and Tübingen, 1883), pp. 250–317.

——, ed. *Die Schweizer Minnesänger*. Frauenfeld, 1886. Reprinted Darmstadt, 1964.

Baskervill, Charles Read. "English Songs on the Night Visit," *PMLA*, XXXVI (1921), 564–614.

Baudelaire, Charles. *Les Fleurs du Mal*, ed. Ernest Raynaud. Paris: Garnier, 1954.

Bauss, Hermann. *Studien zum Liebesdialog in der höfischen Epik*. Würzburg, 1937.

Bec, Pierre, ed. *Petite Anthologie de la Lyrique Occitane du Moyen Age*. 4th ed. Avignon, 1966.

Becker, Philipp August. "Vom christlichen Hymnus zum Minnesang," *Historisches Jahrbuch im Auftrage der Görres- Gesellschaft*, LII (1932), 1–39. Reprinted in Becker's *Zur romanischen Literaturgeschichte: Ausgewählte Studien und Aufsätze* (Munich, 1967), pp. 14–77.

——. "Vom geistlichen Tagelied," *Volkstum und Kultur der Romanen*, II (1929), 293–302.

——. "Vom Morgenhymnus zum Tagelied," in his *Zur romanischen Literaturgeschichte: Ausgewählte Studien und Aufsätze* (Munich, 1967), pp. 149–73.

Beeson, Charles H. *A Primer of Medieval Latin*. New York, 1925.

Belperron, Pierre. *La Joie d'Amour: Contribution à l'étude des troubadours et de l'amour coutois*. Paris, 1948.

Bernard of Clairvaux. *Sermones de diversis. P. L.*, CLXXXIII, cols. 537–748.

——. *Sermones in Cantica Canticorum. P. L.*, CLXXXIII, cols. 785–1198.

Bernart de Ventadorn. *Bernart von Vantadorn: Seine Lieder*, ed. Carl Appel. Halle, 1915.

Bezzola, Reto R. *Les Origines et la formation de la littérature courtoise en Occident, 500–1200.* IIe partie: *La société féodale et la transformation de la littérature de cour*. Paris, 1960.

Blumenberg, Hans. "Licht als Metapher der Wahrheit: Im Vorfeld der philosophischen Begriffsbildung," *Studium Generale*, X (1957), 432–47.

Boas, George. *The Acceptance of Time*. University of California Publications in Philosophy, Vol. XVI, No. 12 (Berkeley, 1950), pp. 249–70.

Böhme, Franz Magnus, ed. *Altdeutsches Liederbuch*. Leipzig, 1877.

Bömer, A. "Das Vagantenlied von Phyllis und Flora nach einer Niederschrift des ausgehenden 12. Jahrhunderts," *ZfdA*, Neue Folge, LVI (1919), 217 ff.

Boestfleisch, Kurt. *Studien zum Minnegedanken bei Wolfram von Eschenbach*. Königsberger Deutsche Forschungen, No. 8. Königsberg, 1930.

Bohn, Emil. "Zwei Trobadorlieder," *Archiv*, CX (1903), 110–24.

Bolte, Johannes. "Zum deutschen Volksliede: 36–42," *Zeitschrift des Vereins für Volkskunde*, XXI (1911), 74–84.

——. "Zum deutschen Volksliede: 53–66," *Zeitschrift des Vereins für Volkskunde*, XXXV (1925–1926), 25–37.

Brabant, Frank Herbert. *Time and Eternity in Christian Thought*. London, 1937.

Brachmann, Friedrich. "Zu den Minnesängern," *Germania*, XXXI (1886), 443–86.

Brinkmann, Hennig. *Entstehungsgeschichte des Minnesangs. DVLG*, Buchreihe, No. 8. Halle, 1926.

——. *Geschichte der lateinischen Liebesdichtung im Mittelalter*. Halle, 1925.

——. *Zu Wesen und Form mittelalterlicher Dichtung*. Halle, 1928.

Bumke, Joachim. *Wolfram von Eschenbach*. Stuttgart, 1964.

Cadenet. *Der Trobador Cadenet*, ed. Carl Appel. Halle, 1920.

Callahan, John Francis. *Four Views of Time in Ancient Philosophy*. Cambridge, Mass., 1948.

Cassou, Jean. "Le message spirituel des troubadours," *AIEO*, Fasc. 2 (1949), 115–20.

The Castell of Perseverance, in F. J. Furnivall and A. W. Pollard, eds., *The Macro Plays*, Early English Text Society, Extra Series, No. 97 (London, 1904), pp. 75–186.

Chabaneau, Camille. *Sainte Marie Madeleine dans la littérature provençale*. Paris, 1887.

Chaix-Ruy, J. "Le problème du temps dans les *Confessions* et dans *La Cité de Dieu*," *Giornale di Metafisica*, IX (1954), 464–77.

Chaucer, Geoffrey. *The Works of Geoffrey Chaucer*, ed. Fred N. Robinson. 2nd ed. Boston, 1957.

Chrétien de Troyes. *Le chevalier au lion (Yvain)*, ed. Mario Roques. Paris, 1965.

Cluzel, Irénée M. "Les jarŷas et l'*amour courtois*," *CN*, XX (1960), 233–50.

Conrad-Curtius, Hedwig. *Die Zeit*. Munich, 1954.

Cornelius, Roberta Douglas. *The Figurative Castle*. Bryn Mawr, Pa., 1930.

Crescini, Vincenzo. *Manuale per l'avviamento agli studi provenzali*. 3rd ed. Milan, 1926.

Curtius, Ernst Robert. *European Literature and the Latin Middle Ages*, trans. Willard R. Trask. New York: Harper Torchbooks, 1963.

Damon, Philip. *Modes of analogy in ancient and medieval verse*. Berkeley, 1961.

——. "The refrain of the bilingual Alba," *Philological Quarterly*, XXXIII (1954), 421–23.

Daude de Pradas. *Poésies du Troubadour Daude de Pradas*, ed. Alexander Schutz. Paris, 1933.

Davenson, Henri [Henri Irénée Marrou]. *Les troubadours*. [Paris], 1961.

De anima, Liber Quartus, attributed to Hugh of St. Victor. *P. L.*, CLXXVII, cols. 165–90.

de Boor, Helmut, and Richard Newald. *Geschichte der deutschen Literatur*. Vol. II: *Die höfische Literatur, Vorbereitung, Blüte, Ausklang: 1170–1250*, by Helmut de Boor. Munich, 1953.

——. *Geschichte der deutschen Literatur*. Vol. III, Part 1: *Die deutsche Literatur im späten Mittelalter, Zerfall und Neubeginn, Erster Teil: 1250–1350*, by Helmut de Boor. Munich, 1964.

de Bruyne, Edgar. *Études d'esthétique médiévale*. 3 vols. Bruges, 1946.

Dejeanne, J.-M.-L. "Sur l'Aube bilingue du Ms. Vatican Reg. 1462," in *Mélanges [Camille] Chabaneau* (Erlangen, 1907), pp. 77–80.

Denomy, Alexander J. "Courtly Love and Courtliness," *Speculum*, XXVIII (1953), 44–63.

——. *The Heresy of Courtly Love*. New York, 1947.

de Rougemont, Denis. *L'Amour et l'Occident*. 2nd ed. Paris, 1956.

De S. Guthlaco presbytero, in *Acta Sanctorum*, Aprilis, Vol. II (Antwerp, 1675), 37–50.

Diez, Friedrich. *Leben und Werke der Troubadours*. 2nd ed., ed. Karl Bartsch. Leipzig, 1882.

——. *Die Poesie der Troubadours*. Leipzig, 1883.

Donne, John. *The Poems*, ed. Herbert J. C. Grierson. 2 vols. Oxford, 1912.

Dronke, Peter. *The Medieval Lyric*. London, 1968.

Dürckheim, K. von. "Untersuchungen zum gelebten Raum: Erlebniswirklichkeit und ihr Verständnis," *Neue psychologische Studien*, VI (1932), 383 ff.

Eggers, Hans. "Grundriss und Aufbau von Gottfried Webers Tristanwerk," *Euphorion*, XLVIII (1954), 473–84.

Emerson, Oliver Farrar, ed. *A Middle English Reader*. New York, 1905.

Errante, Guido. *Lirica romanza del primo secolo*. New York, 1943.

——. *Marcabru e le fonti sacre dell' antica lirica romanza*. Florence, 1948.

Faral, Edmond. "La Pastourelle," *Romania*, XLIX (1923), 204–59.

Fourquet, Jean. "Littérature courtoise et théologie," *EG*, XII (1957), 34–39.

——. "Thèses sur le Minnesang," *EG*, IX (1954), 1–15.

Fränkel, Ludwig. *Shakespeare und das Tagelied: Ein Beitrag zur vergleichenden Literaturgeschichte der germanischen Völker*. Hannover, 1893.

Frappier, Jean. *La poésie lyrique française aux XIIe et XIIIe siècles: Les auteurs et les genres*. "Les cours de Sorbonne." Paris, n.d.

Freud, Sigmund. "Formulierungen über die zwei Prinzipien des psychischen Geschehens," *GW*, VIII, 230–38.

——. "Das Ich und das Es," *GW*, XIII, 235–89.

——. "Jenseits des Lustprinzips," *GW*, XIII, 1–69.

——. *Neue Folge der Vorlesungen zur Einführung in die Psychoanalyse, GW*, XV.

——. "Das Unbehagen in der Kultur," *GW*, XIV, 419–506.

Frings, Theodor. "Frauenstrophe und Frauenlied in der frühen deutschen Lyrik," in *Festchrift Hermann August Korff* (Leipzig, 1957), pp. 13–28.

Frye, Northrop. *Anatomy of Criticism*. Princeton, 1957.

Furstner, Hans. *Studien zur Wesensbestimmung der höfischen Minne*. Groningen, 1956.

Gent, Werner. *Die Philosophie des Raumes und der Zeit*. 2nd ed. Hildesheim, 1962.

——. *Das Problem der Zeit*. Frankfurt a. M., 1934. Reprinted Hildesheim, 1965.

Gillespie, Gerald. "Origins of Romance Lyrics: A Review of Research," *Yearbook of Comparative and General Literature*, XVI (1967), 16–32.

Gilson, Étienne. *The Christian Philosophy of Saint Augustine*, trans. L. E. M. Lynch. New York, 1967.

——. *La théologie mystique de saint Bernard*. Paris, 1947.

Giraut de Bornelh. *Sämtliche Lieder des Trobadors Giraut de Bornelh*, ed. Adolf Kolsen. 2 vols. Halle, 1907–1935.

Goethe, Johann Wolfgang von. *Gedenkausgabe der Werke, Briefe und Gespräche*, ed. Ernst Beutler. 24 vols. Zürich and Stuttgart, 1949.

Goldin, Frederick. *The Mirror of Narcissus in the Courtly Love Lyric*. Ithaca, 1967.

Gottfried von Strassburg. *Tristan und Isold*, ed. Friedrich Ranke. 9th printing. Zürich and Berlin, 1965.

Gruenter, Rainer. "Bauformen der Waldleben-Episode in Gotfrids Tristan und Isold," in *Festschrift Günther Müller* (Bonn, 1957), pp. 21–48.

——. "Gottfried Weber, Gottfrieds von Strassburg Tristan . . ." [Review], *Deutsche Literaturzeitung*, LXXV (1954), 267–83.

——. "Das *wunnecliche tal*," *Euphorion*, LV (1961), 341–404.

Gruyter, Walter de. *Das deutsche Tagelied*. Leipzig, 1887.

Guilhem Figueira. *Guilhem Figueira, ein provenzalischer Troubadour*, ed. Emil Lévy. Berlin, 1880.

Guitton, Jean. *Man in Time*, trans. Adrienne Foulke. Notre Dame, Indiana, 1966.

——. *Le temps et l'éternité chez Plotin et Saint Augustin*. 3rd ed. Paris, 1959.

Hätzlerin, Clara. *Liederbuch der Clara Hätzlerin*, ed. Carl Haltaus. Quedlinburg and Leipzig, 1840.

Hagen, Friedrich Heinrich von der, ed. *Gesamtabenteuer: Hundert altdeutsche Erzählungen*. 3 vols. Stuttgart and Tübingen, 1850. Reprinted Darmstadt, 1961.

——, ed. *Minnesinger: Deutsche Liederdichter des 12., 13. und 14. Jhdts.* 4 vols. Leipzig, 1838.

Hatto, Arthur T., ed. *Eos: An Enquiry into the Theme of Lovers' Meetings and Partings at Dawn in Poetry*. The Hague, 1965.

Hauser, Arnold. *The Social History of Art.* 4 vols. New York: Vintage Books, n.d.

Heinrich von dem Türlin. *Diu crône*, ed. G. H. F. Scholl, Stuttgart, 1852.

Herbot von Fritzlar. *Liet von Troye*, ed. G. K. Frommann. Quedlinburg and Leipzig, 1837.

Hill, Raymond Thompson, and Thomas Goddard Bergin, eds. *Anthology of the Provençal Troubadours*. New Haven, 1941.

Hölderlin, Friedrich. *Sämtliche Werke*, ed. Friedrich Beissner. 6 vols. Stuttgart, 1946–1961.

Hoepffner, Ernest. "Deux notes sur le troubadour Guiraut de Borneil," *Romania*, LXIII (1937), 204–25.

——. *Les Troubadours dans leur Vie et dans leurs Oeuvres*. Paris, 1955.

Honorius Augustodunensis. *Expositio in Cantica canticorum*. P. L., CLXXII, cols. 347–542.

——. *Speculum Ecclesiae*. P. L., CLXXII, cols. 807–1108.

Hugo of Fouilly. *De claustro animae*. P. L., CLXXVI, cols. 1017–1182.

Hugo von Montfort. [Works], ed. J. E. Wackernell. Innsbruck, 1881.

Ibn Ḥazm, Abū Muḥammad ᶜAlī. *A Book Containing the Risāla, known as the Dove's Neck-Ring, about Love and Lovers . . .*, trans. Alois Richard Nykl. Paris, 1931.

Jackson, William T. H. "The *De Amore* of Andreas Capellanus and the Practice of Love at Court," *Romanic Review*, XLIX (1958), 243–51.

——. "The Epic Center as Structural Determinant in Medieval Narrative Poetry," in Robert A. Fowkes and Volkmar Sander, eds. *New York University Department of German Studies in Germanic Languages and Literature* (Reutlingen, 1967), pp. 79–95.

——. "The role of Brangaene in Gottfried's *Tristan*," *Germanic Review*, XXVIII (1953), 290–96.

Jaspers, Karl. *Von der Wahrheit: Philosophische Logik*. Vol. I. Munich, 1947.

Jaufré Rudel. *Les Chansons de Jaufré Rudel*, ed. Alfred Jeanroy. 2nd ed. Paris, 1965.

Jeanroy, Alfred. *Les origines de la poésie lyrique en France au moyen-âge*. Paris, 1889.

——. *La Poésie lyrique des Troubadours*. 2 vols. Toulouse and Paris. 1934.

——. "Studien über das Tagelied . . . von G. Schlaeger" [Review], *Romania*, XXIV (1895), 287–89.

Jolivet, Régis. *Dieu soleil des esprits: La doctrine augustinienne de l'illumination*. Paris, 1934.

Jones, William Powell. *The Pastourelle, a study of the origins and tradition of a lyric type*. Cambridge, Mass., 1931.

Jonin, Pierre. *Les personnages féminins dans les romans français de Tristan au XIIᵉ siècle: Étude des influences contemporaines*. Gap, 1958.

Kaske, Robert E. "The Aube in Chaucer's *Troilus*," in Richard J. Schoeck and Jerome Taylor, eds. *Chaucer Criticism*, II (Notre Dame, 1961), 167–79.

——. "An Aube in the Reeve's Tale," *ELH*, XXVI (1959), 295–310.

——. "January's 'Aube'," *Modern Language Notes*, LXXV (1960), 1–4.

Keferstein, Georg. "Zur Liebesauffassung in Wolframs 'Parzival'," in *Festschrift für Albert Leitzmann* (Jena, 1937), pp. 15–32.

Keller, Adelbert von, ed. *Altdeutsche Gedichte*. Tübingen, 1846.

Knight, George Wilson. *The Shakespearian Tempest, with a Chart of Shakespeare's Dramatic Universe*. London, 1960.

Kobel, Erwin. *Untersuchungen zum gelebten Raum in der mittelhochdeutschen Dichtung*. Zürich, 1951.

Kochs, Theodor. *Das deutsche geistliche Tagelied*. Münster i.W., 1928.

Kolb, Herbert. *Der Begriff der Minne und das Entstehen der höfischen Lyrik*. Tübingen, 1958.

———. "*Der Minnen hus*: Zur Allegorie der Minnegrotte in Gottfrieds *Tristan*," *Euphorion*, LVI (1962), 229–47.

Koppitz, Hans-Joachim. *Wolframs Religiosität: Beobachtung über das Verhältnis Wolframs von Eschenbach zur religiösen Tradition des Mittelalters*. Bonn, 1959.

Kraus, Carl von, ed. *Deutsche Liederdichter des 13. Jahrhunderts*. 2 vols. Tübingen, 1952–1958.

———. *Walther von der Vogelweide: Untersuchungen*. Berlin and Leipzig, 1935.

Kroes, H. W. J. "Das Tagelied Heinrichs von Morungen," *Neophilologus*, XXXIV (1950). 141–43.

Kück, Eduard. "Zu Wolframs Liedern," *Beiträge*, XXII (1897), 94–114.

Kuhn, Hugo. *Minnesangs Wende*. Tübingen, 1952.

———. "Soziale Realität und dichterische Fiktion am Beispiel der höfischen Ritterdichtung Deutschlands," in *Soziologie und Leben*, ed. Carl Brinkmann (Tübingen, 1952), pp. 195–219. Reprinted in Kuhn's *Dichtung und Welt im Mittelalter* (Stuttgart, 1959), pp. 22–40.

Lachmann, Karl, Moriz Haupt, and Friedrich Vogt, eds. *Des Minnesangs Frühling*. 33rd ed., revised by Carl von Kraus. Stuttgart, 1965.

Lampey, Erich. *Das Zeitproblem nach den Bekenntnissen Augustins*. Regensburg, 1960.

Lavaud, René. "*L'Aube* du Troubadour Cadenet," *AIEO*, Fasc. 1 (1948), 9–11.

Lavelle, Louis. *Du temps et de l'éternité*. Paris, 1945.

Lazar, Moshé. *Amour courtois et "Fin' amors" dans la littérature du XIIᵉ siècle*. Paris, 1964.

Lerch, Eugen. "Trobadorsprache und religiöse Sprache," *CN*, III (1943), 214–30.

Lesser, Ernst. "Das Verhältnis der Frauenmonologe in den lyrischen und epischen deutschen Dichtungen des 12. und angehenden 13. Jahrhunderts," *Beiträge*, XXIV (1899), 361–83.

Lewent, Kurt. "Weitere textkritische Bemerkungen zu den Liedern des Bernart von Ventadorn," *ZfrPh*, XLIII (1923), 657–74.

———. *Zum Text der Lieder des Giraut de Bornelh*. Bibliotheca dell' "Archivum Romanicum," Serie I, Vol. 26. Florence, 1938.

Lommatzsch, Erhard, ed. *Provenzalisches Liederbuch*. Berlin, 1917.

Lot-Borodine, Myrrha. *De l'Amour profane à l'amour sacré: Études de psychologie sentimentale au Moyen Age*. Paris, 1961.

Mackenzie, William Roy. *The English Moralities from the Point of View of Allegory*. Boston, 1914.

Matfré Ermengaud. *Le Breviari d'Amor de Matfre Ermengaud*, ed. Gabriel Azaïs. Béziers, 1862–1866.

Maurer, Friedrich. *Leid: Studien zur Bedeutungs- und Problemgeschichte, besonders in den grossen Epen der staufischen Zeit*. Bern, 1951.

Mayer-Rosa, Norbert. *Studien zum deutschen Tagelied*. Tübingen, 1938.

Mazzeo, Joseph Antony. *Medieval Cultural Tradition in Dante's Comedy.* Ithaca, 1960.

Mechthild von Magdeburg. *Offenbarung der Schwester Mechthild von Magdeburg, oder Das fliessende Licht der Gottheit*, ed. P. Gall Morel. Regensburg, 1869. Reprinted Darmstadt, 1963.

Meiss, Millard. "Light as Form and Symbol in Some Fifteenth-Century Paintings," *Art Bulletin*, XXVII (1945), 175–81.

Meyer, Richard M. "Walthers zweites Tagelied," *ZfdA*, XLIX [Neue Folge, XXXVII] (1908), 385–94.

Mohr, Wolfgang. "Minnesang als gesellschaftskunst," *Der Deutschunterricht*, VI (1954), Heft 5, pp. 83–107.

——. "Wolframs Tagelieder," in *Festschrift für Paul Kluckhohn und Hermann Schneider* (Tübingen, 1948), pp. 148–65.

Moret, André. *Les débuts du lyrisme en Allemagne.* Travaux et mémoires de l'université de Lille, No. 27. Lille, 1951.

——. "Le problème des Origines du Minnesang," *EG*, II (1947) 22–41.

Müller, Günther. "Gradualismus: Eine Vorstudie zur altdeutschen Literaturgeschichte," *DVLG*, II (1924), 681–720.

Muschg, Walter. *Tragische Literaturgeschichte.* 3rd printing. Bern, 1957.

Nelli, René. "De l'amour provençal," *Les Cahiers du Sud*, Special issue: *Le Génie d'Oc et l'homme méditerranéen* (Marseille, 1943), pp. 44–68.

——. *L'Érotique des troubadours.* Toulouse, 1963.

——. "Les grands problèmes de la littérature d'Oc," *AIEO*, Fasc. 7 (1951), 39–47.

——, and René Lavaud, eds. *Les troubadours.* Vol. II: *Le trésor poétique de l'occitanie.* Bruges, 1966.

Neumann, Eduard. "Zum Problem einer mittelaltergemässen Tristan-Interpretation," *Euphorion*, XLVIII (1954), 484–90.

Neumann, Friedrich. "Der Markgraf von Hohenburg," *ZfdA*, LXXXVI (1955–1956), 119–60.

Nickel, Emil. *Studien zum Liebesproblem bei Gottfried von Strassburg.* Königsberger deutsche Forschungen, No. 1. Königsberg, 1927.

Nicklas, Friedrich. *Untersuchungen über Stil und Geschichte des deutschen Tagelieds.* Germanische Studien, No. 72. Berlin, 1929.

Nygren, Anders. *Agape and Eros: A Study of the Christian Idea of Love*, trans. Philip S. Watson. Philadelphia, 1953.

Nykl, Alois Richard. *Hispano-Arabic Poetry and its relations with the Old Provençal Troubadours.* Baltimore, 1946.

——. "Leo Spitzer, L'amour lointain de Jaufré Rudel . . ." [Review], *Speculum*, XX (1945), 252–58.

Ohling, Hertha. *Das deutsche Tagelied vom Mittelalter bis zum Ausgang der Renaissance.* Köln, 1938.

Ohly, Friedrich. *Hohelied-Studien: Grundzüge einer Geschichte der Hoheliedauslegung des Abendlandes bis um 1200.* Wiesbaden, 1958.

Oswald. Der Münchener Oswald, ed. Georg Baesecke. Breslau, 1907.

Oswald von Wolkenstein. *Die Lieder Oswalds von Wolkenstein*, ed. Karl Kurt Klein. Tübingen, 1962.

Ovid. *Heroides and Amores*, ed. Grant Showerman. Loeb Classical Library. London, and Cambridge, Mass., 1914.

The Owl and the Nightingale, ed. Eric Gerald Stanley. London, 1960.

Panofsky, Erwin. *Abbot Suger on the Abbey Church of St.-Denis and its Art Treasures*. Princeton, 1946.

——. *Early Netherlandish Painting, its Origins and Character.* 2 vols. Cambridge, Mass., 1958.

Panvini, Bruno. "Giraldo di Bornelh; Trovatore del Sec. XII," *Siculorum Gymnasium* (Catania), Luglio-Dicembre 1948, pp. 200–67, and Gennaio-Giugno 1949, pp. 32–89.

Parducci, Amos. "Sulla lirica romanza delle origine," *Rendiconto delle sessioni della Accademia delle Scienze dell' Istituto di Bologna, Classe di scienze morali*, Serie 4, Vol. X (1946–1947), pp. 66–71.

Paris, Gaston, ed. *Chansons du XVe siècle*. Paris, 1875.

——. "*Les origines de la poésie lyrique en France* . . . par Alfred Jeanroy . . ." [Review, Part 3], *Journal des Savants* (1892), pp. 155–67.

Peire Vidal. *Les poésies de Peire Vidal*, ed. Joseph Anglade. 2nd ed. Paris, 1965.

Peter Lombard. *Sententiarum libri quattuor*, ed. J.-P. Migne. Paris, 1841.

Poulet, Georges. *Études sur le temps humain.* Paris, 1952.

——. *Les métamorphoses du cercle.* Paris, 1961.

Raby, F. J. E. *A History of Secular Latin Poetry in the Middle Ages.* 2 vols. Oxford, 1934.

Ranke, Friedrich. *Die Allegorie der Minnegrotte in Gottfrieds Tristan.* Schriften der Königsberger Gelehrten Gesellschaft, Geisteswissenschaftliche Klasse, Jg. 2, Heft 2. Berlin, 1925.

——. *Gott, Welt und Humanität in der deutschen Dichtung des Mittelalters.* Basel, 1952.

Rauch, Irmengard. "Wolfram's Dawn-Song Series: An Explication," *Monatshefte für deutschen Unterricht, deutsche Sprache und Literatur*, LV (1963), 367–74.

Riquer, Martin de, ed. *Las albas provenzales.* Barcelona, 1944.

Robertson, Durant W., Jr. "Chaucerian Tragedy," *ELH*, XIX (1952), 1–37. Reprinted in Richard J. Schoeck and Jerome Taylor, eds. *Chaucer Criticism*, II (Notre Dame, 1961), 86–121.

——. *A Preface to Chaucer: Studies in Medieval Perspectives.* Princeton, 1963.

——. "The subject of the *De amore* of Andreas Capellanus," *Modern Philology*, L (1952–1953), 145–61.

Rodrigues Lapa, Manuel. *Das origens da poesia lírica em Portugal na idade-média.* Lisbon, 1929.

——. *Lições de Literatura Portuguesa, Época Medieval.* Lisbon, 1934.

Roethe, G. "Das deutsche Tagelied von Walter de Gruyter" [Review], *Afd A*, XVI (1890), 75–97.

Roncaglia, Aurelio. "Il 'Canto delle scolte modanesi'," *CN*, VIII (1948), 5–46.

Ruh, Kurt. "Das Tagelied Heinrichs von Morungen," *Trivium*, II (1944), 173–77.

Salverda de Grave, J.-J. "Observations sur l'art lyrique de Giraut de Borneil," *Mededeelingen det Koninklijke Nederlandsche Akademie van Wetenschappen, Afd. Letterkunde*, Nieuwe reeks, Deel 1 (1938), 1–131.

Sardemann, Franz. *Ursprung und Entwicklung der Lehre von lumen rationis aeternae, lumen divinum, lumen naturale, rationes seminales, veritates aeternae bis Descartes.* Kassel, 1902.

Sauer, Joseph. *Die Symbolik des Kirchengebäudes.* Freiburg, 1902.

Sawles Ward, in J. A. W. Bennett and G. V. Smithers, eds. *Early Middle English Verse and Prose* (Oxford, 1966), pp. 246–61.

Scheludko, Dimitri. "Beiträge zur Entstehungsgeschichte der altprovenzalischen Lyrik: die arabische Theorie," *AR*, XII (1928), 30–127.

——. "Beiträge zur Entstehungsgeschichte der altprovenzalischen Lyrik: klassisch-lateinische Theorie," *AR*, XI (1927), 273–312.

——. "Beiträge zur Entstehungsgeschichte der altprovenzalischen Lyrik [Die mittellateinische Theorie]," *AR*, XV (1931), 137–206.

——. "Beiträge zur Entstehungsgeschichte der altprovenzalischen Lyrik: Die Volksliedertheorie," *ZfSL*, LII (1929), 1–38 and 201–66.

——. "Ovid und die Troubadours," *ZfrPh*, LIV (1934), 129–74.

——. "Religiöse Elemente im weltlichen Liebeslied der Trobadors," *ZfSL*, LIX (1935), 402–21, and LX (1937), 18–35.

——. "Über die Theorien der Liebe bei den Trobadors," *ZfrPh*, LX (1940), 191–234.

Scheunemann, Ernst, and Friedrich Ranke, eds. *Texte zur Geschichte des deutschen Tagelieds.* Bern, 1947.

Schlaeger, Georg. *Studien über das Tagelied.* Jena, 1895.

Schlösser, Felix. *Andreas Capellanus: seine Minnelehre und das christliche Weltbild um 1200.* Bonn, 1960.

Schmidt, Johannes. "Die älteste Alba," *ZfdPh*, XII (1881), 333–41.

Scholte, Jan Hendrik. "Wolframs Lyrik," *Beiträge*, LXIX (1947), 409–19.

Schröder, W. J. *Der Ritter zwischen Welt und Gott.* Weimar, 1952.

Schultz, Alwin. *Das höfische Leben zur Zeit der Minnesinger.* 2 vols. Leipzig, 1889.

Schumann, Otto. "Das deutsche geistliche tagelied, von dr Theodor Kochs" [Review], *AfdA*, XLIX (1930), 116–20.

Schwietering, Julius. *Die deutsche Dichtung des Mittelalters.* 2nd ed. Darmstadt, 1957.

——. "Einwürkung der Antike auf die Entstehung des frühen deutschen Minnesangs," *ZfdA*, LXI (1924), 61–82.

——. "Der Tristan Gottfrieds von Strassburg und die Bernhardische Mystik," in his *Mystik und höfische Dichtung im Hochmittelalter* (Darmstadt, 1962), pp. 1–35.

Scudieri Ruggieri, Jole M. "Per le origini dell' alba," *CN*, III (1943), 191–202.

Singer, Samuel. *Die religiöse Lyrik des Mittelalters.* Bern, 1933.

Smith, Victor. "Vieilles chansons recueillies en Velay et en Forez," *Romania*, VII (1878), 52–84.

Spitzer, Leo. *L'amour lointain de Jaufré Rudel et le sens de la poésie des troubadours.* Chapel Hill, 1944.

——. "The Mozarabic Lyric and Theodor Frings' Theories," *Comparative Literature*, IV (1952), 1–22.

——. "Salvatore Santangelo, *L'amore lontano di Jaufre Rudel...*" [Review], *Romania*, LXXV (1954), 396–402.

Stengel, E. "Der Entwicklungsgang der provenzalischen Alba," *ZfrPh*, IX (1885), 407–12.

——. "Peire Espagnol's Alba," *ZfrPh*, X (1886), 160–62.

Strecker, Karl, ed. *Die Cambridger Lieder*. Berlin, 1926.

Streicher, Oskar. "Verhältnis zwischen Mann und Frau und dichterische Anschauung in der mhd. Lyrik," *ZfdPh*, XXIV (1892), 171–86.

Stronski, Stanislaw. *La Poésie et la réalité aux temps des troubadours*. Oxford, 1943.

Thomas, Helmuth. "Wolframs Tageliederzyklus," *ZfdA*, LXXXVII (1956–1957), 45–58.

Utley, Francis Lee. *The Crooked Rib: An Analytical Index to the Argument about Women in English and Scots Literature to the End of the Year 1568*. Columbus, Ohio, 1944.

Valency, Maurice. *In Praise of Love: An Introduction to the Love-Poetry of the Renaissance*. New York, 1961.

Wagner, Richard. *Tristan und Isolde*. London, Mainz, Zürich, and New York: Edition Eulenburg, n.d.

Walter of Châtillon. *Die Lieder Walters von Chatillon in der Handschrift 351 von St. Omer*, ed. Karl Strecker. Berlin, 1925.

Walther, Hans. *Das Streitgedicht in der lateinischen Literatur des Mittelalters*. Munich, 1920.

Walther von der Vogelweide. *Die Gedichte Walthers von der Vogelweide*, ed. Carl von Kraus. 12th ed. Berlin, 1959.

——. *Sprüche und Lieder: Gesamtausgabe*, ed. Helmut Protze. Halle, 1963.

Watts, Alan W. *Nature, Man, and Woman*. New York, 1958.

Weber, Gottfried. *Gottfrieds von Strassburg Tristan und die Krise des hochmittelalterlichen Weltbildes um 1200*. Stuttgart, 1953.

——. *Parzival: Ringen und Vollendung*. Oberursel, 1948.

Wechssler, Eduard. *Das Kulturproblem des Minnesangs*. Halle, 1909.

Wehrli, Max, ed. *Deutsche Lyrik des Mittelalters*. Zürich, 1955.

——. "Der Tristan Gottfrieds von Strassburg," *Trivium*, IV (1946), 81–117.

Wettstein, Jacques. *"Mezura": L'Idéal des troubadours*. Zürich, 1945.

White, T. H., trans. *The Bestiary, A Book of Beasts: Being a Translation from a Latin Bestiary of the Twelfth Century*. New York: Capricorn Books, 1960.

Wikman, K. Rob. V. "Die Einleitung der Ehe," *Acta Academiae Aboensis: Humaniora*, XI (1937), 1–384.

Wilhelm, James J. *The Cruelest Month: Spring, Nature, and Love in Classical and Medieval Lyrics*. New Haven, 1965.

Wittenweiler, Heinrich. *Heinrich Wittenwilers Ring*, ed. Edmund Wiessner. Leipzig, 1931.

Wodtke, Friedrich Wilhelm. "Die Allegorie des 'Inneren Paradieses' bei Bernhard von Clairvaux, Honorius Augustodunensis, Gottfried von Strassburg und in der deutschen Mystik," in *Festschrift Josef Quint*, ed. Hugo Moser (Bonn, 1964), pp. 277–90.

Wolfram von Eschenbach. *Parzival*, ed. Karl Lachmann. 6th ed. Berlin and Leipzig, 1926.

Woods, William S. "The *Aube* in *Aucassin et Nicolette*," in *Medieval Studies in Honor of Urban Tigner Holmes, Jr.* (Chapel Hill, 1965), pp. 209–15.

Wulff, August. *Die frauenfeindlichen Dichtungen in den romanischen Literaturen des Mittelalters*. Halle, 1914.

Wynnere and Wastoure, ed. Israel Gollancz. London, 1920.

Zorzi, Diego. "L'*Amor de lonh* di Jaufre Rudel," *Aevum*, XXIX (1955), 124–44.

——. *Valori religiosi nella letteratura provenzale: la spiritualità trinitaria*. Pubblicazioni dell' Università Cattolica del S. Cuore, N. S., No. 44. Milan, 1954.

Zumthor, Paul. "Au berceau du lyrisme européen," *Cahiers du Sud*, XLI (1954–1955), No. 326, pp. 3–61.

INDEX

Abbey of the Holy Spirit, sermon on (Rolle, attrib.), 60, 128–29
Adam of St. Victor: "O Maria stella maris," 276*n*
"Ad ruinas Cumarum, urbis vetustissimae" (Sannazzaro), 197
adultery, 41, 44, 95, 97–106, 242; *alba*, 39–48, 94, 97–100, 122, 147–48, 152, 241; *chanson*, 40; gradualistic explanation, 98–100, 103, 105–06, 242; *see also* love and lovers; love and lovers (*alba*); sexuality
Aeneid (Vergil), 49–50, 62*n*, 111–12, 285*n*
Aeschylus, 58
agape, 221, 222
Alanus de Insulis, 76, 77
Albrecht von Johansdorf: "Swer minne minnecliche treit," 99–100, 100–01, 105
"Ales diei nuntius" (Prudentius): day and night, symbolism and imagery, 68–75, 77, 78, 103, 108, 110, 171; dualism, 93, 98, 103, 106, 112; Christ as watchman, 127–28

allegory, *see* symbolism and imagery; symbolism and imagery, Christian
Ambrose, Saint: dawn-hymns, 68, 214
amor mixtus, 223–27
amor purus, 223, 225
Amores (Ovid), 5–6, 173–77
"Amors, enquera · us preyara" (Bernart de Ventadorn), 233
Amphitruo (Plautus), 285*n*
Andreas Capellanus: *De arte honeste amandi*, 102, 103, 105, 223, 224
Anglo-Saxon narratives, 29–30
Anna Karenina (Tolstoy), 119
Annunciation (Jan van Eyck), 80–81, 82, 87, 88
Antony and Cleopatra (Shakespeare), 211, 212
Appel, Carl, 117, 118
Aquinas, Saint Thomas, 98–99; *see also* gradualism
Arabic literature: possible source for *alba*, 8, 142*n*; portrayal of women, 156
Ariosto, Lodovico: *Orlando furioso*, 221

Aristotle: structural system in Dante's *Paradiso*, 32; concept of permanence, 189

Arthurian romances, 29–30

Astrophel and Stella (Sidney), 2

As You Like It (Shakespeare), 2

aube, 2

Augustine, Saint (and Augustinian thought), 27, 103; on Fall of Man, 13, 181, 182, 183–84, 188; *Confessions*, 168–72, 172–73, 175, 176, 177, 191–92, 204n; divided will, 168–72, 172–73, 175, 176, 177, 183, 191–92, 204n, 241; concept of time, 180–92 *passim*, 196, 204n, 205–06, 212, 213; *De civitate dei*, 181–182, 183, 184; on sexual lust, 183–84, 184–85, 238; *In Joannis Evangelium*, 190–91; *De trinitate*, 191, 286n

awakening, spiritual: symbolism and imagery, 67, 68, 75, 171

Bartholomew, Saint, 78–79

Bartsch, Karl, 141n

Baudelaire, Charles: "Recueillement," 110–11, 112

Bede, Saint: *Ecclesiastical History of the English Nation*, 29, 61

"Be m'an perdut lai enves Ventadorn" (Bernart de Ventadorn), 217

"Bem platz longua" (Folquet de Marselha), 276n

Benoît de Sainte-Maure: *Roman de Troie*, 282n

Beowulf, 29

Bernard, Saint, 12, 22, 28, 81

Bernart de Ventadorn: "Tant ai mo cor ple de joya," 53–54, 234; "Be m'an perdut lai enves Ventadorn," 217; "Lo gens tems de pascor," 217; "Pois preyatz me, senhor," 222–23; "Lo tems vai e ven e vire," 231, 232; "Amors, enquera · us preyara," 233

"Be vei e conosc e sai" (Giraut de Bornelh), 92–93, 94

birds: dawn announced by, in *alba*, 1, 6, 148–50

Boccaccio, Giovanni: *Filostrato*, 2, 5–6

Bruno von Hornberg: "Swer tougenlîcher minne pflege," 98

Cadenet; 147; "S'anc fui belha ni prezada," 42, 114–19, 120, 121, 160, 161

Cambridge Songs, 23, 53

Canterbury Tales (Chaucer), 226–27

castle, 28, 29, 30; allegories, 24–30 *passim*, 59–60, 128, 130; *alba*, 27–28, 56, 228; *see also* court and courtly life

Castle of Perseverance, The, 119–20, 166, 168

Castrum humani corporis, 25, 60

Cervantes Saavedra, Miguel de: *Don Quixote*, 158n

chamber, enclosed (*alba*), 1, 14, 19, 20, 23, 24, 35, 143, 228; as paradise, 23, 24; analogy with Garden of Eden, 23–24, 182; analogy with *hortus conclusus*, 24; analogy with castle allegory, 27–28; sexual analogy, 33–34; in *chanson*, 229, 234

change, *see* time, change

chanson, 2, 3, 216–17; influence of, 2, 3, 4; lady, 2, 12, 40, 42, 216–17, 217–18, 220, 221, 222, 224, 227, 228, 229, 230, 232, 233, 238; lover, 2, 216, 217, 220, 221–22, 228, 229, 230, 232, 233, 234, 237; lovers, 2, 216–23 *passim*, 227, 229, 230; *eros* and *agape*, 221–22; comparison with *alba*, 2–4, 216–39; and mysticism of Saint Bernard, 12; adultery, 40; *mal mariée*, 42, 118; spying, 127, 227–28; sexuality, 222–23, 224–25, 227; conflict of pleasure and reality, 227–28, 234–39 *passim*; vertical relationship, 217, 220, 221; concept of space, 228–30; separation, 229, 236; concept of time, 231–37 *passim*; dream as device, 234–35

Chaucer, Geoffrey, influence of *alba* on: *Troilus and Criseyde*, 2, 28, 57, 84, 85, 86, 213–14, 249–53 (text of *alba*-scene); *Canterbury Tales* (*Reeve's Tale*), 226–27; *Compleynt of Mars*, 238

Le chevalier au lion (*Yvain*) (Chrétien de Troyes), 281n

Chinese poetry, 90

choice, problem of, 158–77 *passim*

Chrétien de Troyes, 218; *Le Chevalier au lion* (*Yvain*), 281n

Christ: sacrifice as atonement for Fall, 183, 194, 195

Christ, symbolism and imagery: in Virgin's womb, 24, 82; light, 63–65, 69; dawn as Second Coming, 66–72 *passim*, 74; as watchman, 71, 126–28,